MATHEMATICS
IN ARCHAEOLOGY

COLLINS ARCHAEOLOGY

MATHEMATICS IN ARCHAEOLOGY

CLIVE ORTON

COLLINS
14 St James's Place, London
1980

William Collins Sons & Co Ltd
London · Glasgow · Sydney · Auckland
Toronto · Johannesburg

First published 1980
© Clive Orton 1980
ISBN 0 00 216226 1
Set in Bembo
Made and Printed in Great Britain by
William Collins Sons & Co Ltd Glasgow

EDITORS' FOREWORD

Additions to the large and growing number of books on archaeological subjects may seem at first sight hard to justify; there would appear to be a book to meet every need and answer every question. Yet this overprovision is more apparent than real. Although certain subjects, for instance Roman Britain, are quite well provided for, others have scarcely been touched. But more than that, archaeology is moving so fast on all fronts that the rapid changes within it make it very difficult for the ordinary reader to keep up. In the last twenty years or so there has been a considerable increase in the number of professional archaeologists who are generating a great deal of new knowledge and many new ideas which often cannot be quickly shared with a wider public. Threats to sites by advancing development in town centres, building on new land and road works, as well as from agriculture and forestry, have grown to terrifying proportions, and are being at any rate partially met by extensive rescue operations. The volume of ancient material of all kinds and periods has multiplied enormously, and its interpretation in the light of new knowledge and techniques has altered, in most cases radically, the accepted picture of the past.

There is thus a real danger of the general reader being left out of the new developments while the professionals are absorbed in gathering and processing clues. This series is intended for the reader who wishes to know what is happening in a given field. He may not be a trained archaeologist, although he may be attending courses in some aspect of the subject; he may want to know more about his locality, or about some particular aspect, problem or technique; or he may be merely generally interested in the roots of our civilization, and how knowledge about them is obtained. It is indeed vital to maintain links with our past, not only for inner enrichment, but for the fuller understanding of the present, which will inform and guide the shaping of our future.

The series presents books of moderate length, well illustrated, on various aspects of archaeology, special topics, regions, techniques and problems. They are written in straightforward language by experts in their fields who, from a deep study of their subjects, have something fresh and stimulating to say about them. They are essentially up-to-date and down-to-earth. They point to sites and museums to visit, and to books which will enable the reader to follow up points which intrigue him. Finally, they do not avoid controversy, because the editors are convinced that the public enjoys being taken to the very frontiers of knowledge.

CHERRY LAVELL
ERIC WOOD

Some Forthcoming Titles

HOUSES   R. W. Brunskill
IRON AND STEEL   D. W. Crossley
CHURCH ARCHAEOLOGY   Ann Hamlin
THE FLOATING FRONTIER   Mark Hassall
GLASS   Ruth Hurst Vose
SOUTH WEST BRITAIN   Susan Pearce
PREHISTORIC AND ROMAN
    AGRICULTURE   Peter Reynolds
SETTLEMENT IN BRITAIN
    Christopher Taylor

Published Titles

VIKING AGE SCULPTURE   Richard N. Bailey
THE ARCHAEOLOGY OF THE
    WELSH MARCHES   S. C. Stanford

ACKNOWLEDGEMENTS

I have made extensive use of published work, and I am grateful to the following for permission to use copyright material: Museum of London, Department of Urban Archaeology, (figs 1.1, 1.2, 3.5, 3.9); Professor A. C. Renfrew and C. B. Burgess (fig 2.1); Dr J. P. Gillam (fig 2.2); A. & C. Black Ltd (fig 2.3); P. Davey (fig 2.4); Dr M. J. Fulford (figs 2.5–2.7); Professor F. R. Hodson (figs 2.12, 2.28); The Computer Centre, University of Birmingham (figs 2.13, 5.2); Dr D. Roe (fig 2.15); Dr E. G. Stickel (fig 2.16); Dr J. D. Wilcock (figs 2.17, 2.18); Gerald Duckworth and Co. Ltd (figs 3.6, 3.8, 5.1, 5.9); H. L. Sheldon (figs 3.11, 3.12, 3.27, 8.1); Edinburgh University Press (figs 3.13, 3.18, 3.19); Thames and Hudson Ltd (figs 4.1, 4.2); Cambridge University Press (figs 4.3, 4.9–4.11, 4.14–4.19, 7.5–7.10, 8.14, 8.15); Mrs K. Hartley (fig 4.4); The Institute of Archaeology, University of London (figs 6.4–6.7); Professor B. W. Cunliffe (fig 6.8); J. H. Ashdown (fig 7.1); P. Backman (fig 7.2); Dr R. E. Chaplin (fig 8.6); Dr R. C. A. Rottländer (figs 8.10–8.13).

I am grateful to the following for supplying photographs: N. Plastow (pl 1); Oxfordshire Museums Service (pl 2); T. Hurst (pls 3, 11, 12, 14); Museum of London, Photographic Department (pls 4–8, 13, 15); Colchester Museum (pl 9); Salisbury and South Wiltshire Museum (pl 10); National Monuments Record (pl 16).

Special thanks go to Pat Altham and Robin Densem, who allowed me to use their unpublished results, and to those who commented on sections of the text, including the Winchester Animal Bone Studies Group and Chris Green of the Museum of London, Department of Urban Archaeology. The text was typed by Mary Ferretti, Sally Lancaster and Noreen Smith, and Chris Ratcliffe collated and typed the bibliography. Finally I should like to thank the series editors for their faith in the idea of this book, and for their constant support and encouragement.

7

CONTENTS

LIST OF PLATES

PREFACE

The role of mathematics in archaeology is often seen either as one of a whole bundle of 'scientific methods', like radiocarbon dating, thin-sectioning and so on, or as an adjunct to a particular view of archaeology, sometimes called the New Archaeology. Having been trained as a mathematician and statistician, I have always thought this was a pity. Mathematics can be used as a tool for organizing one's thoughts and data, and as such is of value to any archaeologist, whatever his philosophy, and whether he works in the field, laboratory, study or armchair.

I have approached the subject via the questions that archaeologists and others frequently ask about their finds. Chapter 2 looks at the question 'what is it?' and how artefacts can be sorted and classified; chapter 3 turns to the question 'how old is it?' – ways of looking at stratigraphy and the interpretation of dating evidence. The geographical aspects are dealt with in chapters 4 and 7, and the question of function in chapter 5. A less appreciated problem comes in chapter 6, which deals with the special difficulties of working with broken objects like pots and bones. More general questions of interpretation – what one can or cannot say about a body of data – are met in chapter 8. The final chapter is partly speculative, and tries to pick out some trends for the future.

The aim throughout is to demonstrate the mathematical ideas that sit at the heart of many archaeological ideas and concepts, and to work them out through practical examples. It is not intended to turn the archaeologist into a mathematician or vice versa, but to show what work has been done and to help the reader gain access to it.

The archaeological or general reader may have had no contact with mathematics for many years, and may remember it as a mysterious discipline inflicted on him at school, and with which he never really came to grips. This can lead to a feeling that mathematics is a closed book, and that any attempt to understand it is doomed to failure. I believe that this problem can be overcome by a joint effort on the part of the writer and the reader. The writer can make mathematical ideas more accessible by expressing them in ordinary language rather than in the private language of mathematicians. This I have tried to do, which is why there are few x's, sigma's or other mathematical symbols in my argument. The reader on his part must make an act of faith – in himself. If he can avoid a defeatist outlook, and approach the mathematics with confidence in his ability to grasp it, I believe that he will be able to, and that he will even enjoy it.

CHAPTER ONE

Introduction

To most people, the idea of connecting mathematics with archaeology comes as something of surprise. Mathematics is about numbers, or triangles, or strange things one does with quadratic equations, while archaeology is about digging holes, and finding things – from coins or sherds up to buildings and whole cities – but where is the link? The answer is that both of these descriptions are caricatures: numbers form a relatively small part of mathematics, which concerns itself with the study of patterns and relationships, while a large part of archaeology consists of the interpretation of material evidence, and the actual recovery of the evidence from the ground forms a relatively small part. Now the two subjects begin to edge towards one another. How does the archaeologist go about his task of interpreting his evidence, but by looking for patterns and relationships within it? And here he is within the realm of mathematics.

That may sound too neat, and certainly too general and abstract to be satisfying. What sort of pattern? What sorts of relationships? How can mathematics help detect patterns in archaeological evidence? In the following chapters we shall look at various common archaeological activities – classifying artefacts into different types, using dating evidence, studying the source and function of artefacts, coping with the peculiar problems of pottery and bones (which are so often broken) and looking at distribution maps – and see that there are mathematical ideas underlying each activity. Often, it seems, the archaeologist, rather like *Le Bourgeois Gentilhomme*, has been speaking mathematics all his life without realizing it. If so, he may have much to gain by realizing it, and bringing in the particular aspect of mathematics explicitly. After all, someone may already have studied that topic as mathematics in more depth, and he can save himself much work by drawing on the mathematician's experience. This does not mean that the mathematician's job is to tell the archaeologist what to do – the archaeologist maintains his responsibility for what he does – but to help him decide how to do it. On the other hand, mathematics does have its rules, which cannot be flouted simply because the archaeologist does not like them, or finds them inconvenient. Mathematics has been described as the 'Queen and Servant of Sciences' and it is this dual role that we shall examine.

For this reason, some of the archaeology of the following chapters may seem distinctly old-fashioned to the more 'trendy' or 'scientific' reader. Rather than get embroiled in arguments about what archaeologists ought to be doing, whether that be formulating lawlike generalizations, 'General Systems Theory' or whatever, I have stuck to the sort of problems facing ordinary archaeologists in their everyday work, and tried to show the extent to which mathematical ideas permeate these problems. The bigger, strategic, questions are left to those better qualified or more confident to deal with them: my concern is with the tactical, day-to-day problems of extracting information from data.

Archaeological evidence

Before proceeding to specific topics, it will be worth looking first at the general nature of archaeological evidence on the one hand, and of the mathematical and statistical approach to evidence on the other. The first thing to note about archaeology is that its evidence is material, not written. We shall keep well clear of the specialized areas of documentary interpretation in all its forms. Attempts have been made to use mathematics in studying, for example, different versions of the same text in order to establish as authentic a version as possible, and in historical analysis; but they are outside the scope of this book.

Even with this restriction, archaeological evidence comes in a wide range of forms. There are archaeological deposits in the widest sense – soils, ditch fills, etc. – representing man's impact on his surroundings; artefacts of all sorts, from humble pottery sherds and waste flints up to palaces and cities, and biological evidence – bone, seeds, pollen, etc., which can tell us more about man's environment and his interaction with it. Also, we must not forget evidence from fieldwork other than excavation – aerial photographs, plans, surveys and so on. Most important of all, and frequently the least understood, are the relationships between these different forms of evidence: which artefacts are from which deposit, for instance. Objects lose much of their value when dissociated from their provenance. Similarly, there are the relationships between one deposit and another (*stratigraphy*) and between one artefact and another. The amount of evidence which must be marshalled and analysed is enormous.

What is more, the evidence is not straightforward. Sometimes it is fragmentary – the complete pot or bone comb, for example, is the rare exception – which may cause us difficulties in deciding to which 'type' it belongs. It is almost always disturbed – in the very nature of things archaeological deposits tend to be disturbed by later activity, and the evidence either destroyed or mixed up. One must always be on guard too against evidence that is downright misleading. For example, an Iron Age shuttle of a type previously only found in Wessex was recently found during excavation of a site in Mitcham, Surrey (*pl 1*).

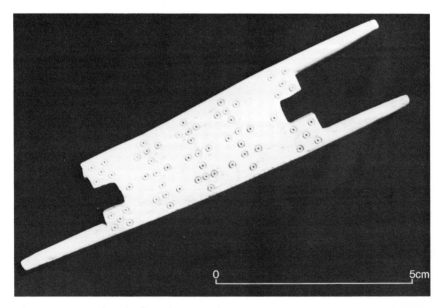

Plate 1   Bone shuttle found at Mitcham Grove, Surrey, but of 'Wessex' type.

Treated uncritically, and plotted on a distribution map, it would of course considerably extend the range of this type of object. But in fact it was found in an eighteenth/nineteenth-century context, in a house which had been owned by Samuel Hoare the banker, who was related to Colt Hoare the archaeologist, who had excavated extensively in Wessex. . . .

Finally, the evidence may be correct as far as it goes, but not be fully understood. As an illustration, take the line of the Roman wall around the City of London (*fig 1.1*). The line had been known for many years, but no one had ever satisfactorily explained the curious

17

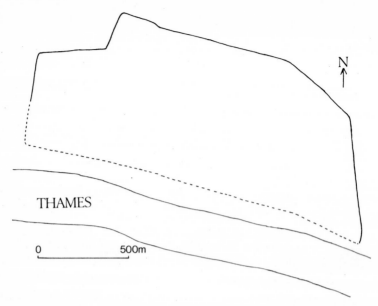

Fig 1.1   Line of the wall around Roman London prior to discovery of the Cripplegate fort.

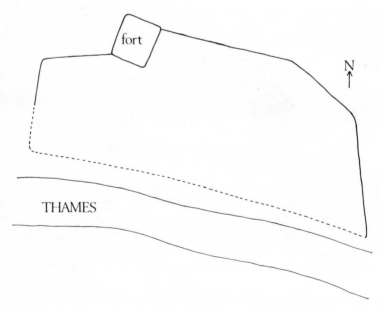

Fig 1.2   Line of the wall around Roman London after the discovery of the Cripplegate fort.

re-entrant in the north-west sector. It was only when excavations in the 1940s and 1950s revealed the existence of an earlier fort (the 'Cripplegate' fort) here (*fig 1.2*) that it all became clear. The later city wall had 'taken in' two sides of the earlier fort wall, presumably to save time and stone.

To sum up, the archaeologist must cope not only with large masses of evidence, but with large masses of 'low grade' evidence. It may be full of gaps and errors and there may be nothing he can do to collect more or to improve the quality of what he has.

The statistical cycle

The role of mathematics, and especially of statistics, is to provide a framework within which this mass of evidence can be sifted, and useful information detected. The archaeologist will naturally have his theories and hypotheses, which he will wish to test in the light of his evidence. Unfortunately, there often seems to be a link missing between the theory and the real world of data. For example, suppose the hypothesis is that the main method of transport of Romano-British pottery from the north Oxfordshire kilns was by water, while the data consist of the percentages of that sort of pottery at a number of sites in southern England (see chapter 4, p 122). Clearly, the data do not provide a direct test of hypothesis. What we need is some deduction

Plate 2   Romano-British pottery from north Oxfordshire.

19

from the hypothesis which concerns the sort of information we have to hand – in this example perhaps that the percentages would be higher at sites that can be reached along rivers from Oxford than at sites which cannot. We can now compare this idea with the actual percentages and see whether they support it or not. What we have done is to take one aspect of the hypothesis and put it into mathematical form so that a comparison with the evidence is possible.

In statistical jargon, this idea is called a model. It represents, in mathematical form, the feature of the hypothesis which seems most directly related to our data. In archaeology, 'model' is an over-worked word, and can mean almost anything. But it is almost always a simplification or idealization of the original hypothesis. The models encountered in this book will all be mathematical models, that is, they will all be expressed in mathematic terms. Generally, they will be implicit and will not be announced with a big label saying 'MODEL'.

If the model acts as a link between theory and the real world, we need to be able to proceed from theory to model and from model to real world, and then back again. This process has been called the Statistical Cycle, and is illustrated in *fig 1.3*. It may look rather formidable at first, so let us consider it bit by bit, starting at the top left-hand

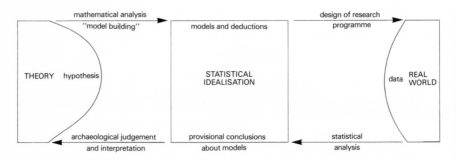

Fig 1.3   The 'Statistical Cycle'.

corner. We start – at least in this ideal situation – with the archaeologist's hypothesis, which we have to simplify and turn into a mathematical form. This task is known as model-building. A good model has to strike a balance between being (a) complicated enough to represent the real world adequately and (b) simple enough to be amenable to statistical analysis. This balancing act is never easy, and in the hands of a skilled practitioner can approach the status of a creative art. Not surprisingly, it is the part of the cycle most often missing, or inadequate, in archaeological applications of statistics. The temptation is always to pick a model 'off-the-shelf', as it were, without particular regard to whether it is suitable for the task in hand. Sometimes it is not even appreciated that there *is* a model underlying a chosen statistical technique, and therefore no assessment is made of whether the technique really fits the problem. But there is always a model of some sort present, and the need for some resemblance between the real-life problem and the mathematical model must be kept in mind. In practice, some techniques are more tolerant of discrepancies between real life and the model than others – they are called 'robust'.

Having settled on our model, we naturally turn to the collection of data. With a good choice of model, we should get some guidance from it as to how much and what sort of data we need. For example, a statistician's model of the voting habits of the electorate may lead him to suggest that a sample of only 2000 voters may be sufficient for an opinion poll, provided that they are carefully chosen with respect to age, sex and constituency. In our archaeological example (p 122) our model of the distribution of north Oxfordshire pottery may lead us to decide that we need to know the proportion of that sort of pottery at (let us say) fifty sites, of which so many are less than twenty miles from the kilns, so many are between twenty and fifty miles, etc., and there are roughly equal numbers north, south, east and west of Oxford. Of course, it is not always that easy: there may not be enough sites in a particular sector, or they may not have yielded enough pottery to be reliable, or someone may have thrown away the coarse ware sherds, or . . . But whatever the practical snags, the principle is clear enough: a carefully thought out programme, based on the chosen model, can help to ensure that one's results are neither (a) inconclusive through lack of data (though of course they may be inconclusive because of the very nature of the data) or (b) expensive because of a super-abundance of data.

This leads us to the thorny question of cost: research costs money, or at least time if undertaken by voluntary organizations, and using time or money in one way means that it is not available for use in a different way. In practice, therefore, designing an experiment or research programme is yet another balancing act, between the need to collect information and the need not to spend resources. It usually comes down to either doing one's best on a fixed budget or achieving a required level of precision as cheaply as possible. Good design is essential in either case.

Sampling

In recent years some archaeologists have come to realize that because so much archaeological field work is, in effect, sampling (whether it be sampling a site by excavation or a parish by field-walking), the statistical theory of sampling might have something to offer them. Provided that they can frame their questions in a numerical way, and have some idea of the accuracy required of the results, then in principle sampling theory can tell them how to collect the information they need as cheaply as possible, or how to get as much information as possible on a fixed budget. In other words, it can help their research design.

So far, this approach has been applied at three different scales: regional, site and assemblage. An example of the first might be the intensive study of selected small areas of a region in order to say something about the region as a whole. Of the second, one can think of excavating selected parts of a site (perhaps because time to excavate the whole site is not available) to draw conclusions about the whole site, or of excavating chosen sites in a town to draw conclusions about the town (after all, a town is just one big site). In the third category comes the selection of a sample of artefacts for more detailed study than is possible to apply to a whole assemblage – for example, detailed measurements on flint waste flakes, or the sorts of scientific methods discussed in chapter 4.

The link between theory and real life is not as simple as it might seem. For one thing, the use of sampling theory demands that there should be a population from which one selects a sample, and that the members of this population should be identified and enumerated (i.e. listed in some sort of order). This rules out the sampling of sites directly (since the archaeologist cannot enumerate, say, all the round barrows in his county, but only the ones he knows of) but it does permit the sampling of land, since that can be enumerated (for example, by listing of Ordnance Survey grid squares). Secondly, the sample must be random, that is we must be able to specify in advance the probability of selection of any member of the population. This may be possible for selecting blocks of countryside from a map, but not for selecting sites in a town (where site selection may depend mainly on the friendliness of developers, and very little on sampling theory). The relevance of strict statistical sampling theory to archaeology is therefore still a matter for debate, and is likely to remain so for some time.

The statistical cycle again

Something that a statistician learns slowly, and often painfully, is not to take his data for granted. There are rarely such things as 'objective' facts: more often the data are a record of the relationship between the recorder and the recorded. To return to our example, the answers obtained from an opinion poll can be influenced by the phrasing of the questions, and even their position on the question-naire. In chapter 6 we shall see how different approaches to archaeological recording can lead to different answers, even when based on the same material. Consistency in recording, and a clear statement of how the recording was done, are as important as the data themselves.

If we have persevered this far, the 'statistical analysis' link of the cycle is, the statistician will tell us, 'a formality'. He is right in the sense that we have little choice in what is done here – that has all been settled long ago by the choice of model and the design of our research programme. All we have to do is perform the appropriate calcula-tions, and provided we get our sums right there are no problems. It may be extremely tedious, and we may be able to avoid the tedium by employing a computer.

From all this 'number-crunching', some provisional conclusions should emerge. They may be that x% of the population say they will vote for Bloggs, or that the percentage of north Oxfordshire pottery falls off twice as quickly for sites with no access by river as it does for sites with access. In general terms, we can say something about the parameters in the model – in these examples the voting percentages and the relationship between proportion of pottery and distance from the kiln. The conclusion may be less immediately useful: we may discover that our model was inadequate and that we need to think again.

The non-numerate archaeologist may by this stage be feeling distinctly left out. Two links of the cycle have been mathematical, and the third purely automatic. Does he have a role any more? Where does he fit into the picture? The answer is that the fourth link is his chance to shine. This is where the decisions have to be made, and the intuition exercised. Will Bloggs win the election? Is Oxfordshire pottery mainly distributed by river, or is there an alternative explanation? He has all the information, and now he must interpret it, deciding which interpretation to choose and how much reliance he can put on it. The rest of the cycle has in no way diminished his responsi-bility: rather, it has organized and presented the issues to him in as clear a way as possible. But now it leaves him to bridge the 'imagination gap', as it has been called, alone. And it is on his performance here that he will be judged.

Now we are 'home', but only for the time being. Soon something will change – perhaps a new theory will arise or a more refined or sensitive model, or perhaps someone will gather some more data. Then we are off again, round the cycle once more. And so it goes on.

Obviously this is a rather idealized account of the statistical cycle. It is rarely so neat and satisfying, particularly in archaeology. We may simply have to use whatever data come to hand, or whatever techniques are available. We may not have the necessary expertise, time or money to build models, design programmes, and so on. Nevertheless, the ideal cycle gives us a standard against which to measure the adequacy of a particular approach to a problem. In the coming chapters we shall be able to judge how much progress has been made towards this ideal in various aspects of archaeological work. We shall see that in some areas one can benefit greatly by using a mathematical approach – interpreting dating evidence and distribution maps, for instance. In other areas there is still nothing to beat the practised eye of the experienced archaeologist – for example in the study of decorated samian pottery, where 'style' is so important. My aim is simply to show where mathematics can help.

CHAPTER TWO

What Is It?

Introduction – the need to classify

One might at first think that the question 'what is it?' in archaeology covered the same ground as 'what was it for?' In identifying artefacts (including structures), are we not trying to describe their function – a certain bronze object is an axe head, a certain pot is a cooking pot or a storage vessel, a certain structure is a kiln, and so on? A quick look at almost any major excavation report or work of archaeological synthesis will show that this is not the case. We soon find, not that 'an axe is an axe is an axe', but that there are flat axes, palstaves, socketed axes, winged axes and, in even more detail, we find 'Group I' to 'Group V' palstaves *(fig 2.1)*. Cooking pots are not just cooking pots, but 'Gillam 138' cooking pots, or whatever *(fig 2.2)*. The kilns, too, come in a surprising multiplicity of shapes – Musty type 1A, 1B, etc. *(fig 2.3)*.

Sometimes prosaic numbering systems are used, as by Gillam, and sometimes rather poetical names – Henshall divides Scottish passage graves into an Orkney-Cromarty-Hebridean (O-C-H) group, a Bargrennan group, a Clava group and a Maes Howe group – but the principle is much the same in each case.[1] A group of objects (or structures) with supposedly similar function has been divided up into sub-groups, generally (but not always – see chapter 4) according to their shape. Sometimes these sub-groups are called types, sometimes groups; if they are of pottery the word 'form' is often used (as in the well-known Dragendorff forms of samian pottery), while 'category' and 'class' also appear on occasions, often to denote rather broader groupings. In mathematical terms they would be called sub-sets. But whatever the label attached to them, these sub-sets seem to follow a common pattern: the objects in a sub-set are, in some way, like each other and, at the same time, unlike (or at least less like) objects in other sub-sets.

Reading more widely, one could soon gain the impression that

25

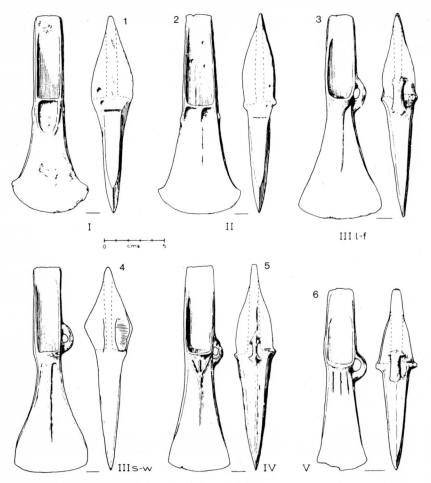

Fig 2.1　Example of different 'types' of an artefact, in this case Anglo-Welsh palstaves (bronze axes). *From Burgess (1974).*

archaeologists must spend much of their time dividing artefacts into sub-sets — in other words, classifying, or constructing typologies – or sorting artefacts into existing typologies. This impression would not be far from the truth – one estimate (probably exaggerated) is that 80 or 90% of an archaeologist's time is spend in classifying his material.[2]

Why, one might ask, do they bother? The cynic might see a sure route to a Ph.D. or a shortcut to immortality (what else did Dragendorff do? and where is Maes Howe?), but there must be more to classification than that. It must offer some advantage over, on the one

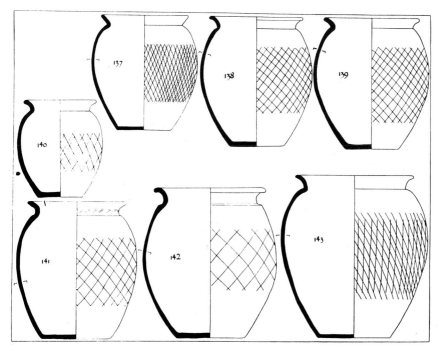

Fig 2.2   Example of different types of artefacts, in this case black-burnished ware
cooking pots. *From Gillam (1970).*

hand, a simple 'an axe is an axe is an axe' approach and, at the other
extreme, the consideration of every artefact as unique, distinct and
(however subtly) different from every other.

The first advantage is purely practical: if every object were treated
as unique, then in order for one archaeologist to convey to another
what he had found at a particular site, he would have to draw and/or
describe every object – every implement, every coin, every sherd of
pottery. Not only would the report consume a vast quantity of paper,
be terribly expensive to buy and incredibly boring to read, but it
would not, in fact, convey the information it set out to convey. The
information might be there, but it would not be conveyed to the
reader. There could be exceptions, of course – a site where every
artefact found really did differ from every other – but they would be
few and far between. Also, much of the information might not
actually be significant. For example, minor variations in the shape of
the rim of a pottery vessel may well simply reflect the variations that
are inevitable in a manual technology.[3] *Pl 3* shows a set of six hand-
made stoneware mugs purchased on one occasion from a craftsman in

27

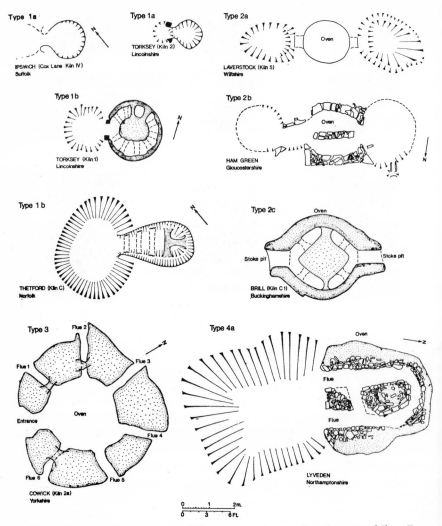

Fig 2.3 The idea of 'types' extended to structures – medieval pottery kilns. *From Musty (1973).*

Wales. There are appreciable differences in rim and handle form, but all were undeniably made by the same man in the same place over a very short period. There is clearly a danger of losing the wood for the trees.

The second advantage is more interesting. The archaeologist is concerned to detect patterns of various sorts: spatial or geographical patterns have been recognized as such for a long time and plotted as

28

Plate 3 Set of six 'identical' hand-thrown coffee mugs. Note the difference in height and diameter, and in the shape of rims, bases and handles.

distribution maps (which will be dealt with in chapters 4 and 7), but patterns in time have been treated less explicitly, perhaps because they are less easily visualized (see chapter 3). In both cases, the amount of useful information available to the reader has increased as techniques of presentation have improved. Distribution maps are progressing from the simple 'point' map, showing where artefacts of a certain type have been found (e.g. *fig 2.4*) to a more quantitative map, showing the proportion of artefacts of a certain type in assemblages at sites of the relevant period. A good example of the latter is a map by Fulford of the distribution of New Forest pottery in Southern England (*fig 2.5*). The traditional pattern in time is scarcely a pattern at all, but simply a statement of the likely date ranges of various 'types', perhaps with areas of uncertainty at each end, as in *fig 2.6*. Again, the trend is towards more quantitative representations, illustrated here (*fig 2.7*) by one of Fulford's results from his study of the Portchester Castle pottery. In all these cases, the breaking down of the material into types enables the archaeologist to make general statements which will be of use to other archaeologists, whether in dating particular artefacts or in studying possible patterns of trade or usage.

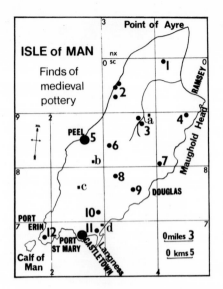

Fig 2.4 Example of simple 'point' type of distribution map,
showing find-spots of medieval pottery on the Isle
of Man. *From Garrard (1977).*

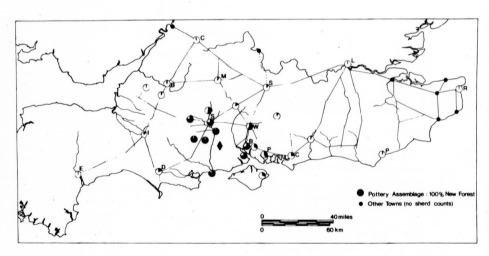

Fig 2.5 Example of a quantitative distribution map, showing proportions of
New Forest pottery at sites in Southern England. *From Fulford (1975).*

Fig 2.6 *Opposite:* Chart showing date ranges of various 'types' of pottery.
From Fulford (1975).

TYPE	275	300	325	350	375	400
1						
2						
3						
4						
5						
6						
7						
8						
9						
10						
11						
12						
13						
14						
15						
16						
17						
18						
19						
20						
21						
22						
23						
24						
25						
26						
27						
28						
29						
30						
31						
32						
33						
34						
35						
36						
37						
38						
39						
40						
41						
42						
43						
44						
45						
46						
47						
48						

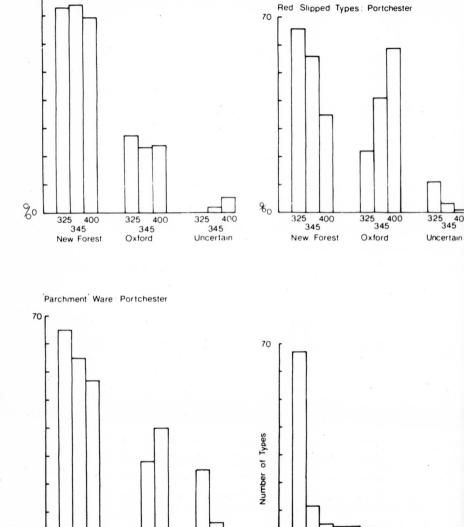

Fig 2.7 A more quantitative presentation, showing percentages of different types of pottery at different dates. *From Fulford (1975).*

Criteria – what makes a 'good' classification?

Whatever the needs, the archaeologist knows that he must have a good classification system if he is to obtain useful results. If pressed to explain what he means by 'good', he will probably produce a list of requirements something like the following:

(i) objects belonging to the same type should be alike in some way (the way will be specified: it might be shape, chemical composition or some other characteristic);

(ii) objects belonging to different types should as a rule be less alike than objects belonging to the same type (these two conditions are sometimes called the definition of a 'natural' classification);

(iii) the types should be properly defined, that is, if the work is repeated, the results obtained should be much the same (except perhaps for some borderline cases);

(iv) it should be possible to decide which type a new object (i.e., one that was not part of the original set used to define the types) belongs to, with relative ease.

The intuitive approach

In looking at ways in which objects can be classified, it is worthwhile keeping these objectives in mind. The traditional approach is for the archaeologist to organize his material by eye, perhaps by laying it out on large tables, or by laying out drawings of the objects, and moving them about into groups until he is reasonably satisfied. The type is then commonly defined as one object which appears representative of a small group of very similar objects. A good example is Gillam's classic work on Romano-British pottery, which illustrate 350 types of vessel, and gives the provenances of the actual type sherd and other examples of the same type in each case.[4] The intuitive approach often satisfies requirements (i) and (ii) – if the worker concerned is good at this sort of activity – but tends to fall down on (iii) and (iv): on (iii) because a different archaeologist, working on the same material, could get a different result, and on (iv) because the types are defined in terms of their centre or 'typical vessel' so that, presented with a new vessel, it is not easy to decide whether it is more like type X, and should be called 'X', or more like type Y and should be called 'Y'. Also, while this approach is quite successful in classifying shapes, it would not be so good for organizing numerical information, for example, the percentages of different trace elements in bronzes (see pp. 108–9).

An alternative approach, which satisfies (iv), is to define the types in terms of a simple numerical or geometric criterion. In mathematical terms these would be called the frontiers of the sub-sets. As an example I have chosen some of the definitions of classes of vessel employed by Webster:[5]

jar: 'vessel with constriction at the neck whose width is usually less than its height . . . This term in general excludes flagons and beakers'.

bowl: 'a neckless vessel, which can be conveniently defined as having a height more than one third but not greater than its diameter'.

dish: 'a shallow vessel, which can be conveniently defined as having a height less than a third of but greater than a seventh of its diameter'.

plate or platter: 'a shallow vessel, in height not greater than a seventh of its diameter'.

It is clear that a suitable vessel could be placed readily in one of these four classes by simply measuring its height and rim diameter, and dividing one by the other. More elegantly, an overlay in the form of fig 2.8 can be placed on a drawing of the vessel and its class read off, according to the sector in which the rim falls when the base is placed in the base line.★

In this case, the class is defined (at least in part) in terms of its frontiers. The question arises – having gained on (iv), have we lost

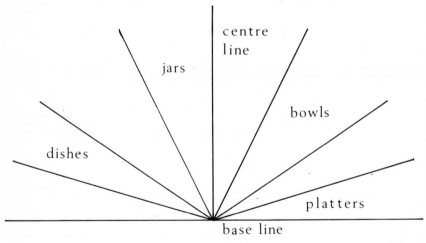

Fig 2.8   Simple template for assigning pottery vessel shapes to jar, bowl, dish or platter classes.

★I am grateful to Miss Alison Laws for this idea.

elsewhere? In particular, do we now have (for example) jars that look like bowls, or bowls that look like dishes? Fortunately, Gillam groups his types into classes which can be compared with Webster's definitions. *Fig 2.9* shows the rim diameter/height ratios of Gillam's jars, while *figs 2.10 and 2.11* do the same for his bowls and dishes.

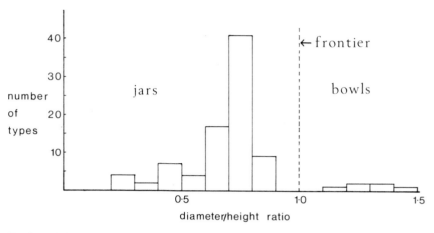

Fig 2.9 Histogram showing the rim diameter/height ratios of jar types in Gillam.

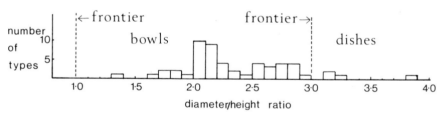

Fig 2.10 Histogram showing the rim diameter/height ratios of bowl types in Gillam.

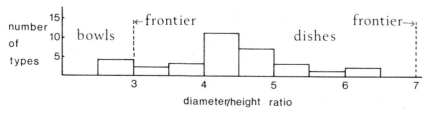

Fig 2.11 Histogram showing the rim diameter/height ratios of dish types in Gillam.

35

Fig 2.9 shows a good agreement between the two definitions, with only a few vessels lying outside the frontier. On examination, they are found to be 'wide-mouthed jars or bowls' (Gillam) which can be squeezed into Webster's 'jars' by suitable interpretation of the word 'usually' in his definition. The bowl/dish frontier is not so easy – four (out of nine) of Gillam's 'segmental bowls' stray across the frontier into the dish zone, while four of his 'dishes' err in the other direction. There does seem to be some splitting of natural groupings, but not much.

The mathematical approach

Why then, do we bother with mathematical approaches to this task? Why not just obtain an expert's view on the classification, study it to find where the frontiers are, and use them? There seem to be a number of reasons:

(i) Pot shapes are relatively simple. More complicated shapes, e.g. of metalwork, may not lend themselves so readily to an intuitive approach. A good example are the much-studied brooches from Münsingen, some of which are shown in *fig 2.12*. Imagine trying to find frontiers between these: and suppose there were 300 rather than thirty.

(ii) Of at least equal importance to the definition of types is some statement of the relationships between them. This is more difficult to achieve intuitively.

(iii) Since archaeologists are almost certain to disagree about definitions of types and relationships between them, it would be useful to be able to pin down the causes of such disagreements. One way of doing this is to use a method which is based on a set of explicit assumptions, but once started proceeds automatically – i.e. two archaeologists starting from the same premises will arrive at the same answer.

(iv) The business of classification is in fact a mathematical activity, whether or not this is explicitly expressed. What is going on is the partition of a set (e.g. of all Roman pots from Hadrian's Wall, or all brooches from Münsingen) into sub-sets according to certain criteria (see above). It seems sensible to make the mathematics explicit – and automatic – and to narrow down the areas of disagreement to a discussion of the characteristics that matter to a particular classification – is, for example, the length of the brooch's bar more/equally/less important than the number of coils in its spring? And why?

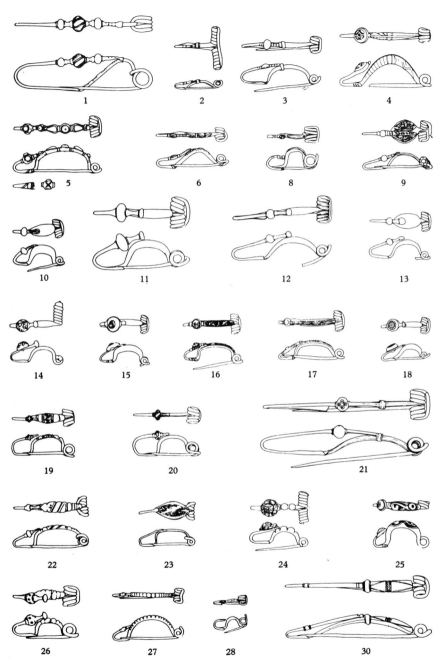

Fig 2.12 Some of the brooches from the much-studied Iron Age cemetery at Münsingen, used as data for experiments in classification. *From Hodson, Sneath and Doran (1966).*

37

A variety of mathematical techniques has been developed which have broadly the same function: given certain data, chosen by the archaeologists to represent the characteristics of the objects being studied, the technique operates on these data in order to display in a useful fashion the relationships between the objects – their similarities and dissimilarities. Before going on to look at some of these techniques it will be helpful to examine some of the ways in which the shape of an object can be represented in simple mathematical terms.

Describing the shape of an object in mathematical terms

The first way is as a number of key measurements. For example, Barker described the shape of an iron weapon point in terms of eleven measurements (*fig 2.13*). Densem, in a study of Roman spearheads, used seven measurements (*fig 2.14*), of which six are equivalent to those of Barker's measurements that are appropriate to spearheads (see *pl 4* for a 'typical' example). Barker suggests reducing all measurements to ratios by dividing them by total length, so making the numerical description more dependent on shape and less on sheer size. We shall meet Densem's spearheads later in this chapter. In a similar fashion, Roe has described hand-axes by a number of ratios (*fig 2.15*).

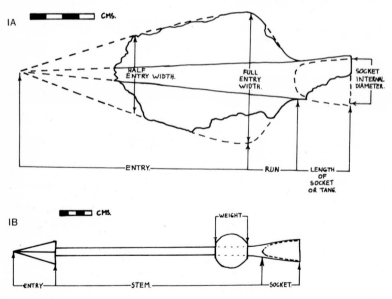

Fig 2.13   Measurements used to describe the shape of an iron weapon point. *From Barker (1975).*

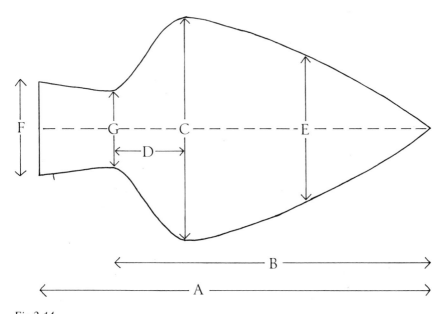

Fig 2.14
The seven measurements used by Densem
to describe the shape of Roman spearheads.
Key (Barker's terms in brackets):
A = total length (ditto)
B = length of head (length of run plus entry)
C = widest width of head (width at full entry)
D = distance from waist to widest width of
   blade (length of run)
E = width of blade halfway between tip and
   widest width (width at half entry)
F = socket diameter at mouth – external
   (ditto but internal)
G = measurement across waist (no equivalent)

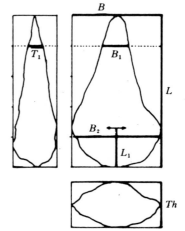

Fig 2.15 Ratios used to describe
shape of flint hand axe.
From Roe (1968).

Plate 4 Typical Roman spearhead.

Plate 5   Selection of Palaeolithic hand-axes from Yiewsley, Middlesex.

Ericson and Stickel suggested breaking down relatively complicated shapes (for example of a pot or metal vessel) into a set of simple
geometric shapes (*fig 2.16*). This could be useful if a numerical
interpretation of the shape could then be made, as has been done by
Shennan and Wilcock in two different ways. The 'sliced' method is
illustrated in *fig 2.17*, and the 'mosaic' method in *fig 2.18*. Both
methods can be used to describe the shape of a vessel with circular
symmetry to any required degree of accuracy, by taking thinner and
thinner slices or smaller and smaller sub-units. Asymmetric features –
like handles, spouts, feet – could cause problems.

These methods have all been used in more or less routine ways on
archaeological applications. Two promising methods which are not
(as far as I know) routine in archaeology are 'splines'[6] and
'linces',[7] both of which can be used to describe shapes of great
complexity. The former basically consists of approximating to a

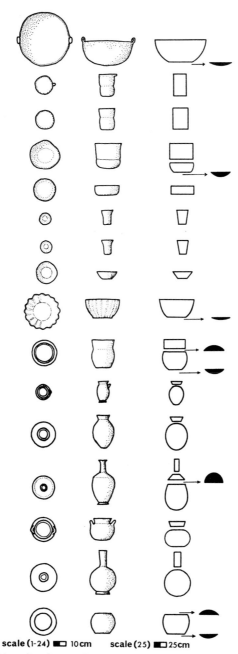

scale (1-24) ■◻ 10cm   **scale (25)** ■◻ 25cm

Fig 2.16 Describing the shape of a pottery vessel by breaking it down into a number of simple shapes. *From Ericson and Stickel (1973).*

41

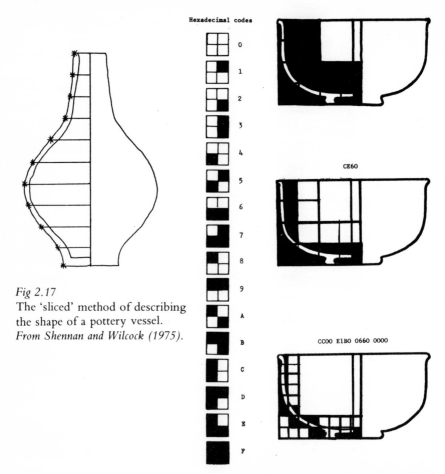

Hexadecimal codes

0
1
2
3
4

CE60

5
6
7
8
9
A

CCOO E1BO 0660 0000

B
C
D
E
F

Fig 2.17
The 'sliced' method of describing
the shape of a pottery vessel.
From Shennan and Wilcock (1975).

Fig 2.18 The 'mosaic' method of describing
the shape of a pottery vessel.
From Shennan and Wilcock (1975).

complex shape by a series of overlapping simple shapes, each of which can be represented by a mathematical equation. The latter is perhaps more elegant and certainly more difficult to explain. Essentially it transforms a complicated curve into a more simple one (and one therefore more suitable for numerical description) by relating its length and curvature.

In general, ratio-type methods are commonly used to describe shapes which do not possess circular symmetry (e.g. brooches, hand-axes), while more geometric methods can be used on the shapes that do (e.g. most pots).

Similarities between the shapes of different objects – the similarity (and dissimilarity) coefficient

Having described our set of objects in numerical fashion, what do we do with them? I have already mentioned (p 33) the requirement that objects belonging to the same type should be alike in some way, while objects belonging to different types should be less alike. What we need, then, is a way of measuring the 'alikeness' of two different objects. This measure is usually called a dissimilarity coefficient, and for a set of objects there will be a coefficient for each pair, measuring the dissimilarity between two objects forming the pair. Sometimes the exact opposite – a similarity coefficient – is calculated. Either coefficient can be used in practice: I have chosen to use the dissimilarity coefficient here, but the choice is arbitrary.

Many ways of calculating a similarity or dissimilarity coefficient have been devised, depending partly on the nature of the characteristics measured and partly on the precise demands that will be put on the coefficient. The distinction that will chiefly concern us now is that between coefficients based on the presence or absence of certain characteristics or attributes in the objects concerned – for example, a certain style of decoration (qualitative data) and the other on numerical values relating to the object (quantitative data). The latter can be further divided between discrete characteristics (for example, the number of coils in the spring of a brooch, which can take only one of a fixed number of values – 0, 1, 2, 3, etc.) and continuous characteristics (for example, the lengths and ratios in the above examples, which can take any value in a certain range). Various arguments have been put forward about the superiority of coefficients based on one or other of these sorts of data, but they seem in practice to miss the point, as in general an object may require all three sorts to describe it. The real problem is how to combine the three into one useful coefficient, and on this point there is no general agreement. The archaeologist is being asked by the mathematics to make explicit his value judgements which are usually either implicit or unrecognized – for example, how important in terms of similarity is the presence or absence of a certain attribute as compared with differences of 10%, 50% or 100% in a certain ratio? Certainly this is not an easy question to answer.

Other problems can arise from the often fragmentary nature of archaeological data. If (say) a particular characteristic is 'incised decoration on handle', how does one treat a pot whose handle is missing? If one chooses to ignore it, then one is throwing away a large proportion of one's data, because complete and perfect objects are relatively rare

ins
cm

Plate 6   Medieval bone comb. The classification of such objects is difficult because they are almost always found broken.

in archaeology. This problem has recently been studied by Galloway in the course of her work on medieval antler combs from Trondheim, Norway.[8]

The dissimilarity matrix

Let us suppose that the archaeologist somehow manages to overcome or avoid these problems, and calculates his dissimilarity coefficients. They are best displayed in the form of a dissimilarity matrix, a simple example of which is shown in *fig 2.19*. Here the coefficients have, for convenience, been converted to percentages – 100% indicating complete dissimilarity and 0% complete similarity. For example, the dissimilarity between objects 1 and 2 is 10%, while between 1 and 5 it is 60%. Two points are worth noting: (i) the coefficient between an object and itself is always 0% (but, depending on the coefficient used, the coefficient between two identical fragments might not be, since they might differ in the missing parts); (ii) the coefficient of dissimilarity between objects 1 and 2 is the same as that between 2 and 1. It is common to leave out the latter from a matrix because it tells us nothing more and only makes the matrix more difficult to read (compare *fig 2.19* with *fig 2.20*).

   In mathematical terms, the archaeologist has turned his amorphous set of objects into a space: the dissimilarities between them are

	1	2	3	4	5	6	7
1	0	10	20	35	60	60	70
2		0	15	40	65	70	70
3			0	50	70	75	80
4				0	30	40	45
5					0	5	20
6						0	20
7							0

Fig 2.19

	1	2	3	4	5	6	7
1	0	10	20	35	60	60	70
2	10	0	15	40	65	70	70
3	20	15	0	50	70	75	80
4	35	40	50	0	30	40	45
5	60	65	70	30	0	5	20
6	60	70	75	40	5	0	20
7	70	70	80	45	25	20	0

Fig 2.20

represented by distances between points in the space. Each object can be thought of as a point in a space, closer to objects which are more similar (that is which have lower dissimilarity coefficients) and further from objects which are less similar (i.e. which have higher dissimilarity coefficients). Among the objects represented in *fig 2.19*, the closest are 5 and 6 (dissimilarity coefficient 5%), the next closest are 1 and 2 (dissimilarity coefficient 10%), and so on. One can soon detect one close sub-set (1, 2, 3) and a second (5, 6, 7) and one rather isolated object (4). Of course, with only seven objects this is a rather trivial example – in practice one might be dealing with dozens or even thousands of objects.

One might at this point be tempted to think that all one has to do is to draw a map or plan of this space with all the objects plotted in as points, examine it and divide it up into the required types. This optimistic view is represented in *fig 2.21*. But real life is not so simple:

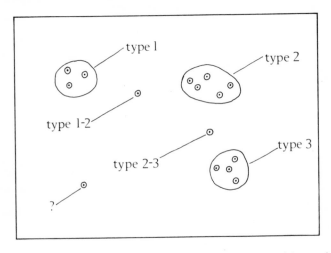

Fig 2.21   Optimistic idea: division of space into types by visual inspection.

if we actually try to draw such a map on a piece of paper, we find – usually at the fourth point – that the distances do not 'fit' or, in other words, the point does not lie on the page at all (try it on the coefficients in *fig 2.20*, using them as distances. 1 and 2 can be drawn in ten units apart; with a pair of compasses, 3 can be drawn in at a distance of 20 from 1 and 15 from 2, and 4 can be drawn in at 35 from 1 and 40 from 2, but its distance from 3 will *not* be 50 – see *fig. 2.22*). If, however, we allow point 4 to lie off the page, we can make all the distances fit – until, that is, we try to locate point 5 (the ambitious can try this as an experiment with small pieces of wood cut to length and stuck together to represent the distances). Clearly the space in which our objects lie cannot be visualized or used by the human mind without considerable simplification. The problem – one that has received much attention in recent years – is to simplify the picture into one that can be understood and used, while not distorting it so much that it becomes unreliable. Three groups of techniques have been developed to a useful level – (i) clustering methods, (ii) scaling methods, (iii) principal components. Each will be discussed below.

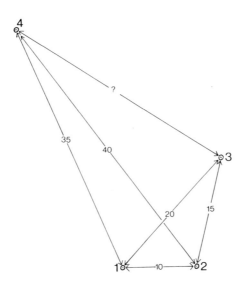

Fig 2.22
Attempt to represent
dissimilarities between
four objects as distances
between four points
on a 'map'.

(i) Clustering methods

The general idea behind this group of methods is to produce a sort of family tree or dendrogram of the objects concerned. In a dendrogram, similar objects appear on close branches of the tree, and dissimilar objects on widely separated branches.

There are many methods available: most work by forming small clusters of very similar objects, gradually merging them together to form larger and larger clusters of less and less similar objects. A particularly straightforward method is that known as single-link cluster analysis, which works as follows:

1. The dissimilarity matrix is searched for the smallest coefficient. The two objects to which it relates are grouped together in the first cluster.

2. The matrix is searched for the next smallest coefficient. If it is between one of the objects in the first cluster and a third object, that object joins the cluster. If it is between two objects, neither of which belongs to the first cluster, they are grouped together to form the second cluster.

3. As the next smallest, and then the next, coefficient is found, objects are added to clusters, or new clusters are formed. If the smallest coefficient is between one object in one cluster and one object in another cluster, then those two clusters are merged.

4. The procedure continues until the dendrogram is complete.

As a practical example, the dendrogram of the matrix shown in *fig 2.19* is drawn below:

	1	2	3	4	5	6	7
1	0	10	20	35	60	60	70
2		0	15	40	60	70	70
3			0	50	75	75	80
4				0	30	40	45
5					0	(5)	20
6						0	20
7							0

Fig. 2.23(a)

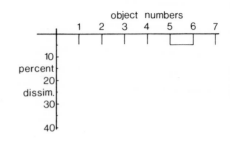

	1	2	3	4	5	6	7
1	0	(10)	20	35	60	60	70
2		0	15	40	60	70	70
3			0	50	75	75	80
4				0	30	40	45
5					0	(5)	20
6						0	20
7							0

Fig 2.23(b)

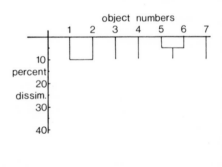

	1	2	3	4	5	6	7
1	0	(10)	20	35	60	60	70
2		0	(15)	40	60	70	70
3			0	50	75	75	80
4				0	30	40	45
5					0	(5)	20
6						0	20
7							0

Fig 2.23(c)

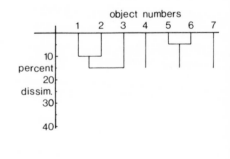

	1	2	3	4	5	6	7
1	0	(10)	(20)	35	60	60	70
2		0	(15)	40	60	70	70
3			0	50	75	75	80
4				0	30	40	45
5					0	(5)	(20)
6						0	(20)
7							0

Fig 2.23(d)

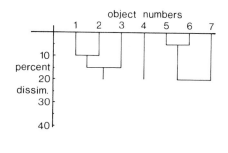

	1	2	3	4	5	6	7
1	0	(10)	(20)	35	60	60	70
2		0	(15)	40	60	70	70
3			0	50	75	75	80
4				0	(30)	40	45
5					0	(5)	(20)
6						0	(20)
7							0

Fig 2.23(e)

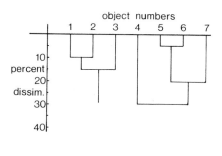

	1	2	3	4	5	6	7
1	0	(10)	(20)	(35)	60	60	70
2		0	(15)	40	60	70	70
3			0	50	75	75	80
4				0	(30)	40	45
5					0	(5)	(20)
6						0	(20)
7							0

Fig 2.23(f)

The main drawback is fairly easy to see: objects 1, 2, 3 are all dissimilar to objects 5, 6, 7 (the smallest coefficient is 60%), and yet they all belong to the same cluster at a dissimilarity coefficient of only 35%, via the intermediate object no. 4. This may not be serious in this simple example, but in a larger problem (perhaps one in which these objects were just a small part) this phenomenon of chaining, as it is called, can cause serious difficulties.

There are various ways of overcoming this difficulty: an object might be required to have a certain dissimilarity coefficient with two objects in a cluster before it joined that cluster (double-link), or with all objects in the cluster (total link). One method that has been much used is to require the average coefficient to have a certain value (average link). This requires more computation, as the following example (based again on *fig 2.19*) shows. On the other hand, the dendrogram appears to represent the situation better.

	1	2	3	4	5	6	7
1	0	10	20	35	60	60	70
2		0	15	40	60	70	70
3			0	50	75	75	80
4				0	30	40	45
5					0	(5)	20
6						0	20
7							0

Fig 2.24(a)

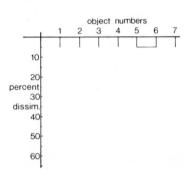

	1	2	3	4	(5,6)	7
1	0	(10)	20	35	60	70
2		0	15	40	65	70
3			0	50	75	80
4				0	35	45
(5,6)						20
7						0

Fig 2.24(b)

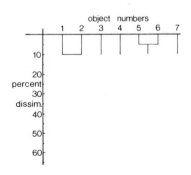

	(1,2)	3	4	(5,6)	7
(1,2)		(17.5)	37.5	62.5	70
3			0	50	75	80
4				0	35	45
(5,6)						20
7						0

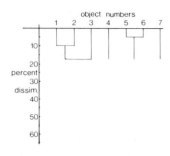

Fig 2.24(c)

	(1,2,3)	4	(5,6)	7
(1,2,3)		41.7	66.7	73.3
4			35	45
(5,6)				(20)
7				0

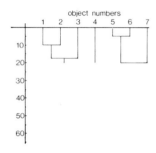

Fig 2.24(d)

	(1,2,3)	4	(5,6,7)
(1,2,3)		41.7	68.9
4		0	(38.3)
(5,6,7)			

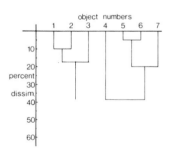

Fig 2.24(e)

	(1,2,3)	(4,5,6,7)
(1,2,3)		62.2
(4,5,6,7)		

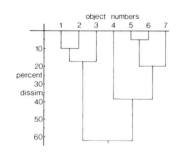

Fig 2.24(f)

Although the order of clustering is in this case the same, the dendrogram gives a much more realistic picture of the relationship between the objects: (1, 2, 3) form a 'tight' cluster, as do (5, 6, 7). No. 4 is probably an intermediate object, and clustering is not completed until a dissimilarity level of over 60% is reached.

In an early paper on the subject, Hodson, Doran and Sneath compared these two methods on a sample of seventy brooches from Münsingen, and concluded that the average-link method had produced groups of archaeological significance, while the single link had not.[9] The main drawback to cluster analysis apparent at that time was the amount of computer storage space occupied by a dissimilarity matrix – for example, 100 objects need about 5000 coefficients, while 500 objects need 250,000 coefficients, each of which has to be stored individually – an enormous amount of computer storage then, and even today.

However, a more fundamental objection to average-link cluster analysis was raised by Jardine et al.[10] They pointed out an important theoretical difficulty: in mathematical language, the technique was 'discontinuous', meaning that a small change in one of the coefficients could affect the dendrogram, not only in the immediate vicinity of the two objects, but also in some circumstances right across the pattern. This is an undesirable characteristic, especially as the question of the best choice of coefficient has still not been settled. Two ways of calculating the coefficients might give very similar similarity matrices and yet rather different dendrograms. The single-link method did not suffer from this theoretical disadvantage, but had already been rejected as being of little practical use in archaeology. The Jardine paper marks something of a turning-point – moving away from average-link methods to newer methods that would be both more acceptable to the mathematicians and if possible less heavy in their demands on computer space and time, while retaining their usefulness to the archaeologist.

The most successful of these methods has become known as the 'k-means' technique, the first archaeological application of which appeared in a paper by Hodson in 1970, where it was tried out experimentally on small sets of test data. Further experiments were published in the following year and the technique now seems well established.[11] It differs from both single- and average-link cluster analysis in that it splits up one initial cluster (containing all objects) into a specified number (k) of clusters, producing an answer which approximates to the 'best' division into that number of clusters ('best' according to the criteria set out on p. 33). The answer is approximate because to find the absolutely best division (which could be done, by trial and error) would take a very long time, even on a computer. However, experience indicates that it is likely to be a good approximation. The actual procedure appears much more complicated than single-link or even average-link cluster analysis.[12] To the computer it has one enormous advantage – it makes it unnecessary to store the distance (or similarity coefficient) between every pair of objects, since the computer can calculate the distances it actually needs (e.g., between one object and the centre of a cluster) as and when it needs them. This frees a great deal of storage space and allows more objects to be handled at once.

The end product is a series of divisions of the objects into approximately the best two clusters, the best three clusters, and so on up to the maximum number likely to be required. Because the different clusterings are done independently there is no reason why two objects which belong to the same cluster when there are, say, four clusters, should still belong to the same cluster when there are only three. For this reason the results cannot usefully be expressed as a dendrogram.

A simpler approach is just to list the membership of each set of clusters, and to show how cohesive the best clusters actually are, by means of a graph showing the 'percentage error of fit' for two clusters, three clusters, and so on. The percentage error of fit is simply the average (squared) distance of the objects from the centres of their respective clusters, expressed as a percentage of their average (squared) distance from the centre of the whole group of objects, thought of as one single cluster. This has a value of 100% when there is only one cluster, and decreases as the number of clusters is increased.

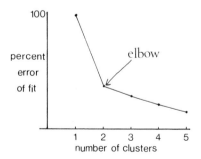

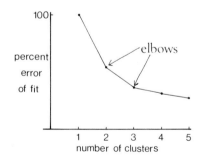

Fig 2.25
Graph of percentage error of fit for one, two, three, four and five clusters. 'Elbow' at 2 clusters.

Fig 2.26
Graph of percentage error of fit for one, two, three, four and five clusters. 'Elbows' at 2 and 3 clusters.

If, for example, there were really only two clearly distinct clusters, the percentage error of fit would drop sharply between one cluster and two, and slowly for three, four or more clusters (see *fig. 2.25*), while if there were three, it would drop sharply between one and two, and again between two and three clusters, and very slowly for four or more clusters (see *fig. 2.26*). As can be seen from *figs 2.25* and *2.26*, there is a distinct 'elbow' in the graph when the right number of clusters is reached (if there is a right number). This graph is therefore a very useful diagnostic tool – it can tell us whether the data are really suitable for clustering at all, and if so, the number of clusters that there should be.

This technique has so far proved to be the most successful for classifying individual objects.

A practical example – classifying Roman spearheads

An example, a dendrogram of Densem's Roman spearheads, is shown as *fig 2.27*. How does one 'read' this illustration? It is clear first

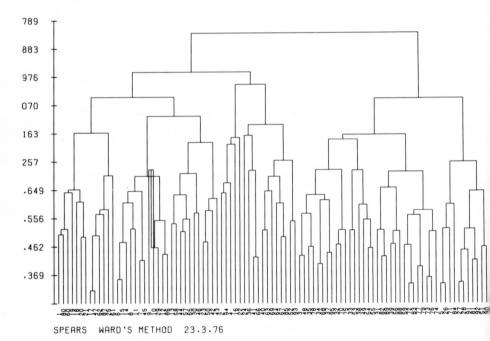

SPEARS   WARD'S METHOD   23.3.76

Fig 2.27   Example of a dendrogram, grouping Roman spearheads according to their shape. *From Densem (unpublished).*

of all that certain pairs of spearheads must be similar to each other – e.g. 17 and 47, 6 and 15, 72 and 83, and that some are not very similar to any others, e.g. 16, 22, 24. Working down from the top, rather than up from the bottom, we can see that there is first a division into two groups – 1 to 93 and 3 to 90; the first then splits into two – 1 to 43 and 2 to 93, and so on. But how do we choose the groups that will be our types? One way would be to choose a certain number of types, say five, and move down the dendrogram until it has just five branches, which would then form the types (in this example, they are 1 to 61, 6 to 43, 2 to 22, 24 to 93 and 3 to 90). The result can be checked by sliding a ruler down the figure until exactly five branches can be seen. Alternatively, we might choose what appear to be good clusters (thus substituting mathematical for archaeological intuition). A 'good' cluster would seem to be one whose objects come together well down the dendrogram (i.e. they are reasonably similar), but which does not join with another cluster until well up the dendrogram (i.e. the objects are not very similar to objects in other clusters). Taken together, these two requirements point to clusters with long 'stalks' – for example, 5 to 90 or 6 to 86, but not 3 to 55. Using this intuitive approach, one might be satisfied with seven clusters – 1 to 61, 6 to 86, 13 to 43, 2 to 22, 24 to 93, 3 to 74 and 5 to 90. No way of dividing them up will be completely satisfactory. In other words, the objects do not necessarily fall into neat clusters, although we can always create clusters if we want to. A check on the validity of our clusters is therefore valuable – perhaps a visual check or perhaps another mathematical technique, looking at the data in a different way.

An alternative approach – multidimensional scaling

We have already seen (p 46) that we cannot in general draw a 'map' of the objects, with their dissimilarities represented by distances – they simply do not fit. But suppose we were prepared to tolerate some distortion in the distances, could we then make them fit? That all depends, one might reply, on what distortions we are asked to accept. It has been suggested that one might be prepared to accept a distortion which would preserve the rank-order of the distances, that is if the dissimilarity between objects 1 and 2 is greater than that between 2 and 3, then the distance between 1 and 2 on our 'map' should be greater than the distance between 2 and 3 on the map, and so on for every possible pair of objects.[13] It may be necessary to distort even the rank-order to make the points representing the objects fit our map – the measure of distortion necessary is known as 'strain'. The technique proposed was called multi-dimensional scaling (MDSCAL, or 'mud-scale' for short) and was first applied in psychology. An early archaeological application concerned the brooches from Münsingen already mentioned.[14] A sample of thirty brooches was studied and the results presented as two- and one-dimensional maps (*fig 2.28*). The map indicates possible trends as well as clustering relationships, and the report concluded that 'the computed configurations come out as well or better than the best of the intuitive analyses'. This technique does, however, demand much computer time if more than a small number of objects are studied.

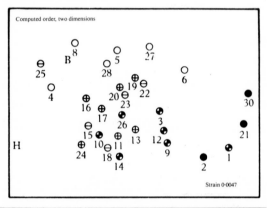

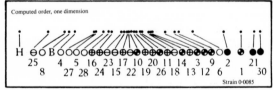

Fig 2.28   An application of MDSCAL to archaeology. 'Maps' showing the similarities between the thirty brooches illustrated in Fig 2.12. *From Hodson, Sneath and Doran (1966).*

Many archaeological applications of MDSCAL have followed, on topics as diverse as microlithic assemblages[15] and Central German bell beakers.[16]

Principal components analysis

A useful auxiliary technique is that known as principal compo-nents analysis (p.c.a.). The idea behind this technique is to find which variable (or combination of variables) contributes most to the variabil-ity between the objects under study – this is known as the first principal component. The combination of variables contributing most to the variability after allowing for the first p.c. is called the second p.c., and so on. There are as many p.c.s as there are variables, but it is often found that most of the variability is contributed by only the first few principal components.

In Densem's work on Roman spearheads, p.c.a. was used to throw light on the results of the cluster analysis. The daunting results are shown in *fig 2.29*.

The first table shows the correlations between the seven measure-

Numerical variable correlations

	1	2	3	4	5	6	7
1	1.0	0.98	0.53	0.65	0.50	0.49	0.46
2		1.0	0.53	0.67	0.47	0.41	0.41
3			1.0	0.49	0.91	0.69	0.75
4				1.0	0.48	0.28	0.31
5					1.0	0.64	0.73
6						1.0	0.84
7							1.0

Percentage variance

64.4	19.0	8.2	4.8	2.2	1.3	0.2

Cumulative variance

64.4	83.4	91.6	96.4	98.5	99.8	100

Eigenvectors – by rows

Vector 1	0.38	0.37	0.42	0.32	0.40	0.37	0.38
Vector 2	−0.43	−0.48	0.23	−0.43	0.25	0.36	0.40
Vector 3	0.34	0.27	−0.34	−0.50	−0.45	0.44	0.23
Vector 4	−0.20	−0.28	−0.32	0.68	−0.33	0.39	0.23
Vector 5	−0.10	0.07	−0.17	0.01	−0.06	−0.61	0.77
Vector 6	0.17	−0.11	−0.71	−0.02	0.67	0.06	−0.04
Vector 7	−0.70	0.68	−0.16	−0.00	0.11	0.11	−0.01

Fig 2.29

ments or variables. For example, there are very high correlations between variables 1 and 2 (total length and length of head), and between variables 3 and 5 (widest width and width halfway between top and widest width) – correlations that one might guess anyway – and most correlations are fairly large. The smallest correlations are between variable 4 (distance from waist to widest width) and 6 (socket diameter) or 7 (measurement across waist).

We next see that 64.4% of the variability between the spearheads is contributed by the first principal component, which from the bottom table we see is made up from

0.38 × variable 1 + 0.37 × variable 2 + 0.42 × variable 3 + 0.32 × variable 4 + 0.40 × variable 5 + 0.37 × variable 6 + 0.38 × variable 7.

What does this mean? The first p.c. consists of almost equal parts of each variable, so it must represent overall size, with large examples at one end of the scale and small examples at the other.

Similarly, 19% of the variability is contributed by the second p.c., which is

−0.43 × variable 1 −0.48 × variable 2 + 0.23 × variable 3 −0.43 × variable 4 + 0.25 × variable 5 + 0.36 × variable 6 + 0.40 × variable 7.

Picking this component to pieces, we note that it consists of negative contributions from variables 1, 2, 4 (all lengths) and positive contributions from variables 3, 5, 6, 7 (all widths), suggesting that it represents a general width/length ratio. Short wide spearheads would score highly on this component and long thin ones lowly.

A further 8% comes from the third p.c.:

0.34 × variable 1 + 0.27 × variable 2 −0.34 × variable 3 −0.50 × variable 4 −0.45 × variable 5 + 0.44 × variable 6 + 0.23 × variable 7.

This is more difficult to interpret, but positive contributions from overall and head length, and socket and waist diameter, and negative contributions from widest width, distance from widest width to waist and width halfway between tip and widest width, indicates a sort of 'pointedness' variable. Examples of spearheads with high and low values on each of the three first p.c.s are shown in *figs 2.30, 2.31* and *2.32*. Between them these three components account for nearly 92% of the variability. The remaining components, apart from contributing little to the overall variability, are very hard to interpret.

A way of checking these conclusions is to draw examples of spearheads with high and low values on each of the first three principal components. *Figs 2.30–2.32* show examples of these.

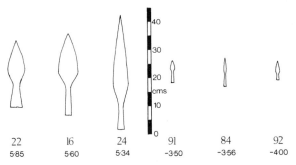

Fig 2.30   Outlines of spearheads with the three highest and three lowest values of the first principal component (representing overall size). Value of component given below spearhead number.

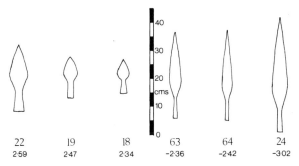

Fig 2.31   Outlines of spearheads with the three highest and three lowest values of the second principal component (representing width/length ratio). Value of component given below spearhead number.

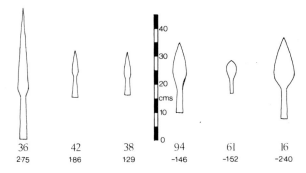

Fig 2.32   Outlines of spearheads with the three highest and three lowest values of the third principal component (representing 'pointedness'). Value of component given below spearhead number.

59

These illustrations certainly help us to understand the nature of the possible variations in shape – from large to small (*fig 2.30*), from short and wide to long and thin (*fig 2.31*) and from 'pointed' to 'blunt' (*fig 2.32*). Can they also help us understand the nature of the clusters we have discovered?

To answer this, I drew up the following table (*fig 2.33*), which shows the highest and lowest values of each principal component in each cluster defined on p 55. These results are presented in a more visual form in *fig 2.34* (compare this with the dendrogram *fig 2.27*).

cluster	1		2		3	
spearhead numbers	1–61		6–86		13–43	
principal components	max	min	max	min	max	min
1	2.29	−0.42	0.96	−0.01	2.31	−0.(
2	2.47	0.55	−0.13	−1.15	1.00	−1.(
3	1.88	−1.52	0.77	−0.65	1.86	0.⁴

Fig 2.33

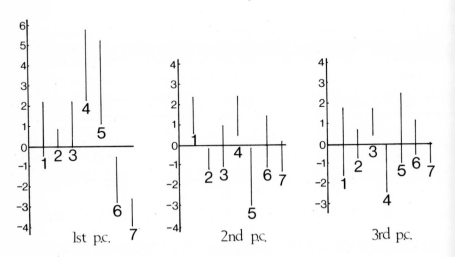

Fig 2.34 Ranges of values of principal components for spearheads in clusters 1, 2 . . . 7, for first, second and third principal components.

We can see from *fig 2.34* that we have two clusters of very large spearheads (Nos. 4 and 5), three of large spearheads (Nos. 1, 2 and 3), one of small (No. 6) and one of very small (No. 7) spearheads, and that size (the first principal component) seems to be the most important factor in distinguishing the clusters, because there is less overlap between the different ranges for this component than for either of the others. The second and third p.c.s distinguish well between clusters 4 and 5 – spearheads in 4 are broad and blunt. The distinctions between 1, 2 and 3 are less clear cut, but in general terms 1 seems to

4		5		6		7	
2–22		24–93		3–74		5–90	
ax	min	max	min	max	min	max	min
.85	2.27	5.34	1.08	−0.47	−2.85	−2.60	−4.00
.59	0.44	−0.04	−3.02	1.52	−1.09	0.22	−1.36
.05	−2.40	2.75	−0.91	1.29	−0.55	0.08	−0.93

consist of broader spearheads than 2 or 3, but 2 and 3 overlap considerably on all three components. *Fig 2.23* shows that 2 and 3 are in fact the most similar of all our clusters, so one could make a case for merging them together.

Given a table showing the principal component values of *all* spearheads (which is too long to publish here), one could work through the whole dendrogram in this way, deciding just why each division occurs where it does. However, a return to archaeological reality is needed now – having seen how different mathematical approaches relate to each other, how do they relate to the archaeological facts?

As well as the shape of each spearhead, Densem recorded (i) its supposed date, (ii) its find-spot, (iii) the nature of the military unit with which it was thought to be associated (if known). To make comparisons between the clusters easier, I then coded these as follows:

(i) date: according to century

(ii) find-spot: 1 = Scotland and Hadrian's Wall; 2 = other N. England; 3 = Midlands; 4 = Wales; 5 = S.W. England; 6 = S.E. England.

(iii) military association: 1 = legionary; 2 = auxiliary ala; 3 = auxiliary part-mounted unit; 4 = auxiliary infantry.

The results are presented in tabular form in *fig 2.35*, showing numbers of spearheads coded to each category (note: some are coded half-and-half to two categories, e.g. first–second century; some are not coded at all because of unknown date, etc.).

It is difficult to make a statistical comment on either (a) or (c), because of the high proportion of uncoded spearheads, which could belong to any of the other columns of the tables. Certain patterns are however apparent in (a) – clusters 3 and 5 seem to be relatively early for instance, but clusters 2 and 7, which might appear to be late, have too many uncoded spearheads for comments to be made with safety. In (c), the numbers in columns 3 and 4 are too small to comment on, and in general the high proportion of uncoded spearheads makes it difficult to say anything about this table.

In (b) we are on surer ground – all the spearheads have a find-spot and regional patterns can be seen – notably concentrations of cluster 2 in Wales, cluster 3 in S.W. England and cluster 7 in S.E. England. But even these apparent patterns are not statistically significant, i.e. they could simply reflect the fact that these ninety-four spearheads are only a small sample of all spearheads found and to be found.

To sum up, the cluster analysis has produced a pattern that suggests a division into 6 or 7 clusters would be reasonable. The main factor in this division appears to be overall size, with breadth/length and pointedness/bluntness as secondary factors. The clusters can be roughly described as

1   : fairly large, broad
2/3 : fairly large, moderate shape
4   : very large, broad, blunt
5   : very large, narrow, sharp
6   : small, moderate shape
7   : very small, fairly narrow and blunt.

There is however no strong correlation between the clusters and the recorded archaeological information about the spears. The clusters, although useful for descriptive purposes, do not seem to be analytically useful – i.e. they do not raise questions which could lead to fruitful developments.

Conclusion

We have seen that archaeologists can spend a great deal of their time in classifying artefacts, which is essentially a mathematical activity – or rather two activities, one of which is mathematical. Firstly, the archaeologist must decide what is important for the task in hand – for

		century					
		1st	2nd	3rd	4th	not coded	total
	1	1½	5½	2½	½	3	13
	2	1	1	4	—	5	11
	3	8	—	—	1	2	11
cluster	4	—	3	1	—	1	5
	5	8½	½	—	1	2	12
	6	18½	3½	2	1	6	31
	7	1	1	—	2	7	11
	total	38½	14½	9½	5½	26	94

Fig 2.35(a)

		region						
		1	2	3	4	5	6	total
	1	5	—	—	5	1	2	13
	2	—	—	—	8	2	1	11
	3	1	—	2	2	6	1	11
cluster	4	1	—	—	3	—	1	5
	5	6	—	—	—	3	3	12
	6	9	—	5	3	7	7	31
	7	3	3	—	—	—	5	11
	total	25	3	7	21	19	19	94

Fig 2.35(b)

		military association					
		1	2	3	4	not coded	total
	1	7	2	1	1	2	13
	2	9½	½	—	—	1	11
	3	4	3	—	1	3	11
cluster	4	2	1	—	—	2	5
	5	4½	3½	—	—	4	12
	6	13½	9½	—	1	7	31
	7	4	1	½	½	5	11
	total	44½	20½	1½	3½	24	94

Fig 2.35 (c)

example, is a difference in size more or less important than a difference in shape? – and secondly, the space of the objects under study must be divided up into sub-units (types, classes or whatever) so as to meet certain criteria necessary for a good sub-division. The first task is pure archaeology and the second is mathematics, and there are advantages in treating them as such. Of course, the outcome of the second may not be entirely to the archaeologist's liking – as in the example of the spearheads – in which case he can adjust his ideas and try again. For example, one might decide that too much emphasis had been placed on size in classifying the spearheads. In this way, the neutrality of the mathematics forces the archaeologist to examine and re-assess his basic assumptions very carefully, while carrying out the purely automatic aspects of the task with a minimum of fuss. The use of a computer may speed the work, but it is by no means essential, unless particularly sophisticated techniques are requested. In fact an *interactive cycle* is built up, with the problem moving back and forth between the archaeology and the mathematics, until (one hopes) a solution is reached. Neither can function without the other – the average (or any?) archaeologist does not possess the geometrical intuition needed to perform the mathematical parts of the task, while unthinking application of numerical techniques will merely confirm the computer man's saying 'garbage in, garbage out'.

Work on devising and assessing the necessary mathematical techniques continues but much progress has been made. The various clustering techniques have suffered from their tendency to create clusters which may or may not really exist: the most recent development, the k-means method, contains a useful internal check on the 'naturalness' of the clusters. The MDSCAL technique provides a result which may be more readily grasped by some users (depending on their geometrical/algebraic intuition), but is expensive in terms of computer time. Various ancillary techniques – for example, principal components analysis – may help us to understand better the underlying structure of the problem, and so come to a better interpretation of the results.

1. *Henshall 1974*, 148–55
2. *Chang 1967*, 71
3. *Young 1973*, 109
4. *Gillam 1970*
5. *Webster 1976*
6. *Boneva, Kendall and Stefanov 1971*
7. *Biek 1976*, 69
8. *Galloway 1976*
9. *Hodson, Sneath and Doran 1966*
10. *Jardine, Jardine and Sibson 1967*
11. *Hodson 1971*
12. *Doran and Hodson 1975*, 180–4
13. *Shepard 1963; Kruskal 1964*
14. *Hodson, Sneath and Doran 1966*
15. *Bonsall and Leach 1974*
16. *Shennan and Wilcock 1975*

CHAPTER THREE

How Old Is It?

Introduction – relative and absolute dating

'How old is it?' is a question frequently asked on archaeological sites, usually by members of the public and often followed by the corollary – 'How do you know?' Not only the public but also archaeologists occupy themselves with these questions, though in the latter case the motivation is something deeper than curiosity. The writing of history requires a knowledge of the chronology of the events that are being studied, so that cause and effect can be assessed, the spread of influence or fashion traced out, and so on. Archaeology too needs to operate within a timetable of past events, although the events may be of a different nature; for example an invasion may perhaps be mirrored by technological changes rather than accounts of battles. Sir Mortimer Wheeler put the point well when, in *Archaeology from the Earth*, he stressed the need for archaeologists to work towards a 'Bradshaw' of the past.[1] More recently, archaeology has been described as the study of change in 'the laboratory of the past', the idea apparently being that waiting for change to happen in order to study it is too slow a process, so why not use the thousands of years of change that have already taken place?[2] This may be an extreme view, but certainly change is of burning interest to archaeologists – for some views it is worth dipping into the proceedings of a recent conference on the subject.[3] Not only the direction of change is important but also its speed, which may mark the difference between a stagnating, slowly developing society and one in which innovation is rapid.

From all quarters, then, we hear the cry for Bradshaw. But how is Bradshaw to be written? The answer is slowly: by the gradual piecing together of information of different sorts from different sites into a coherent and cumulative pattern. The evidence can be divided into (a) evidence relating to objects – pottery, iron, bone, etc., and (b) evidence relating to archaeological contexts – walls, floor, pit fills, etc., and also into (i) relative dating evidence – one object or context is later than another, (ii) absolute dating evidence – the date of an object or context is such-and-such. The latter can be subdivided into 'internal' methods, where the evidence comes from within the object or context itself (e.g. radiocarbon dating) and 'external' methods, where the evidence comes from the object's (or context's) relationship with other objects and/or contexts (e.g. the use of samian for dating associated finds). Most problems are approached via a combination of these sorts of evidence: nevertheless, it is important to consider them separately and to combine the evidence systematically, or confusion and contradiction can easily arise.

In this chapter we shall proceed as follows:

1. relative dating of archaeological contexts (better known as stratigraphy).
2. relative dating of contexts and objects together (seriation).
3. absolute dating by 'internal' (scientific) methods.
4. 'external' dating and the expression of results.

1 STRATIGRAPHY

Archaeological (as opposed to geological) stratigraphy has been put on a systematic basis surprisingly recently. Although an implicit understanding of the principles of stratigraphy is apparent in the work of many archaeologists back at least to Meadows Taylor in 1851, for an explicit statement of these principles we have to look to more recent work, much of which has been done by E. Harris at Winchester. He describes contexts (or layers) as the smallest unit of archaeological identification, possessing three spatial dimensions (length, width and height or thickness) and a time dimension. The last may need to be explained: just as a layer has a beginning and an end in space (e.g. most southerly and most northerly points, or highest and lowest points), so it has a beginning and an end in time. They might be the times at which it started and finished accumulating, or, in the case of a negative feature like a pit (not the fill of the pit, but the pit itself), the time it was dug and the time it was filled in. These give the context its temporal dimension.

Harris goes on to express the startlingly obvious: the direct (time) relationship between two layers, say 1 and 2, can be expressed in one of only four ways:

(i) 1 is later than (above) 2
(ii) 1 is earlier than (below) 2
(iii) 1 and 2 are contemporary
(iv) there is no direct relationship between 1 and 2.

These four situations can be represented symbolically as in *fig 3.1*.

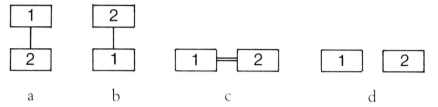

| a | b | c | d |

Fig 3.1   Representations of the four possible direct relationships between two
layers, 1 and 2:
(a) 1 is later than 2
(b) 1 is earlier than 2
(c) 1 and 2 are contemporary
(d) no direct relationship between 1 and 2

The mathematician pricks up his ears at this point, because, as he
will be quick to point out, these relationships means that the layers of a
site form what he would call a partially ordered set, or lattice.[4] This
being so, a great deal of the theory about the relationships (direct and
indirect) between the contexts can be adapted from the corresponding
mathematical theory.

First, though, the direct relationships must be right. Every direct
relationship between one context and another must be observed and
recorded if the stratigraphic sequence is to be correctly constructed. If
also contoured plans of the top of every layer are drawn, the site can be
reconstructed and, in effect, re-excavated. Easy enough to say, but in
practice there are always problems – where exactly does one layer end
and the next start? Or, the relationship has been destroyed by a later
intrusion that cuts both layers; or 'it's in the baulk!' Some can be
overcome by improvements in excavating technique, but some will
remain and give an air of uncertainty to the stratigraphy in places. For
the time being, however, we shall assume that these problems can be
solved and the relationships accurately determined. The problem of
uncertainty, or fuzziness, will be met again in chapter 9.

Using common sense, or the rules governing partially ordered
sets, we can start to put together our observed direct relationships into
one master stratigraphic sequence. The rules are very simple:

(i) transitive relationships: 1 later than 2 and 2 later than 3 implies 1
later than 3.

(ii) antisymmetric relationships: 1 later than 2 and 2 later than 1
implies 1 and 2 contemporary.

These, and other ways of combining information, are shown in *fig 3.2*.

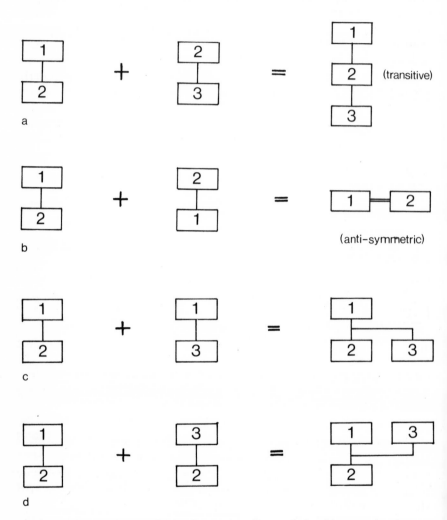

Fig 3.2 Representations of rules for putting direct relationships together into one sequence.
(a) 1 is later than 2 *and* 2 is later than 3 *implies* 1 is later than 2 is later than 3.
(b) 1 is later than 2 *and* 2 is later than 1 *implies* 1 and 2 are contemporary.
(c) 1 is later than 2 *and* 1 is later than 3.
(d) 1 is later than 2 *and* 3 is later than 2.

Fig. 3.2(c) shows how the relationship '1 is later than both 2 and 3' is expressed, while *fig 3.2(d)* shows '1 and 3 are both later than 2'. From these simple rules for adding together observed relationships, a stratigraphic sequence covering the whole site can be pieced together. One has to be careful with the more complicated relationships; for example, *fig 3.3(a)* shows the incorrect addition of two relationships and *fig 3.3(b)* their correct addition, because the right-hand side implies that 2 is later than 4, which information is not contained in the left-hand side, and need not be true.

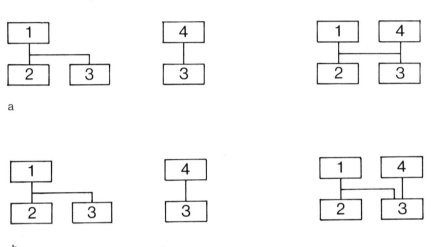

a

b

Fig 3.3   Representation of putting together 1 is later than 2 and 3 *and* 4 is later than 3.
(a) incorrect
(b) correct

In this way one can, step by step, build up a picture of the stratigraphy of a whole site, with no more equipment than patience, pencil, rubber and a large sheet of paper (provided that the direct relationships were correctly recorded at the time of excavation). It should also be apparent that, unless the direct relationships are recorded while excavation is in progress, they cannot be recovered afterwards. The complete picture is known as the sequence diagram, or Harris matrix, although the latter is a misnomer: strictly speaking it is a lattice, and it is certainly not a matrix. Examples of the sequence diagram of a simple site (Burleigh Avenue)[5] and a more complex site (Billingsgate Building)[6] are shown in *figs 3.4* and *3.5* respectively. In each case they are compared with the main section of the site.

Fig 3.4 shows that, for a simple site like this one, there is little to be gained by presenting the stratigraphic sequence in diagrammatic form: a few layers that do not appear in the section are 'captured', but some immediacy is lost. The sequence diagram does however high-light some stratigraphic questions – where in the sequence do layers 16 and (in particular) 7 and 17, belong? All we know about the latter two is that they lie above 5 and below 3, 2 and 1.

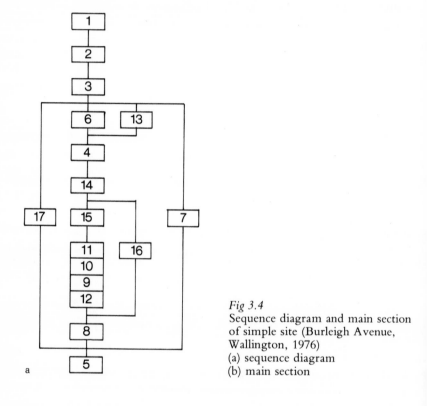

Fig 3.4
Sequence diagram and main section of simple site (Burleigh Avenue, Wallington, 1976)
(a) sequence diagram
(b) main section

a

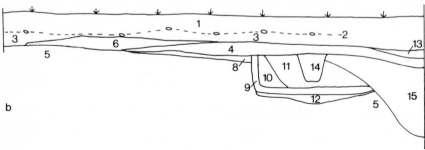

b

At a more complex site like Billingsgate Buildings (*fig 3.5*), the sequence diagram begins to come into its own, but even here the main section is still at least as useful in the interpretation of the site, chiefly because the site consists of one deep narrow trench. It is really on the large extensive site that the sequence diagram scores – on sites where no one section can encompass more than a small fraction of the total number of layers. It was for such sites that the technique was originally developed (large urban sites like Lower Brook Street in Winchester).

There are various conventions that are usually observed when preparing a sequence diagram. Layers that form part of a single feature, as 11, 10, 9 and 12 in *fig 3.4*, which together form an oven or hearth, are grouped together as a single block, without the usual intervening vertical lines. It is also a convention that the lines in the diagram do not cross each other: this is seen as a check on the accuracy of the diagram because if the relationships have been correctly expressed then there is never a need for the lines to cross. However, it is possible for a sequence diagram to express all the relationships correctly and to have crossing lines (which could be straightened out if one wished), and, on the other hand, an incorrect diagram might have no crossing lines. The value of this test as a check therefore seems to be limited, but it is certainly useful in preventing the confusion that might arise if two crossed lines were mistaken for two connected lines. One convention that has not achieved universal support is the treatment of 'negative' features. Harris recommends that these features, which result from the removal of earlier layers (pits, ditches, post-holes, etc.), be given context numbers in the usual way and treated like any other contexts.[7] This has proved too radical for some, but it seems to make good sense.

This is not the place to go into Harris' work in further detail. Since its effects on archaeological practice are far-reaching and profound, the reader is recommended to follow up this section with at least one of Harris' papers referred to above.

The use of computers in preparing sequence diagrams

The value of computers in assisting in the preparation has been hotly debated. Harris, working at Winchester, considered that 'computers should not be used in site analysis of archaeological stratification, on philosophical and practical grounds'[8] and that 'computers should be confined to the post-excavation period where the quantity of the material, for example pottery, suits the quality of the machine'.[9] On

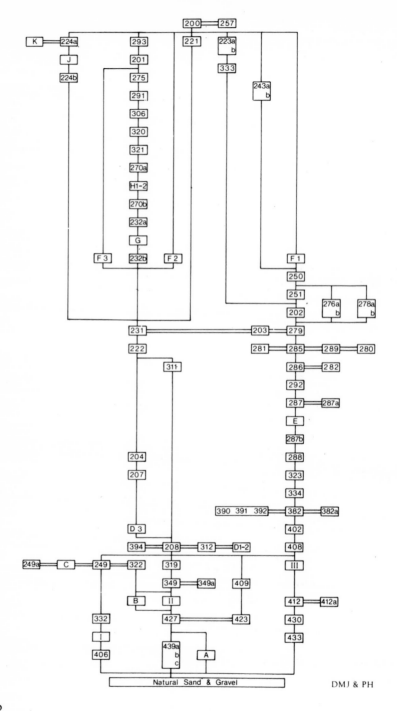

DMJ & PH

East Section

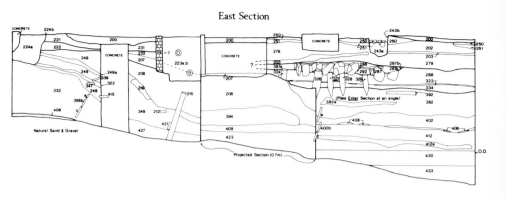

West Section
(Mirrored)

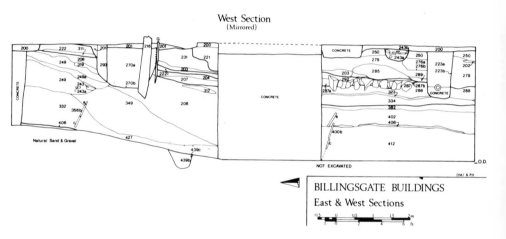

BILLINGSGATE BUILDINGS
East & West Sections

Fig 3.5   Sequence diagram and section from a more complicated site,
Billingsgate Buildings. *By permission of the Museum of London.*

the other hand, Wilcock, working on similar problems from sites in
York, wrote that 'the drawing of phase diagrams for such a site entails
months of work for someone (usually the site supervisor) and is
probably the greatest bottleneck in the work of the (York Archaeological) Trust. This is a job well suited to machine methods . . .'[10] The
debate will no doubt continue, but meanwhile those of us who do not
have access to a computer may draw comfort from Harris' comments.

2 THE RELATIONSHIP BETWEEN STRATIGRAPHY AND THE FINDS

So far I have deliberately not mentioned the role of finds in this analysis. It is now time to examine the relationship between the stratigraphy of the site and the finds associated with each layer, still (for the time being) in the context of relative and not absolute dating. The simplest situation occurs when the site has a relatively straightforward sequence diagram. We can show the presence of artefacts of different types in successive layers in a number of ways:– perhaps as a simple bar diagram like *fig 3.6*, or perhaps by using symbols to represent different artefacts, placing them in the 'boxes' of the sequence diagram itself, as in *fig 3.7*.

What can we see from this representation? Several points are made by the diagram:

(i) Roman and Saxon pottery 'start' lower in the sequence (layer 8) than either medieval (layer 14) or post-medieval (layer 4).

(ii) one type of pottery does not disappear from the sequence when another starts, but occurs right through to the top of the sequence (although not necessarily in every layer).

(iii) the presence of different types of pottery could help us to locate the 'floating' layers 7, 16 and 17 in the sequence. Unfortunately, these three layers contained no pottery at all.

From (i) we could deduce (if we did not already know) that Roman and Saxon pottery pre-dates medieval pottery, which in turn pre-dates post-medieval pottery. We might think that (ii) shows that once a pottery type is made, it continues to be made up to the present day. But this is nonsense, so how do we account for the presence of Roman pottery throughout the Saxon, medieval and post-medieval layers? The site notes show that layer 8 is probably a soil layer, and could represent a long period of accumulation or formation, possibly spanning the Roman and Saxon periods. This explanation cannot be used for the other layers, e.g. 4 which is a floor. The answer is that the earlier material is residual in the later layers at the time of their formation. For example, the Roman pottery in layer 14 was probably originally laid down in layer 8, but was disturbed when the cut for layer 14 was dug through it, and finally ended up in 14 when the cut was filled in. The possibility that finds may be residual is a constant problem, and causes difficulties in both dating layers from the finds in them and vice versa (see below). A similar problem is caused by finds which have a long life – perhaps as heirlooms – and which are therefore already old when first incorporated into a layer.

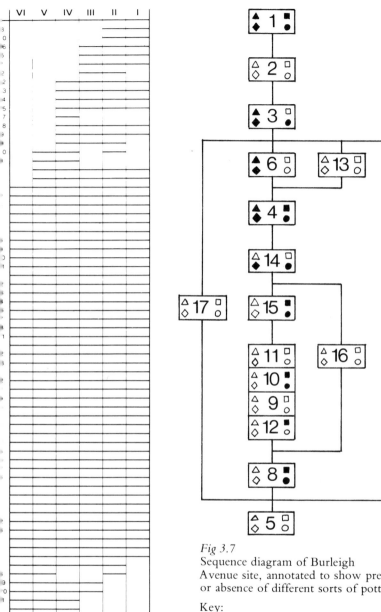

Fig 3.6
ar diagram showing the presence
artefacts of different types in
ccessive layers of a site.
om Mortensen (1973).

Fig 3.7
Sequence diagram of Burleigh
Avenue site, annotated to show presence
or absence of different sorts of pottery.

Key:

	present	absent
post-medieval pottery	▲	△
medieval pottery	◆	◇
Saxon/early medieval pottery	■	□
pre-Roman or Roman pottery	●	○

75

One approach, which helps to reduce this problem and makes better use of the information represented by the finds, is to express not merely presence or absence in each layer, but the percentage of the finds in each layer that belong to each type. An example is given in *fig 3.8* – in this case the artefacts are different types of flint tools.

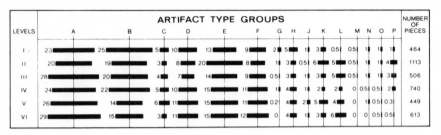

Fig 3.8   Chart showing the percentage of finds in each layer that belong to each type. *From Mortensen (1973).*

Obviously, the number of finds in each layer must be large enough for percentages to be sensible. This does not mean that each total must be greater than 100. If the numbers are small, either (i) selected layers can be used as a 'statistical' sequence for further statistical study, – or (ii) two consecutive layers can be grouped into 'blocks' to give large enough groups of finds for statistical work or (iii) the percentage can be expressed in rounded form, e.g. rounded to the nearest 5% or 10%. Not all sites will be suitable for statistical treatment.

The percentages can be represented visually in the form of a histogram running across the page, as in *fig 3.9*, which shows the percentages of different types of pottery in the 'statistical sequence' of a site in London, Angel Court. Here it can be seen that 'Highgate' and 'Brockley Hill' pottery types are common only in the first two layers (16 and 18) and are scarce (but still present) in the last two (9 and 7). One would probably be prepared to say that these types are residual when found in these layers. An alternative presentation is to make the histogram run up the page (thus reflecting the stratigraphy), with the blocks double-ended, as in *fig 3.8*. Such figures are sometimes called 'battleship curves', although it is difficult to imagine the direction one is viewing the 'battleship' from. The term 'popularity curve' is also used. It seems to be common practice to expect such curves to follow one of three patterns: (i) steady rise, peak or plateau, steady fall, (ii) steady rise to peak or plateau at end of period of study, (iii) steady fall from peak or plateau at beginning of period of study (*see fig 3.10*). This assumption is intuitively reasonable, but does not appear to have been critically tested in practice, and it ignores the problem of residuality.

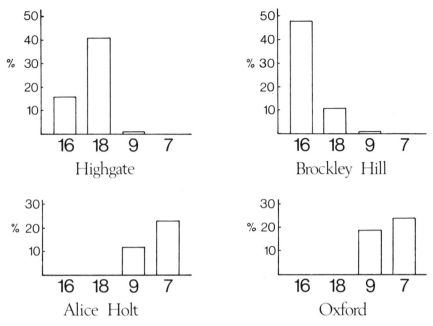

Fig 3.9   Histogram showing percentages of different types of pottery in the main
layers in the sequence at the Angel Court, Walbrook, site. *By permission
of the Museum of London.*

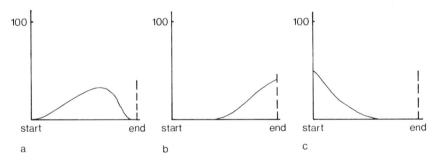

Fig 3.10   Three hypothetical 'popularity curves' (based on Robinson, 1951)
(a) steady rise, peak, and steady fall,
(b) steady rise to end of period of study,
(c) steady fall from start of period of study.

These popularity curves look very nice, and may in some circumstances be a convenient way of publishing the quantitative aspects of a
site pottery report, but they do not in themselves advance the study of

77

the site. So far, all the information has come from the site and has pointed towards the finds. But suppose the sequence diagram consisted, not of one simple sequence (perhaps with a few minor 'branches' as in *fig 3.4*), but of several separate sequences, probably linked at the top and bottom and possibly elsewhere, but basically independent. Such a situation could arise if the site were dug in a 'grid' system of trenches and the baulks were not removed (a practice condemned by Harris[11]) or if it were divided up by modern foundations, which could not be removed or undermined, or if modern disturbances had destroyed parts of the strata, leaving isolated 'islands' of archaeological deposits. The last two are common problems on urban sites. An example is shown in *fig 3.11*. (This site, Mark Brown Wharf, has really three sequences – north, central and south.) It would obviously be extremely useful in the interpretation of the site if we could link the sequences in some way, and say which layers in (for example) the central and southern areas were contemporary with a certain layer in the northern area. Here the finds can perhaps help us if we are prepared to suppose that the finds from contemporary layers are samples from the same 'parent' population of artefacts – namely those in use on the site at that time. This being so, the layer should be at about the same point on the popularity curves, and within a margin of variation that could loosely be called 'sampling error', should have roughly the same proportions of the various types (e.g. of pottery). So, by matching the popularity curves from each sequence, one could 'interleave' them (or 'interdigitate', as I have seen) into one master sequence for the whole site. This master sequence would suggest contemporary groups of layers, across the whole site.

This sounds simple, but what are the practical snags? Firstly, many layers will simply not contain enough finds (even pottery) for a statistical approach to be valid – the 'sampling errors' could swamp the underlying pattern. Secondly, differences in function of different parts of the site could mask the chronological pattern – for example, a sequence of floor layers in a kitchen might contain very different pottery to a contemporary sequence in a dining hall. Nevertheless, it often happens that the sequences can be linked, though not as precisely as one would wish. *Fig 3.12* shows an attempt to link the sequences in *fig 3.11*, based on the evidence of clay tobacco pipes. Pipes are particulary suitable because they can be readily divided into well-established types,[12] easily counted (see chapter 6 for problems of counting pottery) and the types are thought to be reliably dated. Even so, the best we can do is to divide the site into five phases, each including parts of two or more sequences. The five phases are: (A) no

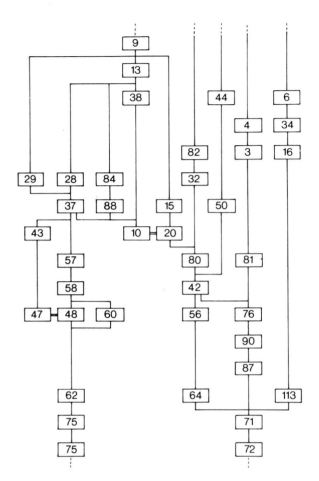

Fig 3.11 Example of sequence diagram, based on
Trench B of site at Mark Brown's Wharf,
Southwark, 1973.

pipes, (B) types 10 and 12 (*ca* 1640–60), (C) types 13, 15 and 18 (*ca*
1660–80), (D) types 19, 20 and 21 (*ca* 1680–1710), (E) types 25 and 26
(*ca* 1730+). The sequence could suggest that type 15 started slightly
earlier than 13 and 18, thus splitting phase (b) (dotted lines). The
linkage is not as precise as it appears, since contexts near the 'top' of a
phase could be contemporary with the next phase but contain none of
the 'right' pipe bowls. Finally, the suggested phases must be checked
against the sequence and the section drawings, to make sure there are
no nonsenses. The last word is still with the site and its stratigraphy.

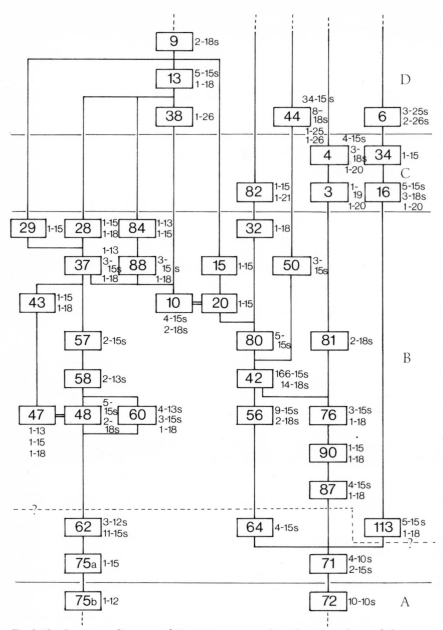

Fig 3.12   Sequence diagram of Fig 3.11, annotated to show numbers of clay
pipes of different types in each context (e.g. context 71 contains 4 type
10 pipes and 2 type 15s). Divided into four phases (A, B, C, D) on the
basis of the clay pipe types (see text). Pre-pipe phase not shown. Phase
B *could* be sub-divided (see broken line).

Seriation

We now move on to a problem that is in one way more difficult and in another more amenable. Suppose that there are no (or very few) stratigraphic relationships. Perhaps the site consists entirely of isolated pits or graves, or perhaps, becoming ambitious, we wish to construct a sequence based on a several sites at once. Without our sequences to help us we are deprived simultaneously of an aid and a constraint – we can manipulate the evidence of the finds without constantly remembering to check whether we have violated any of our fundamental stratigraphic relationships. Mathematically speaking, it is usually easier to solve a problem in an unconstrained situation (e.g. no stratigraphy to worry about) than in a constrained situation (e.g. when only some of the many possible sequences are allowed because of what we know about the stratigraphy of the site). For these reasons, far more work has been put into devising techniques which will order deposits (e.g. graves, which are particularly suitable because the problem of residuality does not usually arise) with no constraints than into techniques which use both finds evidence and stratigraphy simultaneously. These techniques, which go by the collective name of seriation, have gained a bad reputation in some quarters: their use may have encouraged the idea that it is not necessary to worry too much about stratigraphy on site, because one can sort it out by seriation afterwards (usually on a computer). Nothing could be further from the truth. Any information which is lost on site cannot be recovered in the laboratory or study.

Seriation has a long history, going back at least to Flinders Petrie's work on Egyptian cemeteries in the nineteenth century. He attempted to put the pottery and the other finds from 900 Egyptian graves into chronological order (or rather, into a sequence of eighteen groups of fifty graves each, such that the groups were in chronological order). These groups were called sequence-dates, as they formed an arbitrary system of relative dating. Their numbers ranged from 31 to 80, so to say that a certain pottery type has a sequence-date range of 35–50 means that it first appears in a grave in group 35 and last appears in a grave in group 50. Flinders Petrie's work is very sophisticated (and correspondingly hard to follow), but in essence he appears to rely on what Kendall calls the Concentration Principle, summarized by Kendall as '*if* the typology is "chronologically significant", and when the graves have been correctly ordered, then the "sequence-date" *ranges* for the individual types will be found to have been individually *or in some communal way* minimized'.[13] This may not be easy to grasp at first; it is based on the intuitive idea that each pottery type is produced over a well defined period of time, before which and after which it is not made, but during which it is made regularly and available for use. Therefore, of all the graves that do not possess that type, as many as possible should occur either before the first grave to possess it, or after the last grave to do so, and as few as possible should occur chronologically between those two. In other words, the sequence-date range should be minimized. Since minimizing the range for one type may lengthen it for another, they must all be considered simultaneously – hence Kendall's *'in some communal way'*.

Having studied Flinders Petrie's work, Kendall developed a mathematical method for solving the problem (or at least suggesting possible solutions), known as the HORSHU method for reasons which will soon appear.[14] The starting point is an abundance matrix (see *fig 3.13*) which shows the number of artefacts of each type (pot type, brooch type or whatever) that are present in each grave.

		artefact type no.		
		1	2	3
	1	4	2	0
	2	1	3	0
grave	3	1	4	2
no.	4	0	4	2
	5	0	1	5
	6	0	1	5

Fig 3.13

From the abundance matrix a similarity matrix, which is the exact opposite of the dissimilarity matrix (see p 44), is then calculated, expressing the similarity between each pair of graves in relation to the artefacts found in them. An argument due to Kendall shows that this can suitably be done by taking the two rows representing a pair of graves, then for each artefact taking the smaller number of it present, and adding together these numbers. For example, in the matrix shown in *fig 3.13*, the coefficient for graves 1 and 2 is:–
'smaller of 4 and 1' + 'smaller of 2 and 3' plus 'smaller of 0 and 0', i.e. $1 + 2 + 0 = 3$

while the coefficient for grave 1 with itself is:–
'smaller of 4 and 4 + 'smaller of 2 and 2' + 'smaller of 0 and 0', i.e.
4 + 2 + 0 = 6
If we calculate all the coefficients we obtain the matrix:–

		grave no.					
		1	2	3	4	5	6
	1	6	3	3	2	1	1
	2		4	4	3	1	1
grave no.	3			7	6	3	3
	4				6	3	3
	5					4	4
	6						6

Fig 3.14

This differs from the similarity matrix encountered in chapter 2 in which all the coefficients were percentages, but it can be used in a very similar way. In fact, if instead of numbers in the abundance matrix we had used percentages, the resulting similarity matrix would be in the familiar form (see *fig 3.15*).

		artefact type no.		
	1	67	33	0
	2	25	75	0
grave no.	3	14	57	29
	4	0	67	33
	5	0	25	75
	6	0	17	83

Fig 3.15(a)

		grave no.					
		1	2	3	4	5	6
	1	100	58	47	33	25	17
	2		100	71	67	25	17
grave no.	3			100	84	54	46
	4				100	58	50
	5					100	92
	6						100

Fig 3.15(b)

Having got our similarity matrix, what can we do with it? There are two broad directions that can be followed: (i) manipulation of the matrix itself to produce a 'best' order and (ii) use of MDSCAL (see p 55) and related techniques.

Seriation by direct use of the similarity matrix

Techniques in the first category were first proposed by Robinson.[15] They rely on reordering the graves (or whatever the rows and columns of the matrix represent) to produce a 'best' matrix, which it is assumed will give the 'right' order. But what do we mean by 'best'? Well, suppose that the differences in the artefacts contained in the graves were solely due to the differences in artefacts in use at their time of deposition, and that the use of these artefacts followed 'popularity' curves like those described above (p 76). Then, if the graves were thought of as being in a straight line representing time (see *fig 3.16*), the distances along this line would be mirrored by differences in the contents. So we could say that grave no. 1 is most like no. 2, next most like no. 3 and least like no. 6. In the same way, 2 is most like 1 or 3, less like 4 than it is like 3, and so on. In other words, the similarity between 1 and 2 is greater than the similarity between 1 and 3, which is greater than the similarity between 1 and 4, and so on. If the similarity coefficients, whatever they are, are arranged in a matrix (as in *fig 3.15(b)*), then the coefficient will be highest along the diagonal (running from top left to bottom right), lowest in the corner (that is the top right hand corner) and will decrease as one moves away from the diagonal towards any one of the edges along a row or column. Matrices of this special type are called robinson, and if we are fortunate enough to be able to manipulate our similarity matrix into that form (and it cannot always be done) then we have found one of the best orders.

Fig 3.16   Theoretical idea: six graves in time sequence. Distances between graves along this line represent differences in time between the graves.

Most similarity matrices will not become robinson, no matter what order the graves are arranged in. For example, the dissimilarity matrix shown in *fig 20* of chapter 2 (p 45) is very nearly robinson, but not quite (a dissimilarity matrix is robinson if the numbers are lowest on the diagonal, highest in the corner and increase steadily from diagonal to the edges along a row or column). It fails because (a) there is a decrease from row 2, column 6 (70%) to row 1, column 6 (60%), when there should be an increase and (b) because there is a decrease from row 3, column 7 (80%) to row 2, column 7 (70%) when again there should be an increase. No amount of re-ordering the seven artefacts will give a 'better' matrix, so we can conclude that the 'best' order of those seven artefacts is 1, 2, 3, 4, 5, 6, 7.

So even if the situation is not quite ideal, and the matrix not perfectly robinson, we can still produce a quite respectable order. There are many ways of doing this: mostly they rely on a form of intelligent trial-and-error which can be done with pencil and paper if there are not too many graves (or whatever) and on a computer if there are. Methods which can be used with pencil and paper in simple cases like the above (which is just a set of data for purposes of illustration) will be impossible in a real case with, say, sixty rows and seventy columns.

A dilemma now appears – given that our matrix is not likely to be exactly robinson, how nearly so must it be for the 'best' order to be reliable? or indeed, for it to be an order at all? This difficulty is analogous to the one we encountered in cluster analysis, where we found that the techniques tended to produce clusters whether or not they actually existed. In this case, seriation by juggling with the similarity matrix will produce an order whether or not one really exists.

Seriation by use of multi-dimensional scaling

In chapter 2 we found that one answer was to use MDSCAL (p 55) so that one could see whether the clusters actually existed. It seems reasonable to try MDSCAL in the new situation, and to see whether an order exists or not. This was first tried in the late 1960s and at that time yielded a rather surprising result: if there was an order, it appeared not as a straight line (as one might expect) but in a 'horse-shoe' shape.[16] The reason is as follows: at a point in time represented by (for example) a certain grave, a certain set of the artefact types was in use. By a subsequent date, all these types will have gone out of use. The similarity between the chosen grave and any grave deposited after that date will be zero (since they have no artefacts at all in common). The similarity matrix will therefore look something like *fig 3.17*, with a large block of zeroes in the corner.

		grave no.									
		1	2	3	4	5	6	7	8	9	10
	1	100	50	20	10	0	0	0	0	0	0
	2		100	40	15	5	0	0	0	0	0
	3			100	60	40	20	0	0	0	0
	4				100	50	30	10	0	0	0
grave no.	5					100	45	25	5	0	0
	6						100	50	30	10	0
	7							100	60	20	5
	8								100	40	25
	9									100	55
	10										100

Fig 3.17

In this hypothetical example, graves 5 to 10 all have the same similarity with 1 (i.e. zero) and should all be the same distance from 1 in the MDSCAL 'map'. The actual result of a similar matrix is shown in *fig 3.18*, showing the characteristic horseshoe shape. Real life is more complicated; nevertheless the pattern can still be detected in a MDSCAL map produced for a set of graves from the Münsingen cemetery (see *fig 3.19*). In the paper referred to above, Kendall goes on to discuss the ways in which the horseshoe might be straightened and criteria by which the success of a seriation might be judged. In his later papers Kendall showed how the horseshoe could be 'unbent', and so the name given to his method reflects only an incident in its early history. The techniques discussed by Kendall seem to succeed in their task of producing an order without 'straight–jacketing' the data into that form.

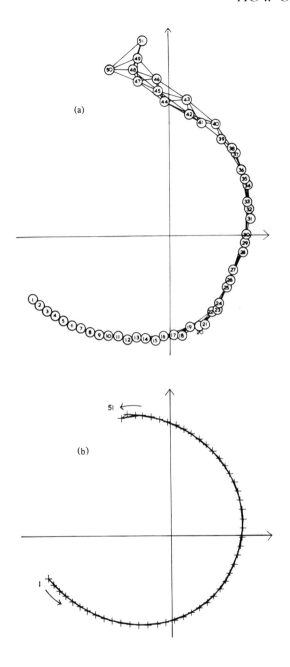

Fig 3.18 Effect of applying MDSCAL to simple, hypothetical similarity matrix. *From Kendall (1971).*

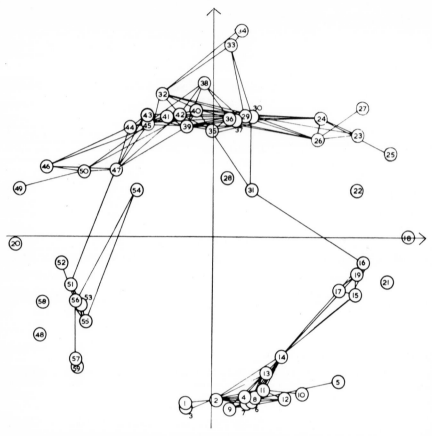

Fig 3.19 MDSCAL applied to a real similarity matrix (of brooches from Münsingen). *From Kendall (1971).*

Problems of seriation

A more fundamental question is 'what does that order represent?' Time is not the only possible dimension. We have seen that if time does underlie the ordering of the graves, artefacts or whatever we are studying, then we may get useful results. But there are other possibilities – a seriation of modern cars (based on their shape) for example, might well order them according to price, while a seriation of modern grave headstones might detect a geographical rather than a chronological trend.[17] To some extent, the association of the order in the data with time rather than some other factor is an act of faith, and must be carefully justified.

3 ABSOLUTE DATING

Perhaps this is a good point at which to pause and scan the ground we have covered. We have seen the underlying mathematical basis of stratigraphy and how mathematics can help when the stratigraphy is lacking. We now have the equipment necessary to construct a chronological sequence from one or many sites. So far though, there are no fixed dates to our sequence; it is, so to speak, floating. In this section, we examine the mathematical problems which arise when we try to pin down our sequence in terms of actual dates.

At the beginning of the chapter we distinguished between internal and external methods of dating, and it will be useful to look at this distinction more closely before moving on to the mathematical problems of the former.

By internal, I mean methods of dating which derive strictly from the object itself, by comparison with a supposedly objective standard. Two examples are radiocarbon and tree-ring dating: in the former case the objective standard is the half-life of the carbon 14 isotope and in the latter it is a master curve of tree ring widths built up from trees of known age. To these scientific methods can be added some rather special historic examples – coins and inscriptions with dates on them come immediately to mind.

By external methods I mean methods which rely on other artefacts or forms of evidence. The most common are the various forms of associative dating – for example, dating finds by association with (a) coins, (b) architectural evidence, (c) documentary evidence, (d) other similar artefacts which are supposed to be better dated (for example dating Roman coarse pottery by its association with samian). One can add to this list the idea of interpolation or extrapolation from known dates in a sequence: for example if a site has five phases of which the first and last can be reliably dated one might provisionally date the intervening phases at regular intervals between the two fixed points.

Another distinction that must be made to prepare the ground before we really start is that between the date of an object and that of a layer or context. Except in rare circumstances an object has a single date which is the date of its manufacture. The exceptions are those objects which can be re-used; for example a timber beam which first forms part of a house, but later is incorporated into a waterfront. An archaeological context, on the other hand, may well not have a single date because it, and the objects it contains, may have accumulated over a long period of time. The usual archaeological practice is to 'date the layer by the latest object found in it', which in effect means that we are estimating the closing date of the context, that is the date at which the last object became incorporated into it. This may, of course, be much later than the date of the last object itself.

Scientific methods

Having dealt with these preliminaries, we now turn to the scientific methods themselves. Although they rely on a variety of physical processes, they all share the characteristic that, at best, they provide an estimate both of date and of the precision of that estimate. By precision, I use the statistical meaning of a measure of the likely difference between the estimate and the true date, based purely on random variation. At worst, and in real life very often, all sorts of biases and non-random effects can distort the picture. Firstly, though, we shall examine what happens when the method can produce an unbiased estimate and an idea of its precision. Because it is the most developed of the scientific techniques, I shall refer throughout to radiocarbon dates: the arguments will generally carry over to other techniques and a lot of vagueness will be avoided.

Radiocarbon dating

A radiocarbon date consists of two parts, the estimate and the precision, measured in statistical terms by the standard deviation of the estimate (called the standard error by some writers). They are usually presented thus:

$$3000 \text{ BC} \pm 100$$

The 3000 BC part is obviously the estimate, but what does the ± 100 mean? It says that the standard deviation of the estimate is 100 years, which means that the probability of the true date lying between two chosen dates (say 'x' and 'y') is given by a statistical formula, which is conveniently represented by the area under a certain curve, shown in *fig 3.20*. This curve, known as a Normal or Gaussian curve, is mathematically constructed so that the whole area beneath the curve (i.e. between the curve and the horizontal straight line or axis) is one unit (e.g. one square inch). The probability that the true date lies between the dates 'x' BC and 'y' BC is the area shown shaded on *fig 3.20*. It can either be measured directly or found in a book of statistical tables such as Lindley and Miller. The position of the curve is fixed by the estimate: in this case the estimate is 3000 BC and the curve is (a) symmetrical about 3000 BC and (b) comes to a peak there. The standard deviation determines the general shape of the curve – a

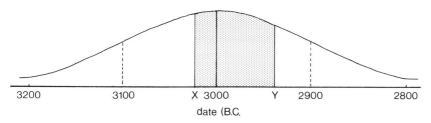

3200   3100   X 3000   Y   2900   2800

date (B.C.

Fig 3.20   Example of Normal or Gaussian curve, as used in interpretation of radiocarbon dates (see text).

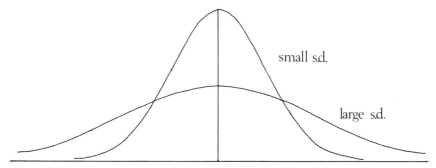

small s.d.

large s.d.

Fig 3.21   Two Normal curves, showing effect of small or large standard deviation (s.d.) on the shape of the curve.

large standard deviation (or s.d. for short) will produce a wide low curve and small s.d. a more peaked curve (see *fig 3.21*) but the total area under the curve will be the same in each case.

Whatever the s.d., the curve always has the characteristic that about 68% of the area beneath it lies between the estimate minus one s.d. and the estimate plus one s.d. (e.g. 3100 and 2900 BC in *fig 3.20*) and about 95% of the area beneath it lies between the estimate minus two s.d.s and the estimate plus two s.d.s, (e.g. 3200 and 2800 BC in *fig 3.20*). In terms of probabilities, there is a 68% chance that the true answer (in our example) lies between 3100 and 2900 BC, and a 95% chance that it lies between 3200 and 2800 BC. By using a book of statistical tables we could, if we wished, calculate the chance of the true date lying between any two chosen dates (e.g. 3400 and 2900 BC, or even 2800 and 2600 BC, though of course the latter chance would be very small), or alternatively, calculate a date-range wide enough to have a chosen chance of including the true date. What we cannot do is find a date range which has a 100% chance of including the two dates. All this information is included in the deceptively simple statement 3000 BC ± 100.

However, since this statement is open to misinterpretation (it might be taken to mean that the date must lie between 3100 and 2900 BC, for example) a more exact, if less familiar, form of shorthand might be preferable, e.g.

$$N \ (3000 \ BC, \ 100),$$

where N refers to the Normal curve and its characteristics (see above) the first number being the estimate and the second its standard deviation.

Often, archaeologists seem to know all about this in an academic sense, and yet still fail to take account of it in their interpretation of the evidence. Mathematical interpretation must here form an integral part of archaeological interpretation. It is an interesting exercise to go through a report which contains radiocarbon dates expressed baldly as (e.g.) '3000 BC ± 100' and turn them into statements like 'with a 68% chance of lying between 3100 and 2900 BC'.

Using radiocarbon results

It becomes more interesting, from the mathematician's point of view if not the archaeologist's, when two or more dates have to be considered at the same time. Three such cases will be examined here: (i) two independent radiocarbon dates for the same feature or object; (ii) two or more dates from different contexts with no stratigraphic relationship between them; (iii) two or more dates from different contexts with stratigraphic relationships between them. A small case-study containing examples of both (i) and (ii) will be examined.

(i) It may happen that a cautious archaeologist has taken two samples from the same feature, or one each from two objects which he thinks should be contemporary. Assuming that the two 'agree' (that is that the standard deviation of the difference between the two estimates is not too large – see (ii) below), he will probably wish to combine the two results to get a more precise result. This can be done by using a weighted average, with the weights depending on the standard deviations. The formula for the weights, and for the standard deviation of the weighted average, is rather complicated. In the simple case where the two results have the same s.d., the 'best' estimate is a simple average of the two, and its s.d. is about 70% of the original. So, for example, original dates of (A) 3100 BC ± 100 and (B) 2900 BC ± 100 can be combined into a joint estimate of 3000 BC ± 70, a useful increase in precision.

(ii) If we have two different contexts, A and B, not related stratigraphically, then a question we shall naturally want to ask is 'is A later than B?' Indeed, one of our aims in taking radiocarbon samples from the two contexts, which could even be from different sites, may have been to answer that question. What we have to do is to calculate the difference between the two dates, and its standard deviation. The former is easy, the latter a little more difficult: the s.d.s cannot be added together, but have to be combined by squaring each, adding the squares, and then taking the square root. In the example above, the different is $3100 - 2900 = 200$ years, and its s.d. is the square root of $100 \times 100 + 100 \times 100$, which is about 140 years, so that it can be written as 200 ± 140 years. Looking up the tables again, I find that this means the chance of A actually being later than B is about 8% – not a large chance but larger than one might expect and not so small that it can be ignored with complete safety. We can reasonably expect that about one out of every twelve interpretations supported by this much evidence will in fact be wrong.

(iii) The combination of internal dates with stratigraphic evidence is perhaps the most difficult of all. Suppose our two contexts A and B are such that B is (stratigraphically) later than A. Previously, we could have represented the dates of A and B graphically as in *fig 3.22(a)* but this no longer holds since we know that B is later than A. Instead, we have a situation like *fig 3.22(b)*, where dates in the shaded area below the diagonal line are forbidden, because in this zone A is later than B. Dates for B before 2900 BC are more likely to be 'forbidden' than

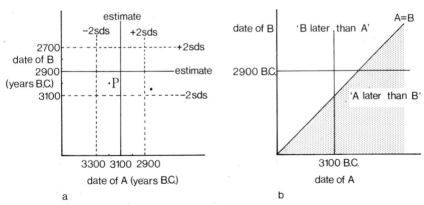

Fig 3.22 (a) the dates of samples A and B can be represented as a point anywhere on this graph, e.g. point P, which is at A = 3200 BC, B = 3000 BC. The joint date is most likely to be near the crossing of the two 'estimate' lines.
(b) The same situation with the additional information that B is stratigraphically later than A. The shaded area is therefore 'forbidden'.

93

those after 2900 BC (because more of the area below the 2900 BC line is shaded than of the area above), which means that the best estimate is a little later than 2900 BC. By a similar argument, the best estimate for the date of A is a little earlier than 3100 BC. The stratigraphic relationship has altered the interpretation of the radiocarbon dates.

A case study

This is taken from an interim report on the Rams Hill excavation.[18] Three phases are discussed, with radiocarbon dates as follows:

first palisade:	1030 ± 70 bc	(Har 461)
	1050 ± 70 bc	(Har 231)
	740 ± 70 bc	(Har 230)
second palisade:	1060 ± 70 bc	(Har 232)
third ('double') palisade:	1070 ± 70 bc	(Har 228)
	1010 ± 70 bc	(Har 229)

If one had to rely on this evidence alone to put these three phases into chronological order, the statistical argument would go like this:

1. Reject Har 230 as an 'outlier', possibly contaminated, since it lies so far from the other two dates from this phase (see (ii) above).
2. Average the dates and combine the standard deviations (see (i) above). The results are:

first palisade:	1040 ± 50 bc
second palisade:	1060 ± 70 bc
third palisade:	1040 ± 50 bc

3. The 'statistical' order is:–

second palisade:	1060 ± 70 bc
first ⎱ palisade: third ⎰	1040 ± 50 bc

4. The difference in estimated date between first and second palisades is −20 ± 86, and the probability that the 'first palisade' is earlier than the 'second palisade' is about 41%, while the probability that the second is earlier than the third is about 59%. The probability that the true order is 'first', 'second', 'third', is even less (in fact less than 25%). If there were no other evidence, we would be tempted cautiously to reject the suggested sequence in favour of that shown above, while if there was stratigraphic evidence for the sequence as suggested, we would have to admit that the radiocarbon dates had not been useful in providing relative dating for the three phases. As a by-product, the stratigraphic evidence would slightly alter the 'best' estimates, based on the radiocarbon figures. There is apparently little use made of the

radiocarbon dates in sorting out the complicated stratigraphy in the final report.[19] Clearly radiocarbon has its limitations for sorting out detailed phasing in this way.

The problems of using carbon-14 dates were recently highlighted by a study of the Cadbury massacre.[20] This is an historical event, securely dated to between 45 and 61 AD. Several carbon-14 samples were taken from deposits that could be associated with the massacre. The results showed a very wide spread of radiocarbon dates, much complicated by the need to calibrate them. Had the historical evidence not been available, the event could have been dated only to 'within several centuries'.

So far we have looked only at the problems of interpretation that arise when we can assume that the data are reliable and unbiased. Unfortunately, life is rarely so simple. There are many possible sources of unreliability in radiocarbon dates, the most important of which is contamination. This problem has been discussed in a practical way by Harkness who shows that even a small percentage of modern carbon can seriously affect the estimated date.[21] There is nothing that the statistician can do about it – the answer lies in careful sampling and close liaison between the archaeologist and the laboratory.

The calibration question

A problem of more interest to the mathematician concerns the fundamental assumptions on which the whole technique is based. The particular assumption which has been found wanting is that the concentration of radiocarbon in the atmosphere has not varied appreciably over the period with which we are concerned (say 50,000 BC–1700 AD). Work carried out in the USA suggests that there have been considerable fluctuations in the past: for example, it seems that the concentration of radiocarbon was higher in the period 5000 BC–1000 BC than previously. These findings have been based on wood taken from the bristle-cone pines of the White Mountains of California.

These extraordinary trees were known to live up to 4500 years and by dendrochronological methods their wood could be dated back beyond 6000 BC.[22] Each sample taken thus had two dates: (i) a 'tree-ring' date, derived from its position in the dendrochronological pattern and (ii) a radiocarbon date. When the two sets of dates were plotted on a graph, it was found that they did not agree, but diverged – the older the samples, the greater was the 'true' (tree-ring) age in comparison with the radiocarbon age. Clearly a correction or calibration was needed in order to convert the now suspect radiocarbon dates into supposedly 'true' dates. Since the problem first appeared there has been enormous controversy about how this should be done, and several rival calibration curves have been produced. The first statistical pit-fall has now been charted and avoided: it concerned whether one should use a so-called calibration function or an inverse calibration function in order to convert radiocarbon dates into 'true' dates. To explain the difference, a calibration function expresses the radiocarbon date in terms of the true date (*fig 3.23(a)*) while the inverse expresses the true date in terms of the radiocarbon date.

To correct a radiocarbon date, one simply looks up the date on the 'radiocarbon' axis, follows the dotted line across or up until the curve is reached, and then down or across to the 'true date' axis, where the date can be read off. If the curve is smooth, the two methods will give similar answers, but if it has 'kinks' or 'wiggles' in it (see below), the calibration curve could give more than one true date for the same radiocarbon date (in *fig 3.23(a)* it gives three) but the inverse curve can only give one because the curve is not allowed to double back on itself. For this reason, the latter seemed preferable from an archaeological point of view. But it has even greater disadvantages than the former: firstly, it expresses a fixed (if unknown) number (the true date) in terms of a known number which contains an element of random variation, which is unsound from a mathematical point of view. Secondly – and this is really a practical demonstration of the first point – it leads to even odder results.

In *fig 3.23(b)*, for example, there could be up to three radiocarbon

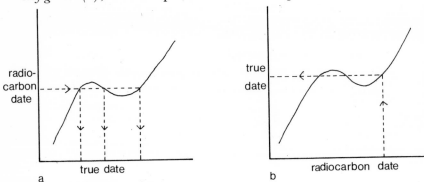

Fig 3.23. Two sorts of calibration function:
(a) calibration function, expressing radiocarbon date in terms of the true date
(b) inverse calibration function, expressing true date in terms of the radiocarbon date

96

dates corresponding to the same true date (even supposing that there were no 'random' errors in the dates). There is therefore a mathematical case for not using the subjectively preferable 'inverse calibration curve', although this means that the archaeologist will have to accept ambiguous results if there are kinks in the curve.

The real debate is – are there kinks in the curve? The first attempt at drawing a calibration curve was made by Suess, who drew a freehand curve passing as close as possible to as many of the points on the graph as possible, a procedure which caused raised eyebrows among interested statisticians.[23] The two sides in the debate can be described as the 'smoothies', who favour a smooth calibration curve, generally with an explicit mathematical formula, and the 'wigglies', who favour a more subjective approach, retaining many, if not all, of the interesting kinks and wiggles in Suess' original curve.

The debate is far from over and it would be rash to try to predict who will win. Two points that are worth making however are: (i) it is a mathematical debate concerning the interpretation of the same data according to different hypotheses; (ii) the onus really lies on the 'wigglies' to demonstrate conclusively that something more complicated than a simple smooth curve is needed. Otherwise support must rest with the simpler hypothesis so long as it remains tenable.

4 'EXTERNAL' DATING METHODS

There are really three different aspects of dating grouped together here:

(i) dating finds from their context;
(ii) dating contexts from their finds;
(iii) dating finds from other finds in the same context (this is a combination of (i) and (ii)).

The nature of the evidence in (ii) differs from that in (i), because the date of a context must be later than that of objects contained in it (if the context accumulated over a period then the closing or terminal date of the context is later than the latest object in it). This means that in case (i) the date ascribed to finds is a *terminus ante quem* (TAQ) – the date before which they must have been made – while in case (ii) the date given to the context is a *terminus post quem* (TPQ) – the date after which it must have been laid down (or at least finished being laid down). In case (iii), there is neither a TAQ nor a TPQ, but only a date which might with good fortune approximate to the date of the object.

A straightforward and comprehensive account of the problems of such dating – chiefly cases (i) and (ii) – from a purely archaeological point of view, was given by Hurst in a paper particularly concerned with medieval pottery, but which is of far more general application.[24] He lists the five criteria for dating medieval pottery, in (his) descending order of reliability:

1 Coins or other small finds
2 Documentary evidence
3 Architectural evidence
4 Comparison with dateable sequences or examples elsewhere
5 Typology

Although coins are one of the few classes of artefact that can (usually) be closely dated, the problem of using them for dating contexts or other objects is that they may have been in circulation or hoarded for a long time before being lost, and could easily have been disturbed from an earlier context into a later (see below). The only really secure association is a coin hoard in a pot, and such finds are very rare. Small finds are rarely as well dated as coins, so the problem is that much more difficult.

In theory it should be possible to obtain a reliable date for pottery associated with a building which is itself reliably dated by documentary evidence, and which had a relatively short life. Also, pottery found under a building of known date should at least have a TAQ and pottery found in such a building a TPQ. But even here, there are problems – it has been known for archaeologists to excavate castles which are not the ones to which the building documents relate (e.g. Faringdon, near Oxford),[25] and the 'patchiness' of surviving medieval records is such that earlier or later building phases may now be undocumented. It is therefore difficult to be certain that the building one is excavating is actually the right phase of the actual building to which the documents relate. However, there are examples of reliable TAQs, e.g. Oxford castle mound.[26]

Architectural evidence can be useful, but one of the problems is that architectural styles are not necessarily contemporary over the whole country, but can spread rather like ripples in a pond, becoming out-of-date in one area before even reaching another.

Hurst points out that medieval coarse pottery rarely travelled more than twenty miles from source to use, and that stylistic trends varied regionally.[27] He gives the example of simple everted rims which may be eleventh century in Sussex, thirteenth century in Gloucestershire or fourteenth century in Devon. Clearly reliable comparisons can only be made over short distances, and the findings of parallels of vessel shape at a considerable distance is not a good guide to dating, except for certain fine wares which were traded over long distances.

The fifth method, typological dating, is really a way of relative and not absolute dating. At its best, it is a sort of seriation based on similarities and differences in technique and style. At worst it can be a largely fictitious exercise, based on unreal assumptions (e.g. that technical skill always improves).

A possible answer

At this point, one might ask 'well, what *can* we do then?' Either we accept the dating evidence and form a hypothesis, remembering Hurst's 'the hypotheses of yesterday become the beliefs of today and the untruths of tomorrow',[28] or we reject it and get nowhere at all. There is apparently no 'middle way'.

A statistical approach can, I believe, put the evidence in a form which gives not only the hypotheses but also the degree of reliability which can be placed on it.

Subsequent evidence can then be 'added' to it; reinforcing it and increasing the reliability if it 'agrees' and modifying it appropriately if not. Direct contradictions will be rare. To get the feel of this approach, we shall first tackle some relatively simple problems, in which the statistical approach tends to urge caution, before looking at the wider implications, which are a largely unexplored field of study.

The dating probability curve

The basic tool in a statistical approach to dating is the dating probability curve, which expresses all that we currently know about the date of an object or context. Three simple examples are shown in *fig 3.24*.

Fig 3.24(a) shows the probability associated with a conventionally-expressed date, in this case '60–90 AD'. The graph shows that the object has an equal chance of having been made in any year between 60 and 90 AD, and no chance of having been made either before 60 or after 90 AD – a rather idealized statement. *Fig 3.24(b)* shows a more realistic dating, in this case '*ca* 60–90 AD'. Any date between 60 and 90 AD is more likely than any date before 60 or after 90 AD, while the 'most likely' date is about 75 AD. There is a high probability that the date of manufacture lies between 60 and 90 AD and a small probability that it does not. *Fig 3.24(c)* shows a TPQ of 60 AD – all dates before this are impossible, dates soon after 60 AD are most likely and the probability falls away the further after 60 AD we look. All these are simply graphical representations of states of

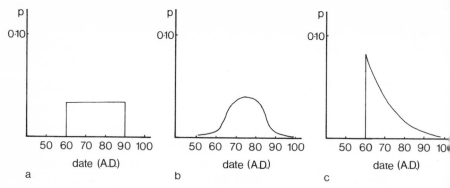

Fig. 3.24 Three examples of dating probability curves:
(a) represents a conventional expression of date, in this case '60–90 AD'
(b) represents approximate dating, in this case *ca* 60–90 AD
(c) represents a *terminus post quem* of 60 AD

belief: there are also algebraic representations (i.e. the equations which represent the graphs shown in *fig 3.24*), but as I am trying to keep algebra as such out of this book, we shall stick to the graphs.

Suppose now we find a coin of 60 AD in a context. What can we say (graphically) about the date of that context? The situation is that of *fig 3.24(c)* but how steeply does the probability fall away? In other words, what is the likely 'life' of the coin, between manufacture and deposition? (The problem of re-deposition complicates things, so for the time being we will ignore it.) A useful way of looking at this is through the branch of mathematics known as renewal theory, which usually deals with topics such as the life-span of a light bulb before it fails. The question of the life of a coin before it is lost, or a pot before it is broken, is analogous and we can use parts of the theory without having to puzzle it out for ourselves. Renewal theory concerns itself with the probability of failure (or loss) given that the object is still functioning. There are three general possibilities (shown in *fig 3.25*) known as positive ageing, no ageing, and negative ageing (a, b and c respectively).

With positive ageing, the object has a greater chance of failure the older it gets, i.e. it is wearing out. In the 'no ageing' model the object has the same chance of failure whatever its age (it does not wear out). Cases of pure accidental loss would seem to follow this model – if we have six coins of different dates in our pocket and drop one, it is just as likely to be the newest as the oldest. 'Negative ageing' is the least likely to happen – the longer an object lasts the less likely it is to fail. The pattern followed by a piece of modern machinery is likely to be a

100

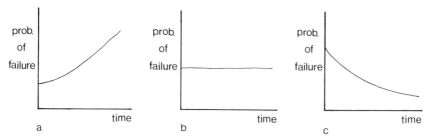

Fig 3.25   Three possible relationships between time and probability of failure
(a) positive ageing (probability increases with time)
(b) no ageing (probability does not change)
(c) negative ageing (probability decreases with time)

combination of all three – first a short period of negative ageing ('running in' or 'teething troubles'), followed by a longer period of no ageing, and then the onset of positive ageing (at which point the owner probably trades it in for a new model). Very little work has been done in investigating the pattern that archaeological artefacts are likely to follow. In the absence of firm evidence, I have chosen the 'no ageing' models for coins and pottery, partly because it seems reasonable, partly because it is a conceptually simple and neutral model, and partly because it makes the mathematics particularly easy.

Two case studies

The next question is – what is the probability of failure (or loss)? Or, looked at another way, what is the average life-span? In two cases where I was involved we first tried to answer this question using (i) dates of samian pottery from two sites – Highgate Wood in North London and Toppings Wharf in Southwark and (ii) dates of Roman coins from a site at Lefevre Road, Bow, East London. The average life of the samian was calculated by examining the date of all sherds, in the same context, working out the average difference in date between the latest sherd and all the others, and making an adjustment to allow for the life of the latest sherd (the statistical theory behind all this is complicated but available on request). The same method was used for the coins. On this basis the average life of the samian was twenty-nine years at Highgate and eighteen years at Southwark, while the average life of the coins was forty-seven years. Even more striking was the discovery that nearly 20% of the samian sherds from Highgate were over fifty years old at their time of deposition.

It was later pointed out by Joanna Bird (who had dated the samian in the first place) that neither of the sites was very suitable for our samian-ageing investigation, as most of the samian there consisted of very small pieces which could not always be reliably dated. Fortunately, I was then asked to look at the same problem from a much more useful site – 93/95 Borough High Street, Southwark – where the samian was in large pieces and came from a well-stratified sequence of stream deposits. The subsequent analysis took into account: (i) the dates assigned to the sherds of samian – where several from one context were given the same date range, they were spread evenly through it (for example four sherds all dated '60–80 AD' were given dates 64, 68, 72 and 76 AD); (ii) the likely 'life' of the latest sherd (see above); and (ii) the sequence itself – the date of deposition of a context cannot be earlier than the one below it. A summary of the results is shown in *figs 3.26 and 3.27.*

context no.	no. of vessels represented	av. date of vessels (AD)	estimated date of deposit (AD)	av. age of vessels (years)
2	5	61	65	4
9	30	67	90	23
18	37	80	110	30
21	10	89	120	31
27	31	100	130	30
31	5	92	140	48
33	16	110	150	40
34	4	135	180	45

Fig 3.26

These results agree well with those based on an independent examination of the coarse pottery. They show an increase in time of the average age of samian at deposition, which can be broken down into three stages:

(i) 'Early' phase. Samian only recently imported, no 'old' samian in use: breakages are therefore of relatively recent vessels. Increasing usage; (*ca* 65–90 AD; average age at deposition less than twenty-five years).

(ii) 'Steady' phase. Breakages balanced by new imports. Some 'old' samian in use, but average age stays much the same. Constant usage; (*ca* 90–130 AD; average age at deposition thirty years).

(iii) 'Decline' phase. Breakages exceed new imports: High proportion of 'old' samian in use, average increasing. Declining usage; (*ca* 130 AD +; average age at deposition forty years).

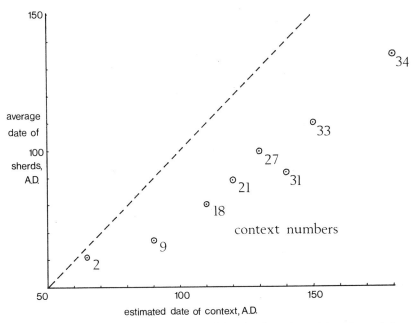

Fig 3.27   Comparison of average date of sherds of samian with estimated date of context in which they were found. Contexts are a sequence of stream deposits at 93/95 Borough High Street, Southwark (Bird *et al.*, 1978).

Clearly one cannot use just one average age, but must consider the factors likely to influence it at any particular time. However, these are the most reliable results that are available to me.

A general approach to the problem

We are now in a position to look at the question posed on p 97 – what does the date of a find tell us about the date of the context? First, suppose there is only one dateable find. If it can be given an exact date (for example a coin, if we are lucky), the dating probability curve (d.p.c.) of the context will look like *fig 3.28(a)*. If it can only be given a range (e.g. a sherd of samian), the d.p.c. will look like *fig 3.28(b)*.

In the first case, the 'most likely' date is the date of the coin, but even this has a very low probability. The 'expected' date (in the sense of an average in a large number of such contexts), is forty years later than the coin, while the 'median' date (that is the date which is as likely to be before the actual date as it is after) is twenty–eight years later than the coin date.

In the second case, the 'most likely' date is the end date of the range; the 'expected date' is forty-five years after the first year of the

103

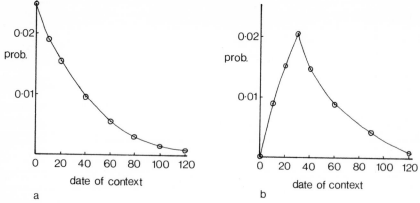

Fig 3.28 Dating a context from *one* datable find
(a) find is given an exact date. 'Date of context' is years after date of find. Average 'life' of find taken to be 40 years (c.f. coins, see above).
(b) find is given a range of dates. 'Date of context' is years after start of date range of find. Range and average 'life' of find both taken to be 30 years (c.f. samian, see above).

range (that is thirty years after the mid year of the range), and the median date is thirty-seven years after the first year of the range.

These results may be interesting and highlight the dangers (not that they should need highlighting) of using single sherds or coins as dating evidence, but they are of limited practical use. More useful results could be obtained by generalizing with the following situations:

(i) more than one dateable object per context,
(ii) stratigraphic relationships taken into account,
(iii) possibility of dating finds from well dated contexts,
(iv) allowing for the possibility of re-deposition, according to the stratigraphy of the site,

which together could lead to a simultaneous probability dating of a whole site. Further evidence (e.g. from other sites) could be incorporated into this framework without causing radical dislocations. This approach could have important consequences for the way in which dating evidence is treated, and in particular, the way in which different pieces of evidence are combined. Much of the essential groundwork remains to be done but some progress has been made with (i): we now have the result that the average age at deposition of the latest dateable find decreases in direct proportion to the number of dateable finds in that context – for example, with two sherds of samian instead of the one in *fig 3.28(b)* the average age at deposition of the later would be fifteen years, with three ten years, and so on.

Summary

In conclusion to this section, we can say that the full potential of dating evidence has not yet been tapped. Advances will come through looking at the whole dating of a site simultaneously in terms of probabilities. An interesting side line is that the closer an object can be dated, the greater seems to be its average age at deposition. One might speculate that the dating information (i.e. the precision of a date as given by 'a range of possible production dates' plus 'life') is the same for all objects. If this were so, it would place an absolute limit on the closeness to which any context could ever be dated, depending on the number of dateable objects in it and in other contexts in its sequence. I offer this as a stimulus to further work rather than a serious suggestion, but some speculation as to where this might lead is found in chapter 9.

Postscript

It would be odd to leave the subject of dating without mentioning the area in which a statistical approach has apparently had its greatest success – the dating of clay tobacco pipe stems by their bore. The original idea is simple enough – that between 1620 and 1800 the stem bore of such pipes decreased steadily. As an empirical observation, so far, so good, although it should be noted that the rate of decrease varied regionally and that even in one place at one time, bore size was by no means consistent (as one would expect from a process of threading in a wire and withdrawing it).

The first statistical approach was to examine a number of large well-dated groups of stems, and to use their measurement to construct a regression equation linking average stem bore with year of manufacture.[29] It was found necessary to assume that

(i) the sample was random and representative
(ii) it was deposited before 1780
(iii) there was a constant rate of deposition throughout the period of accumulation.

Later work demonstrated that a sample of at least 900 fragments was required for a reliable result, that in any case results became less reliable after about 1760.[30] The next step was the the rejection of a single regression equation as inadequate, and its replacement by no less than ten equations, each covering a different part of the period 1620–1800, with considerable overlaps between them.[31] At this point the archaeologist may well ask whether it is worth all the effort. After all, if there are 900 stem fragments, there are likely to be a fair number of bowls, and bowls can be dated typologically with a reasonable degree of accuracy.

There are other more theoretical objections too, concerned with the three assumptions mentioned above. Assumption (i) is an act of faith, but if one cannot make it one may as well give up before spending any time at all on the problem. The worrying assumption is (iii) – it seems inherently rather unlikely and implies that the given date will be the average date of deposition, which is not usually what we want. Contexts are generally dated by the latest find in them, and the value of an average date (especially if expressed as a single year) is uncertain. As an extreme example, a group of early stems (say *ca* 1620) that was re-deposited and mixed with a group of late (say *ca* 1760) stems would be dated to *ca* 1690. Such an obvious situation would no doubt be noticed, but less obvious mixtures could be missed and produce confusing results. A more technical point concerns the equation itself, which is of the form suitable for calculating bore from age, and less suitable for doing the opposite job. There is also the danger that over-enthusiastic users might apply the techniques to groups that are too small.

A more useful approach might be via probability curves, as described above. The probability dating for any given stem bore could be worked out, and these could be used to say as much as one reasonably could from the evidence of one, two or nine hundred stems.

1. *Wheeler 1956*, 38
2. *Plog 1974*, 8–11
3. *Renfrew 1973*
4. *Stoll 1961*, 50
5. *Orton* forthcoming
6. *Jones 1980*
7. *Harris 1975b*, 115
8. *Harris 1975a*, 33
9. *Harris ibid*, 34
10. *Wilcock 1975*, 93
11. *Harris 1977*, 7–8
12. *Oswald 1975*
13. *Kendall 1963*, 659; *1971*, 217
14. *Kendall 1971*
15. *Robinson 1951*
16. *Kendall 1971*, 225
17. *Brothwell 1969*, 674
18. *Current Archaeology IV 1974*, 198
19. *Bradley and Ellison 1975*, 38
20. *Campbell, Baxter and Alcock 1978*
21. *Harkness 1975*, 130–2
22. *Burleigh 1975*, 6–7
23. *Suess 1970*
24. *Hurst 1964*
25. *Hurst ibid*, 141
26. *Hurst ibid*, 141
27. *Hurst ibid*, 147
28. *Hurst ibid*, 149
29. *Harrington 1954*
30. *Hume 1963*
31. *Hanson 1971*

CHAPTER FOUR

Where Does It Come From?

Introduction

This is a less familiar question, and one asked more often by archaeologists than by visitors to sites or museums. The answer satisfies a certain curiosity, of course, but there is more to it than that. Artefacts of similar type (see chapter 2) are frequently found at great distances from each other (dozens, or even hundreds of miles), raising the question 'how did they get there?' Different answers can tell us different things about the contemporary society: for example:

(a) they were made at the same place and traded to the find spot;
(b) they were made by the same person at different places;
(c) they were made in the same style but by different makers in different places (perhaps one was copied from examples of the other, or both from examples from a third source);
(d) their presence is due to the migration of the people who made or obtained them;
(e) the similarity is coincidental and has no significance.

This is not the place to discuss all these possibilities in detail, but it would clearly be very useful to be able to answer the question 'were they both made from the same source material?' if we wanted to choose between them. The source material might be clay and filler (temper) for pottery, ore for metal objects or raw flint for flint tools. Even with the same source material, the artefacts may not actually have been made in the same place, since the material could have been transported in a raw or semi-finished state.

Scientific analysis

Scientific examination of materials to determine their source has been carried out for some years. One of the earliest successes was the identification of sources of a number of types of neolithic stone axes

107

found in south-west England,[1] and which came from sources as far apart as Penzance (Group 1) and Great Langdale, Cumbria (Group VI). Some examples are shown in *pl* 7. More recent studies on the sources of stone implements include work on Near Eastern obsidian by Cann, Dixon and Renfrew and on British flint.[2] In the latter cases, the method used was trace element analysis – that is, determining the proportions of certain rare elements as a means of characterizing particular sources. Trace element analysis has also been extensively used in the study of copper/bronze artefacts of the European Bronze Age. The problem here is rather different, as the artefacts are compared with each other, in order to detect local groupings which might have a common source, and not with parent ore bodies. There is the additional complication that broken bronze artefacts can be melted down (perhaps with other bronzes from other sources) and re-cast, and so on.

Plate 7   Selection of Neolithic polished stone axes.

Pottery is perhaps a less tractable material for this kind of study. However, one notable success has been the tracking-down of the widespread Romano-British pottery known as black-burnished ware type 1 (or BB1 for short) (*pl 8*) to a source in Dorset, by means of heavy mineral analysis. In this case the particular heavy mineral is tourmaline, which is unusually common among the heavy minerals found in BB1.

Plate 8   Three pots of BB1 (black burnished ware, type 1) made in
Dorset, showing the most common forms.

Interpreting the results

Good for the scientists, but where does mathematics come into this
work? So far, in two areas: (i) sorting out large numbers of trace
element analyses (or profiles) into possible 'source' groupings, where
the sources are not known; and (ii) deciding on the most likely sources
for trace element profiles, when the profiles of possible sources are
known.

In category (i) comes the work on copper/bronze artefacts mentioned above and reported by Doran and Hodson. The technique of
k-means cluster analysis (see p 52) is used to try to group the analyses
into significant clusters. Although they describe their work as preliminary, the authors conclude that 'it should eventually be possible to
define definite combinations of trace-elements by cluster analysis. It
should then be possible to distinguish clusters that represent common,
natural and widely-distributed combinations of elements from those
that have at least some regional significance. Within the latter, it might
then be possible to distinguish highly distinctive workshop clusters
from more general ore-clusters that reflect no more than well known
major ore-types'.

An example of (ii) is the obsidian analysis reported by Cann,
Dixon and Renfrew. Their aim was to characterize examples known

to have come from certain sources, so that examples from unknown sources can be identified with the characteristics of the known sources. The first step is to plot the position of each example on a graph showing the proportions of two of the trace elements (see *fig 4.1*) – in this case zirconium and barium – dividing the examples up into ten distinct groups. Some groups correspond to a single source (e.g. group 5 = Kenya), while others (e.g. group 1) correspond to a number of sources. To split up these groups, similar graphs are plotted for other pairs of trace elements (e.g. strontium and iron). To a statistician, it appears inefficient to look at just a pair of trace elements at a time – he wants to look at them all at once. To do so would require a graph in several dimensions, and zones drawn round the various groups just as in *fig 4.1*. This is hard enough to imagine, let alone to do.

Discriminant analysis

The alternative is to find a line which discriminates best between two groups. As a simple example, take groups 1 and 6 (see *fig 4.2*). They cannot be distinguished purely on the basis of zirconium (since there is a considerable overlap), nor on the basis of barium alone (there is almost total overlap – proportions of barium in the two groups are very similar). But they can be distinguished on the basis of a combination of zirconium and barium, and this combination is represented by the line drawn in *fig 4.2*.

Imagine moving along this line from bottom left to top right. One passes quite suddenly from a zone of group 1 to a zone of group 6, with no overlap at all. If all the points were plotted in terms of their distances along this line and at right angles to it, the group 1 and group 6 points would form distinct zones along the line. Such a line is called a discriminant, and the finding of such lines discriminant analysis. In less fortunate cases it may not be possible to find a discriminant that splits the two groups as perfectly as in this example; the aim then would be to find one that does the job as well as possible. A few group 1 specimens may end up in group 6 and vice versa, but the overlap is reduced to a minimum.

In two dimensions, there is little to be gained by using discriminant analysis: it is simple and quicker just to ring the groups as in *fig 4.1*. It is in more than two dimensions that the technique shows to advantage: one can no longer ring the groups but one can still calculate a discriminant and line up the points along it. Analyses of specimens from unknown sources can then be referred to this line to see if they belong to group 1 or group 6. This is not quite as simple as it sounds,

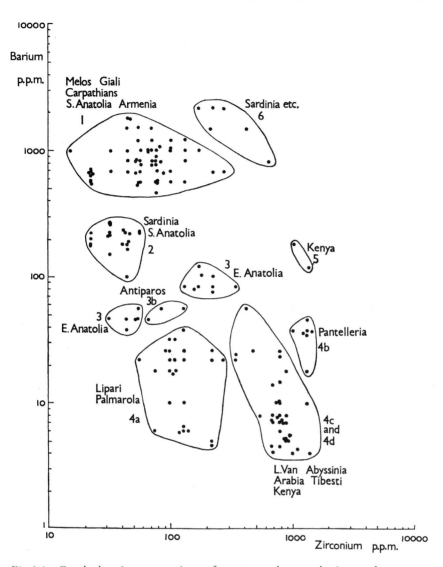

Fig 4.1 Graph showing proportions of two trace elements barium and
zirconium in samples of obsidian. *From Cann, Dixon and Renfrew (1969).*

since each pair of groups will have a different discriminant, and many
comparisons may be needed to track down the required 'matching'
source. Simple tests can help 'filter out' the more obvious choices – for
example, one could distinguish between groups 1 and 6 together and
all the other groups simply on the basis of barium content.

111

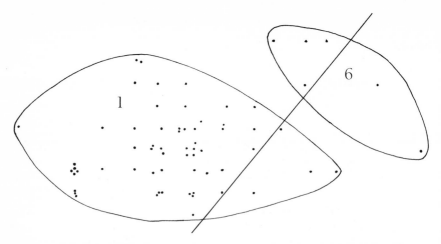

Fig 4.2 Detail from *fig 4.1*, showing groups 1 and 6. The line has been added to show the best discriminant between the two groups. *Adapted from Cann, Dixon and Renfrew (1969).*

Suppose, one might wonder, a new analysis falls between two groups. To which does it belong? Discriminant analysis can help here, too, by telling us which group it is nearer. It helps to define the 'frontiers' between clusters that were discussed in chapter 2.

Summary

The mathematical techniques of cluster analysis and discriminant analysis can help to sort out the results of a scientific study, with the aim of assigning artefacts – perhaps of stone, bronze or pottery – to their place or area of origin. This is interesting information in its own right, and satisfies a certain curiosity, but it is only the beginning of the work so far as the statistician is concerned. The next problem is to interpret the patterns formed when we plot the distribution of artefacts from one or more sources on a map. It is to this problem that we now turn.

MAPS OF ARTEFACT DISTRIBUTIONS

The development of mapping techniques

Distribution maps have a secure and valued place in the archaeological armoury. Maps of the distribution of artefacts can be used for a variety of purposes, either mainly descriptive or to make a particular point (see for example *figs 2.4* and *2.5*). Maps of site distributions will be dealt with later, in chapter 7.

Usually, the purpose of a distribution map is to convince the reader, as cogently and as briefly as possible, of the 'rightness' of a particular point or assertion. The argument has tended to be of the 'any fool can see that . . .' variety. This can be dangerous if the reader cannot see the pattern that is being invoked, or can think of other reasons for its existence.

The simplest and earliest type of artefact distribution map just shows each find-spot of a particular type of artefact as a spot on the map. An example is shown in *fig 4.3*. It tells us very little, except that bronze vessels of a certain rather badly defined class have an apparently wide distribution in Central Europe. There may be possible concentrations in one or two areas, but even they might be due more to variations in the intensity of activity by modern archaeologists than to the activities of prehistoric man. To attempt to argue anything from such a map would be a risky exercise.

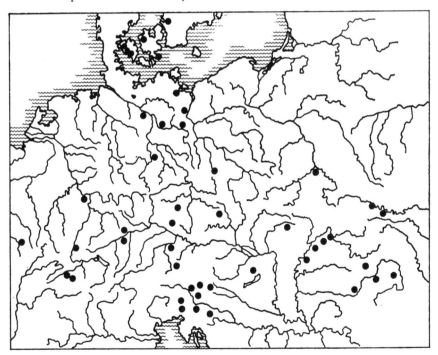

Fig 4.3   Example of an early type of distribution map, giving find-spots of a certain type of artefact. *From Hodder and Orton (1976), after Sprockhoff (1930).*

It is obvious that the amount, as well as the presence, of an artefact type at a certain place is important in studying its distribution. This is particularly so for pottery, where a dot on a simple distribution map might stand for a single sherd or a hundred whole pots. The answer found was to vary the size of the spots: large spots representing large quantities and small spots small quantities, or by putting the number of examples from a site inside the circle representing the site. An example of this form of presentation is shown in *fig 4.4*. Here the kiln site (Colchester) is indicated by a lozenge shape and the pottery is identified by means of makers' stamps (*pl 9*): small dots indicate one stamp found, otherwise the numbers tell the story. There is a very unusual distribution, with two concentrations, one in south–east England and the other in the military zones of Hadrian's and the Antonine Wall. If each find-spot were represented by a plain dot, one might be tempted to discount the scattered northern sites and see the distribution as concentrated in the south–east: the numbers tell us that this is just not so. Clearly the northern users were very important to these Colchester potters. More commonly, quantifying the map in this way would produce the opposite effect – the apparent importance of distant find-spots would tend to be reduced relative to the greater number of stamps (or whatever) found closer to the kiln site.

A map like *fig 4.4* tells us the relative importance of various find-sites, looked at from the point of view of the producer. It does not, however, tell us about the relative importance of various sources, looked at from the point of view of the user. In other words, how much of the pottery at site A came from kiln X? To tell us this, yet another sort of distribution map is needed. A good example is *fig 2.5*, which shows the percentages of New Forest pottery in a number of representative pottery assemblages in southern England. We can see immediately that New Forest pottery (see *pl 10*) is an important part of the assemblage at Salisbury or Winchester, but relatively unimportant at Exeter, London or Richborough. If the total size of the assemblages were also indicated (for example by varying the size of the circles), one could easily turn this map into one of the previous sort, i.e. one showing what proportions of the New Forest products went to each destination.

I have already glossed over one problem here – how does one say that such a percentage of the pottery at a site is of a certain type? More basically, how does one measure quantities of pottery, especially when broken? This is such an important question that it has been given a separate chapter (6) to itself (along with mathematically similar problems about bones), so as not to break up the flow of this chapter.

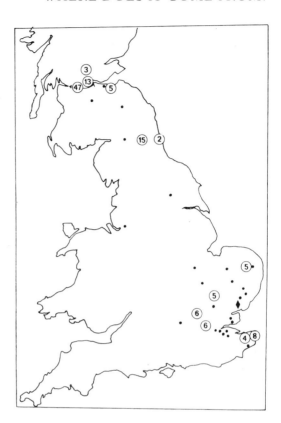

Fig 4.4
More advanced type of
distribution map, showing
numbers of artefacts
found at each find-spot.
From Hartley (1973).

Plate 9   Maker's stamp on mortarium from Colchester. Such stamps
enable products from a particular source to be identified
wherever they may be found.

115

Plate 10   Fourth-century New Forest pottery from Holbury, West Dean.

For the time being, we will suppose that we can measure quantities of pottery.

We now have all the archaeological information we need to study the movements of products from producer to user, by trade or other means. We can now study possible lines and means of transport, the likely value of different types of artefact in the contemporary economy, or possibly means of marketing of products. So far two main techniques have been adapted for these purposes – regression analyses and trend surface analyses.

Current techniques

1 Regression analysis

Regression analysis is an old and well-established statistical technique which has found applications in many fields of study. It is concerned with studying the relationship between two variables, or, more precisely, how one changes as the other is varied. The two variables are not seen as being on an equal footing: one is the independent variable, for which we can choose a value, and the other is the dependent variable, whose value we measure when we have set the first. In a regression analysis one would choose a number of different values for the independent, and study the relationship between the two. Two simple non-archaeological examples may help to make this clear.

An elementary physics experiment, often performed in schools, concerns the extension of a wire when various weights are hung on it. The initial, unstretched, length is measured, a weight of (say) ten grams hung on the end and the length re-measured, and so on for twenty grams, thirty grams, etc. The results usually look like *fig 4.5*. Eventually, of course, the wire will thin out at one point and break, but for some time before this happens, the extension is in direct proportion to the weight. In this situation the weight is the independent variable and the length the dependent, because it makes sense to think of choosing a weight and measuring the corresponding length, but not the other way round.

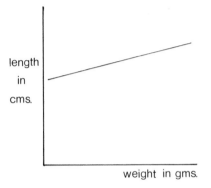

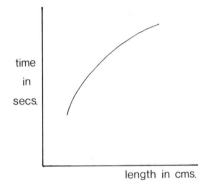

Fig 4.5 Example of linear regression: the relationship between weight hung on a wire and the length of the wire.

Fig 4.6 Example of curvilinear regression: the relationship between length of a pendulum and the time of its swing.

This particularly simple situation, where the change in one variable is in direct proportion to the other, is known as linear regression (because the relationship can be represented by a straight regression line, as in *fig 4.5*). More complicated relationships can occur, as in *fig 4.6*, which shows the relationship between the length of a simple pendulum (the independent variable), and the period of its swing, (the dependent variable). Here again, the status of the two variables is clear-cut: we can choose any length of pendulum (the simplest pendulum is just a weight on a string), but the period of the swing is beyond our control (except via the length). The relationship in this case is not linear, but in general terms it can be called curvilinear (that is, the regression line is curved).

Sometimes regression analysis is used when it is not at all clear which is the dependent and which the independent variable – for example, the heights and weights of schoolchildren, or (to get back to archaeology) the lengths and breadths of flint flakes. This can lead to difficulties, since we can treat (say) height as the independent variable and obtain one regression line, and then treat weight as the independent variable and obtain a different regression line. Which one we choose (or whether we go for a compromise) depends on the precise use that we want to make of the regression relationship.

The most common use of regression analysis in the study of distribution maps is to examine the way in which the density of the distribution of a certain type of artefact decreases as one moves away from its centre of production. One would expect some sort of a decrease, but the pattern it can follow seems to depend heavily on the nature of the artefact and the scale of its production. Firstly, though, there are two ways of measuring the density of the distribution of the artefact: (i) by measuring the proportion of that type of artefact as a percentage of all similar artefacts, at a number of sites around the centre, (ii) measuring the density of sites at which that artefact is found, in zones round the centre. These two approaches are illustrated in *figs 4.7* and *4.8*. In *fig 4.7* we see five sites, A–E, at various distances from the centre. At A (the nearest site), the artefact constitutes 30% of all the artefacts found there, while at E (the furthest site) it is only 1%.

In *fig 4.8* the area around the centre is divided up into zones five kilometres wide. There are five sites with the artefact in the first zone, nine in the second, ten in the third, and seven in the fourth, giving densities of 5, 3, 2, 1 respectively (in terms of sites per area of the innermost zone).

The choice of the measure one uses will depend on each individual situation: as a general rule (i) seems to be more suitable for relatively common or 'bulky' artefacts, like a particular type of pottery, which could be expressed as a percentage of all pottery, or a particular sort of

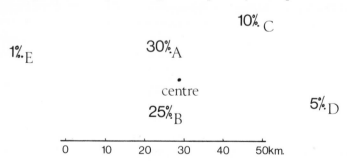

Fig 4.7   Proportions of artefact of a certain type at five sites around the centre of production.

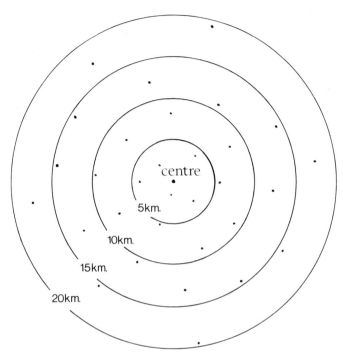

Fig 4.8   Numbers of sites at which a certain artefact is found, in zones around the centre of production.

stone (e.g. obsidian), which could be expressed as a percentage of all stone implements. On the other hand, (ii) seems more suitable for more 'individual' artefacts, for example coins (a particular type is not likely to turn up in great quantity on many sites), although it could also be used for the bulkier sorts of artefacts.

Whichever method we choose, we next have to collect the data we need. For (ii) this may not be too difficult, since we may find it on an existing distribution map: if not, we only need to find out whether or not the particular artefact was found on the chosen sites. We may have more problems with (i): relatively few excavation reports publish the pottery in terms of percentages from different sources (though more are slowly becoming available). Part of the trouble has been in deciding just what is meant by a percentage of what may be a group of sherds of all shapes and sizes. This question is dealt with separately in chapter 6. The data may be more readily available for stone implements.

The next step is to plot the density (however we have measured it) against the distance from the centre of production, since there can be no doubt that distance is the independent variable and density the dependent. The regression line that we obtain is also known as the fall-off curve. Three examples are given in *fig 4.9*: they show the fall off in density of the same class of artefact – Savernake pottery – measured in three different ways. The first (curve 1) is by density of sites (i.e. method (ii) above), the second (curve 2) is by percentage of pottery at each site (i.e. method (i) above), and the third (curve 3) is by percentage of sites possessing Savernake pottery (i.e. the number of sites with Savernake pottery in each zone is divided by the number of sites that could have had Savernake pottery). This figure shows two things – firstly that it would be very dangerous, if we wished to compare two different types of artefact, to measure their densities in different ways, and secondly that fall-off curves can come in a wide variety of shapes.

Fortunately, it has been found that just the shape of a fall-off curve can be described by means of just two parameters – that is, numbers which, by taking different values, can alter the shape of the curve. By convention, they are called '*b*' and α (alpha). The parameter *b* controls the steepness (or gradient) of the curve – large values of *b* mean steep curves and small values mean shallow curves – while α controls the concavity of the curve – a small α means a very concave curve and a high α a less concave curve or even a straight line. Convex fall-off curves appear to be rare. Looking at *fig 4.9*, we can see that curve 1 has a fairly high value of *b* (fairly steep gradient) and a low value of α (concave), curve 2 has a lower value of *b* (less steep gradient) but a higher value of α (less concave), while curve 3 has a very high value of *b* (very steep gradient) and also a very high value of α (straight line).

Some case studies

Our aim now is to be able to interpret the various values of *b* and α in archaeological terms. As a first step, we shall compare the curves obtained for some selected artefacts, and interpret them in terms of what we already know (or suspect) about the artefacts. This can have its dangers: chiefly that one's arguments can tend to become circular. The next step will be to consider theoretical ideas (or models) about how artefacts might become distributed across the countryside, to try to work out what sort of distribution patterns they would give rise to, and finally to compare them with real-life distribution patterns. We will come to this technique (known as simulation) after looking at trend surface analysis (see below). In a comparison of gradients, it was found that coarse, bulky objects (e.g. roofing tiles, Savernake pottery)

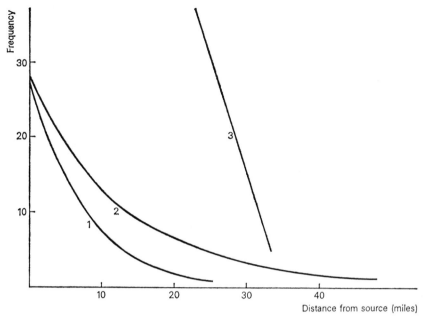

Fig 4.9   Examples of 'fall-off curves' for Savernake pottery. *From Hodder and Orton (1976).*

had a steeper gradient than finer products (e.g. Oxford colour-coated pottery, Iron Age [Dobunnic] coins). Also, larger production centres tended to have a steeper gradient than smaller centres – the higher the percentage at the centre, the further it has to fall, to put it simply. These results are really only what one would expect intuitively. Perhaps more interesting are the values of α, which fall into two distinct groups, as follows:

(i) 'low' values of α (i.e. between 0.1 and 0.6):

Cirencester roofing tiles	: $\alpha = 0.2$
Savernake pottery	: $\alpha = 0.4$
Romano-British Malvernian pottery	: $\alpha = 0.2$
New Forest pottery	: $\alpha = 0.1$
Neolithic picrite axes	: $\alpha = 0.6$

(ii) 'high' values of α (i.e. between 0.9 and 2.5)

Oxfordshire pottery	: $\alpha = 1.0$
Iron Age (Dobunnic) coins	: $\alpha = 1.3$
Anatolian obsidian	: $\alpha = 0.9$
West Cornwall Neolithic pottery	: $\alpha = 1.6$
Neolithic axes from Great Langdale	: $\alpha = 2.5$

121

Ian Hodder has interpreted the 'low' value of α as relating to small-scale 'local' concerns, probably with direct or close contact between the producer and the user. The presence of New Forest pottery in this group may come as a surprise: in fact many of the wares produced there had a very local distribution, and even the finer wares are not as widely distributed as was once thought, and are certainly overshadowed by the larger Oxford potteries. The 'high' values of α were interpreted as relating to large-scale centres manufacturing for a wide area, with more complicated forms of contact between producer and user.

It is always instructive to see whether the data actually fit the pattern that we have tried to impose upon it. In this case – is the fall-off the same in all directions? – because we have tacitly assumed that it is. A good example of this is the Oxford pottery. *Fig 4.10* shows the best fall-off curve drawn through the plot of the percentages at a number of

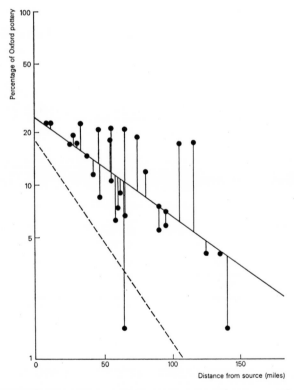

Fig 4.10   Fall-off curve for Oxfordshire colour-coated pottery. The curve clearly does not fit the data well. *From Hodder and Orton (1976).*

sites. It is clear that the curve does not fit the site data well: although they are equally spread above and below the curve, they diverge from it, especially for the greater distances. An examination of the residuals (i.e. the gaps between the points and the curve) indicated that the sites fell into two groups – those that could easily be reached by water from Oxford, and above the curve, and those best reached over land, and generally below the curve (see *fig 4.11*). The two groups of sites now fit their respective curves much better than they fitted the single curve of *fig 4.10*. We can see that where water transport is available, the fall-off rate is very slow indeed, but elsewhere it is much more rapid. There is still one very large negative residual (at about sixty miles from

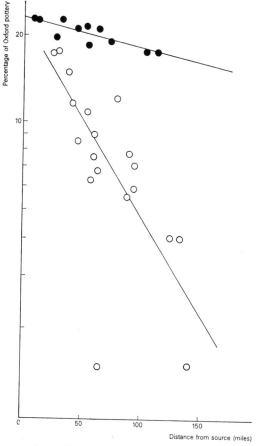

Fig 4.11 The same data, divided into two groups – sites reached by water and sites reached overland. A separate fall-off curve is fitted to each group, giving a much better fit. *From Hodder and Orton (1976).*

Oxford) which is a site very close to the New Forest kilns, and presumably supplied by them in preference to the more distant Oxford centre.

As an archaeological technique, regression analysis is clearly rather crude. In particular the assumption that the fall-off rate is the same in all directions is almost always likely to be an over-simplification. Nevertheless, it does provide a fairly useful basic model with which distributions can be compared, and reasons for the particular shape of the fall-off curve, and for departures from it, can fruitfully be sought.

2 Trend surface analysis

The idea behind trend surface analysis is to produce a 'contour map' of the density of a type of artefact (using density in either of the meanings given above, p 118), in the same way as the Meteorological Office produces a map of atmospheric pressure from readings sent in from weather stations. In industry too the technique has been used for some time, generally under the name of response surface or yield surface techniques.

Grid generalization

The basic idea can be put into practice in one of two ways. The first is an empirical approach in which the map is divided up into a grid of quadrats (usually, but not necessarily, squares), and the density in each quadrat is measured. Since these values would by themselves give, not a smoothed surface, but a pattern like an uneven tiled floor, they are 'smoothed' by averaging the values in four adjacent squares and putting the result at the point where they meet. A smooth 'contour map' can then be drawn. A hypothetical example is shown in fig 4.12. Here (a) shows the original (but imaginary) pattern of sites. In (b) the number of sites is shown in each quadrat, while in (c) the averaged values are given. Note that the map becomes slightly smaller because one cannot average for the points at the very edge of the map. Fig 4.12(d) is the final contour map, with contours drawn in at 'heights' of 2½, 5 and 7½ sites per quadrat. For those who are interested in trying this for themselves, the contours are drawn by taking in turn each line joining each pair of points which have one value greater than 7½ and one less. Find the '7½' point on the line by dividing it in proportion, e.g. the line between 6 and 8 (bottom left-hand corner) divides at ¾ of the way along, because 7½ is ¾ of the way between 6 and 8. All the '7½' points can then be joined up to form the '7½' contour, and so on.

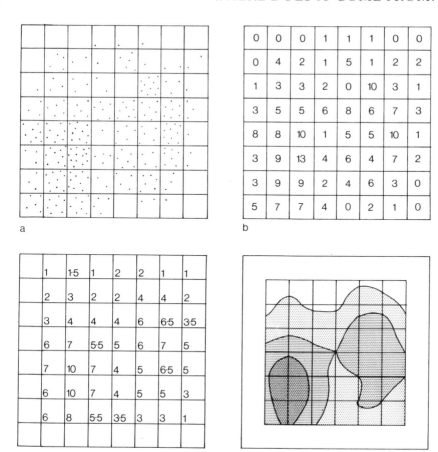

a

b

c

d

Fig 4.12 Example of grid generalization technique.
(a) distribution pattern of sites at which artefacts of a certain type are present
(b) density of such sites per quadrat
(c) 'smoothed' density, averaged from (b)
(d) contour map plotted from (c)

This technique, known as grid generalization, is most suitable for the 'sites per area' definition of density, and the contour map looks as though it could be useful. But there is a hidden problem, because we have had to choose the size of the quadrat, and our choice will have a dramatic effect on the resulting map. To illustrate this point, the same data have been re-analysed with a grid of quadrats twice the size *(fig 4.13)*. In *fig 4.13(b)* a grid of double-size squares (i.e. four

125

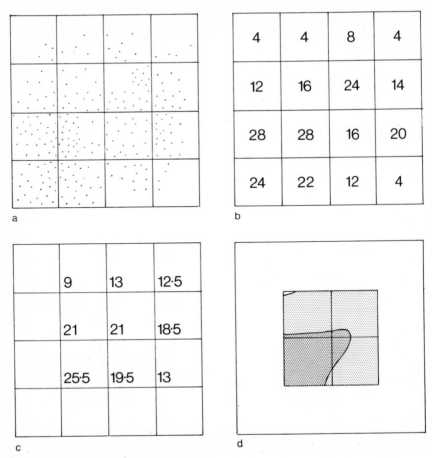

4	4	8	4
12	16	24	14
28	28	16	20
24	22	12	4

a   b

9	13	12·5
21	21	18·5
25·5	19·5	13

c   d

Fig 4.13   Second example of grid generalization technique. The data and the
technique are the same as in *fig 4.12*, but the quadrat-size has been
doubled.

times the area) has been laid over (a) and the sites counted. In (c) they
are averaged, and the resulting contour map is shown in *fig 13(d)*. The
contours are at 'heights' of ten, twenty and thirty sites per quadrat,
because the quadrats have four times the area of those in *fig 4.12*
(4 × 2½ = 10, etc.). The pattern is completely different: instead of a
'twin' peak – one rather higher than the other, we have a single rather
gentle 'plateau'. It is not possible to say that one map is 'right' and the
other 'wrong': they are just different ways of looking at the same data.

One is bound to feel a certain unease about a technique in which an
arbitrary choice can significantly affect the outcome: firstly at the
apparent haphazardness of the final picture, and secondly at the

thought that the quadrat size might be manipulated to produce the desired effect. In a practical example – the distribution of pottery from the Rowlands Castle Kiln in Hampshire – Ian Hodder also found that different quadrat sizes gave very different results. Nevertheless, provided these limitations are understood and allowance made for them, useful results could be obtained.

Regression approach to trend surface analysis

The second technique tries to overcome this difficulty by fitting one simple geometric surface to all the data at once. The methods used are similar to those used in regression analysis (p 116), but work in two dimensions instead of just one. As indicated above, much work has already been done in this area and computer programmes to do the job (which, unlike grid generalization, cannot be done 'by hand') are readily available. Perhaps too readily, because they are based on implicit assumptions which do not seem to match the archaeological reality. To see this, we need to look a little closer at the workings of the technique.

Since there are an infinite number of surfaces that could be used to describe the pattern of artefact densities, we need to narrow the field before asking the computer to find the 'best' one. The first stage is to choose a family of surfaces known as polynomials (because of their description in mathematical terms). They have two main advantages – they are relatively easy to work with and can in practice approximate well to any small part of a large surface. What they cannot necessarily do is approximate well to the whole of a large surface. This is useful for (say) the production engineer, looking (for example) for the optimum setting of temperature and pressure for some process, because he probably already knows the rough limits within which the optimum is likely to lie, and so is only interested in part of the response surface. We as archaeologists are likely to be interested in the whole surface. Within the family of polynomial surfaces, one has to choose whether one wants a second-order, third-order or whatever-order polynomial. The higher the order, the more complicated the surface can become. For reasons of simplicity and expediency, second-, third- and fourth-order polynomials only are commonly considered. The final choice is almost completely arbitrary – none has any grounding in the archaeological situation. The regression analysis was at least based on some idea (however over-simplified) of how real distribution patterns might be expected to look.

The next step is to design the experiment – that is, to choose (in the case of the engineer) combinations of temperature and pressure that we wish to investigate. In archaeology we cannot choose out data points (which might be O.S. grid co-ordinates) but must take (or leave) what we are given by excavation and fieldwork. This means that the fitted surface could at worst be misleading (see comment on *fig 4.16* below) and at best an inefficient use of the data.

It is now a simple matter (for the computer at least) to fit the 'best' surface of the specified family to our data. In doing so, we are assuming that there are no edge-effects, i.e. areas of the map where the usual rules do not apply. There are techniques for dealing with simple edge-effects, e.g. straight line boundaries to 'no-go' areas, but none for the sort of edges, like coastlines, that we are likely to encounter.

After all this, one might despair at getting anything useful out of a fitted trend surface. But it is worth looking critically at a few to see what we can learn from them. To do so we turn again to the Romano-British Oxford potteries. The data already used for *figs 4.10* and *4.11* also formed the basis of a trend surface study. The three 'best' surfaces are shown in *figs 4.14–16: fig 4.14* is the best second-order surface, *fig 4.15* the best third-order surface and *fig 4.16* the best fourth-order surface.

Fig 4.14, the simplest surface, shows an east-west ridge, falling sharply to north and south but rising to the west (and in fact also to the east, although this is not clear from the figure). The south Essex area is in fact on a col (like a mountain pass in shape). An acquaintance with the behaviour of second-order polynomials would tell us that quite small differences in the data can mean the difference between an elongated dome shape (paraboloid) and a 'mountain pass' or 'saddle' shape (hyperboloid). We would expect (or hope for) the former, but have fitted the latter.

The third-order surface of *fig 4.15* is similar: we still have the 'mountain-pass' shape, although now rather curved instead of lying almost directly east-west. Little has been gained in terms of fit or interpretation. The fourth-order surface of *fig 4.16* is much more complicated. It still has a col – now shifted to the Gloucester area – but the main ridge now lies in a north-easterly direction from Oxford to East Anglia and two 'troughs' – one near the New Forest (the other kiln site shown) and one across from Sussex to the Suffolk coast. The whole pattern looks less realistic than the other two. The two ridges seem fictitious – the 'north-easterly' one is almost certainly a product of the lack of sites in this area: since there are no data, any surface will 'fit'. The second trough mentioned is also artificial – probably a compensating effect to the 'peak' in east Kent – (Richborough), but

Figs 4.14–16
Three trend surfaces fitted to
the distribution of Oxfordshire
colour-coated pottery.
All from Hodder and Orton (1976)

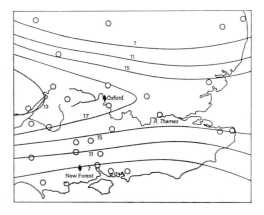

14: the best second-order surface

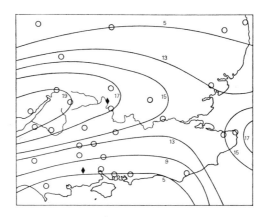

15: the best third-order surface

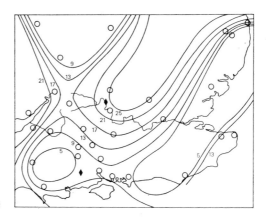

16: the best fourth-order surface

the first is probably 'real', representing an area of scarce Oxford pottery, because of competition from the nearby New Forest kiln (see p 114).

We have had to use our knowledge of the archaeological situation to sort out real features from mathematical features, which rather defeats the object of the exercise. Looking at all three together, the simplest is perhaps the most useful. We can still ask why there is a ridge (even if it is the wrong shape of ridge) and why it lies east-west. If we know about polynomials we will not even be surprised that the ridge is the 'wrong' shape. But somehow all we seem to have done is to substitute mathematical intuition for archaeological intuition, which may be very satisfying to the mathematician but does not help the archaeologist.

Well, where do we go from here? As in regression analysis (p 116), we can examine the residuals, to see which sites fail to fit the general pattern. This would show, for example, the disturbing effect of the New Forest kilns on the simple pattern of *fig 4.14*.

In the longer term, we need to find families of surfaces which could reasonably be expected to look like distribution patterns. One possibility would be a family whose parameters were (i) the distance of the site from the centre of production and (ii) the direction of the site from the centre. We could then have a fall-off curve, but one that varied accordingly to the direction chosen. Although edge effects would still be a problem, the model seems more realistic than either of those described above.

Simulation of artefact dispersal

You may have noticed that there is a gap between the idea of the dispersal of artefacts from a production centre and the two methods used to examine it – regression analysis and trend surface analysis. There is 'something missing' between the idea and the technique – some sort of justification for why that particular technique should be expected to fit a particular sort of distribution pattern. In part this reflects the second-hand nature of many statistical techniques used in archaeology: they have been borrowed from some other discipline because they look promising, and may have no real theoretical underpinning in archaeology itself.

To try to bring the archaeological ideas and the mathematical techniques closer together, Ian Hodder carried out experiments in the computer simulation of artefact dispersal which are worth discussing briefly here.

The first part of the experiment was to simulate (or imitate) the dispersal of artefacts from a single centre. It was assumed that the artefacts were moved in a number of discrete 'steps' before reaching their final resting place. The steps might represent (for example) change of ownership of the artefact, or movement of the owner(s). The steps could take place in any direction, but in different experiments different conditions were imposed on the number and length of the steps. For example, for 'curve no. 1' the number of steps was fixed at 5 and the step length at 0.5 units (actually centimetres in the computer program), while for 'curve no. 2' the number of steps could be 1, 2, 3, 4, 5 or 6 (with equal chances), and the step length was fixed at 1.0 units. The computer then followed the instructions – in the case of curve no. 1 (for example) this involved plotting five successive random steps from the centre, giving one final 'find-spot'. This was repeated a chosen number of times, building up a distribution pattern which followed the rules laid down at the beginning. An example, where the process has been carried out ten times, is shown in *fig 4.17(a)*, and the final distribution pattern in *fig 4.17(b)*. In practice not ten but 100 'walks', as they are called, were made to generate each distribution pattern. Five such patterns were generated for each set of rules, to see the variability that could be expected to exist between different patterns generated under the same set of rules.

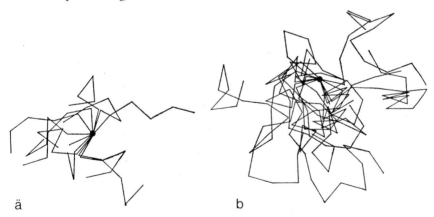

ä   b

Fig 4.17   Example of simulation of dispersal of artefacts from a centre. *From Hodder and Orton (1976).*

To compare these hypothetical distribution patterns with real ones, their fall-off curves (see p 120) were plotted, and their α's and b's calculated (just as for the real-life distributions). Twelve different sets of rules are shown in *fig 4.18* and the corresponding fall-off curves in

Curve no.	No. of steps		Step length (cm)		Comments	α	b
1	5	(fixed)	0.5	(fixed)		2.5	—0.098
2	1–6	(equal probability)	1.0	(fixed)		2.4	—0.047
3	1–3	(equal probability)	0–1	(equal probability)		2.2	—0.130
4	1–2	(equal probability)	0–1	(equal probability)		1.3	—0.152
5	2	(fixed)	0.5	mean (exponential distribution)		1.1	—0.076
6	1–14	(equal probability)	0.5	(fixed)		2.1	—0.077
7	1–10	(equal probability)	0.5	(fixed)		1.9	—0.077
8	1–6	(equal probability)	0.5	(fixed)		1.8	—0.112
9	1–14	(equal probability)	0.5	(fixed)	Barrier at 1.5	2.3	—0.072
10	1–6	(equal probability)	0.5	(fixed)	Barrier at 1.5	1.7	—0.107
11	1–14	(equal probability)	0.5	(fixed)	Barrier at 0.75	2.1	—0.072
12	1–6	(equal probability)	0.5	(fixed)	Barrier at 0.75	1.4	—0.114

Fig 4.18 Twelve possible sets of rules for simulating the dispersal of artefacts from a centre. *From Hodder and Orton (1976).*

fig 4.19. The resulting values of α and b are shown in *fig 4.18*. Two main points emerged from this study:
(i) very different sets of rules (processes) can give rise to very similar fall-off curves;
(ii) parameter α seems rather more sensitive than b to changes in the process. High values of α seem to be related to large numbers of relatively small steps, while low values of α seemed to correspond to fewer, but possibly longer, steps. In general, high values of α seem to relate to costly moves.

The second stage of the experiment was to simulate redistributive processes, that is systems in which artefacts move from producer to user via a central place (e.g. a market town) rather than directly from

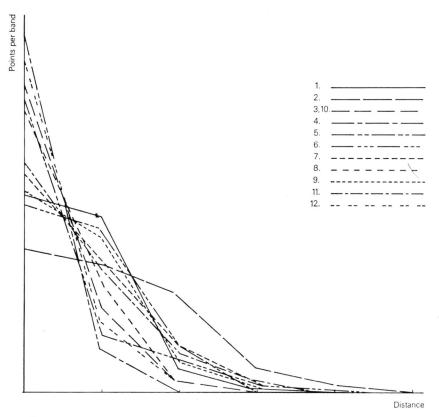

Fig 4.19 The fall-off curves corresponding to the set of rules in *fig 4.18*. From Hodder and Orton (1976).

producer to user. There are important archaeological implications in being able to distinguish between redistributive and other forms of artefact dispersal. Hodder found that, although in ideal circumstances redistributive processes gave rise to distinctive fall-off curves (e.g. curves that rose to a peak before falling away), in real life their distinctive nature was likely to become blurred, and not easy to distinguish from other processes. He concluded that a study of fall-off curves is probably not the best way to sort out redistributive from other processes, and recommended trend surface analysis.

Conclusions

The systematic quantitative study of artefact distribution patterns is still in its early stages. The main techniques used so far – regression

133

analysis and trend surface analysis – have been adopted from other fields of study and have their limitations in archaeological situations. Nevertheless, provided the limitations are properly understood, they can provide useful results. So far, the results obtained have been rather obvious and 'common-sensical'. Future advances will depend on:

(i) the development of techniques more directly related to the archaeological situation, perhaps via computer simulation;

(ii) the creation of a larger body of reliable spatial data, for example percentages of pottery of different types at sites. Some of the problems involved here will be discussed further in chapter 6.

1. *Evens et al. 1962*
2. *Sieveking, Craddock, Hughes, Busch and Ferguson 1972*

CHAPTER FIVE

What Was It For?

On the face of it, you would not expect mathematics to be able to help towards an answer to this question. Surely the question of the function of an artefact is one to be settled by observation, experience and archaeological commonsense? Here at least the 'archaeologist's thumb' still reigns supreme, you might think. On the whole, you would be right – this is the area of the 'imagination gap' (p 24), which calls for a flash of intuition as much as a rigorous analysis.

Interpretation in terms of function

However, mathematical techniques have been used in arguments about function – not the function of an individual artefact or group of artefacts, but the wider question of whether a functional explanation is the correct sort of explanation in a particular problem. The question in which they have become involved concerns differences in assemblages of flint implements in south-west France in the Mousterian period. Before going into this in detail, it may be worth considering a simple hypothetical example. Suppose that, at the excavation of a cemetery, it was found that there were brooches (fibulae) present in each burial. Suppose too that some of the fibulae were heavy and strongly made, while others were lighter and less strong physically (although just as well made in a technical sense). The excavator would naturally ask 'why the difference?' One answer might be that they served a different purpose – perhaps the heavier ones were dress fasteners while the lighter ones were purely decorative – while an alternative might be that the difference was a matter of style or fashion, representing perhaps chronological differences. The former is a 'functional' explanation and the latter a 'stylistic' or 'cultural' explanation. The chosen answer may tell us more about the psychology of the excavator than anything else.

But now let us suppose that buttons were found in some of

the burials, in those that did not have a heavy fibulae (this is a very hypothetical example). In statistical terms there is a perfect (negative) correlation between heavy fibulae and buttons, but no correlation between light fibulae and buttons. This would strengthen the functional argument, because one could argue that heavy fibulae and buttons were alternatives, and that since buttons are obviously dress fasteners, heavy fibulae probably are too. Light fibulae are uncorrelated with buttons, and probably fulfil some other function. To be more realistic, now suppose that the correlation is not perfect, that is not all burials without buttons have heavy fibulae and vice versa. Nevertheless, we suspect that there is some degree of correlation between the two, which we measure by a correlation coefficient. We can then test this coefficient statistical to decide whether the degree of correlation we have observed could have arisen by chance, or whether it is statistically significant. A high level of statistical significance would, probably, be taken as evidence supporting the functional argument. In this way, a mathematical technique has contributed to the argument for (or against) the functional explanation.

A classic example

Let us now tackle the much more difficult case of the Mousterian flints. Fortunately, there is little argument about the basic problem, which has been summed up by Bordes. He divides the broad Mousterian culture into four more specific cultures, the 'Mousterian of Acheulian tradition', the 'typical Mousterian' the 'Charentian Mousterian' and the 'denticulate Mousterian'. Since we are here concerned with the arguments rather than the actual cultures, I will simply call them A, B, C and D respectively. He then examines the stratigraphic sequence at sites in south-west France, four of which are shown in *fig 5.1*.

He rejects the much earlier idea of a simple chronological sequence – A, B, C – and poses the question – what does this strange interstratification of the four 'cultures' mean?

Before comparing his answer with that of Lewis Binford, we need to look at the differences between these four types of Mousterian. Each type of Mousterian is a generalization, based on a number of similar assemblages (that is, contemporary deposits of flint tools) from different sites and phases. Each assemblage can be divided into different tool types (Bordes' 'tool list'), the numbers of which can be expressed as percentages of all tools in the assemblage. The differences between assemblages, and hence between the types of Mousterian, lie

			site		
glaciation	phase	Combe Grenal	Pech de l'Azé II	Pech de l'Azé I	Moustier
	VIII	A			
	VII	B			
	VI	B			B?
Würm II	V	D		?	
	IV	D,C		A	B
	III	D,C			B?
	II	C		A	A?
	I	C,B,C		A	A
	VII	B	—		A
	VI	D	—		A
	V	B	C		A
	IV	B	C		—
Würm I	III	B	B		—
	II	B	B,D,B		B
	I	B	B		

Fig 5.1

chiefly in the percentages of different tool types in different assemblages. For example, hand axes, which are common in A, are rare in B, C and D (which is why A was originally thought to be earlier than the others).

This statement of the problem (which is very brief and much simplified, but I hope contains the bare essentials) sets the scene for the rival explanations. Of the two main protagonists, Bordes favours a cultural explanation: the four types of Mousterian are four 'cultures', and represent different groups of people occupying different areas at different times, in a complicated shifting pattern. To Binford, on the other hand, the differences are functional, and represent different activities carried out by the same people in different places at different times. Different activities require different tool-kits (associated sets of tools) and differences between assemblages reflect varying proportions of different tool-kits. This is again a tremendous simplification, but it will be adequate for our purposes. The arguments put forward range far and wide, touching on topics like seasonal versus all-year round occupation of the sites, but the one which interests us is the overtly mathematical one, which led Binford to put forward his functional view in the first place.

What Binford noticed was that certain groups of tool-types varied in a similar way from one assemblage to another: if one type in the group was more frequent in certain assemblages than in others, then other types in the group would tend to follow the same pattern. What was more, these patterns of covariation, as he called it, extended right across all the four types of Mousterian. The groups of tool-types, which became known as tool-kits, were found by subjecting the lists of percentages of different tool-types in different assemblages to what is called factor analysis. Unfortunately, this technique tends to arouse strong emotions in the hearts of statisticians. Cynics have suggested that the reason is that the technique was originally developed by psychologists for dealing with particular problems in psychology (for example the analysis of scores of groups of individuals in different 'intelligence' tests), and not by 'real' statisticians. Certainly, some of the earlier exponents of the technique seem not to have fully understood its mathematical basis and gave the technique a bad name in the process.

From a user's point of view, factor analysis attempted to explain the variability in the scores of a number of individuals in different tests by hypothetical scores on a smaller number of 'factors'. For example, if people who did well on test A also did well on test B, but did not necessarily do well on tests C, D or E, then tests A and B were correlated and could be represented in whole or part by a 'factor', say Factor 1. By examining the patterns of correlation between all the tests (and there would be far more than the five of this simple example), the researcher would hope to extract a small number of factors which would account for (and therefore, he hoped, explain) the variability in the original scores. In practice it would be found that several tests contributed to the same factor, while any particular test might contribute to more than one factor. The aim was to reduce a large number of tests to a much smaller (and therefore more manageable) number of factors. There are some deep mathematical problems in the theory of the technique – for example, does one choose the number of factors in advance or does it emerge from the data in the course of the analysis? The glossing over of these problems may have led to the hostility of some statisticians. But more likely it was the interpretation that was put on the factors, which were seen as innate characteristics of the individuals, like 'intelligence', 'introversion–extraversion' and so on. Subsequent work revealed that intelligence testing was not that simple, and the whole idea tended to fall from favour, taking factor analysis down with it. Nevertheless, the underlying mathematical idea of factor analysis, the factor model, remained. It has its problems, but provided they were properly understood it was still a potentially useful technique.

Binford's particular insight was to see that the technique had an application in the Mousterian problem; in other words, the factor model was a possible way of approaching the vast amount of data embodied in the tool lists and percentages. In the archaeological version of the model, the tests are replaced by tool-types, the individuals by assemblages, and the scores by the percentages of types in the assemblages. Factor analysis demonstrated the existence of factors which could account for the variations in the percentages between one assemblage and another. These factors were groupings of tool-types which in Binford's interpretation became the tool-kits mentioned above. From a purely statistical point of view this seems a reasonable interpretation, assuming that the mathematics is correct and the technical problems of factor analysis have been taken into account. There was, however, much opposition to these ideas from his fellow archaeologists. It seems to an outsider to consist partly of misunderstandings about what factor analysis is and what it does, partly of distrust of new and unfamiliar techniques, and partly of defence of rival hypotheses.

It is not my concern here to try to say whether Binford was right or wrong, or even to give the reader enough evidence to make that decision for himself. The point is that he has advanced the argument a step: any account of the Mousterian must now seek to explain, not only the patterns shown in *fig 5.1*, but also the covariations between various sets of tool-types, whether they are expressed as factors or just as observed patterns of variation. Not all of his opponents have yet come to grips with this further development of the problem.

Conclusions

Perhaps the main benefit of Binford's work has been the stimulus it has given to the development of methods that could be used to check, or throw further light on, the 'functional argument'. A need for an independent check is obvious: one must also remember that, to some, factor analysis is a suspect technique and not one on which to build archaeological explanations. These methods have been concerned with the distribution of artefacts on an archaeological horizon, for example a paleolithic living floor. Briefly, the argument runs that if certain tool types are associated together in tool kits, serving a common function or perhaps different aspects of the same function, then their distributions on the horizon should be associated, that is the tools should on the whole be found nearer to each other than one would expect if either (or both) was distributed randomly. There is a problem here – first raised by Binford – concerning the attitude of the user towards his tools. Binford contrasts 'expedient' with 'curated' technologies: in the former tools are made as and when required, and are discarded after use, while in the latter they are carefully kept from one occasion of use to the next, and only discarded when broken or completely worn (or by accidental loss). In practice, the cultures under discussion are likely to lie somewhere between these extremes, but differences in emphasis can be expected. Nevertheless, it seems to be the general opinion that patterns of artefact distribution should in some way reflect patterns of use, and that studies of these patterns could be of great value, not only in the restricted area of the Mousterian debate, but more generally in the interpretation of 'open' archaeological sites.

Distribution patterns of artefacts on a site

Initially, methods of studying these distribution patterns (known in the jargon as intra-site spatial analysis) were adopted from geography and plant ecology, where they had been in use for some time. They have not proved to be particularly successful, since the assumptions underlying, say, the distribution of different species of plants in their habitat do not carry over well to archaeological situations. More recently, techniques based specifically on the needs of archaeological problems have begun to be developed. Examples of both early and later techniques will be discussed below.

First, however, a digression to a question which, with hindsight, should have been asked before all this effort started. Is the problem posed by Bordes and answered by Bordes, Binford and others, a real problem? In *fig 5.1,* which is a much simplified statement of the problem, we see sequences of flint assemblages which have been classified by Bordes into different types of Mousterian. Put at its crudest, one could ask – did Bordes get it right? Are all his type A cultures really type A, and so on? Or could one produce an explicable chronological or geographical pattern by re-assigning some assemblages to different types?

An attempt to answer this question has recently been made by Callow and Webb, who studied ninety-six assemblages of Mousterian flints from south-west France, most of which had been classified by Bordes. The division into types of Mousterian was as above, except that the 'Mousterian of Acheulian Tradition' was split into two sub-types, A and B, and the 'Charentian Mousterian' was split into 'Ferrassie' and 'Quina' sub-types, making six in all. One approach would have been to study the percentages of all the different tool types in all the assemblages, but since there are no fewer than sixty-three tool types in Binford's work (some of which are very rare) the study would have been difficult and perhaps inconclusive. Instead they used as their data nine of Binford's indices (measures of various technical and typological characteristics of the tools – for example, degree of retouch on flakes) and two particular types of tools, which are diagnostic for the Denticulate and Quina respectively. Put in mathematical terms, their aim was to see if Bordes' six types of assemblages formed discrete groups, or whether there was overlap between them.

This might seem to be a 'classification' problem, as discussed in chapter 2, and one which might be solved by some sort of cluster analysis. But in fact this problem, although related to classification, is closer to the problem of discrimination, which was discussed near the beginning of chapter 4 (p 110). The method chosen was that of canonical variates analysis, a complicated statistical technique which presents the data given to it in such a way as to bring out visually the differences between the suspected groupings. It does not create divisions if none really exists, since it is a way of looking at the data rather than actually manipulating them, but it does show the divisions between the suspected groups in the best possible light. When the analysis was attempted on all ninety-six assemblages, the results clearly showed the Quina group standing out from the rest (see *fig 5.2*). When the remaining assemblages were re-analyzed, the Mousterian of Acheulian Tradition 'B' formed a clearly distinct grouping. The next step was to analyse yet again the assemblages belonging to the four remaining types: this time the Denticulate stood out from the others. The authors were less happy with the results for just the M.A.T. 'A', 'typical' and Ferrassie Mousterian, as there seemed to be some confusion at the frontier between the typical and Ferrassie groups. This was put down to the rag-bag nature of the typical group: an assemblage which did not possess well-defined characteristics in a particular direction tended to end up as 'typical'. The statistical difficulties could be resolved by re-allocating a few assemblages from one group to another: these changes also made sense in terms of the flint assemblages themselves and the stratigraphy of the sites where they were found.

Thus the canonical variates analysis confirmed Bordes' classification of the assemblages, with a few minor changes. It has of course a wider role than this particular study: it is of use in checking the distinctness of suspected groups, for example those coming from a

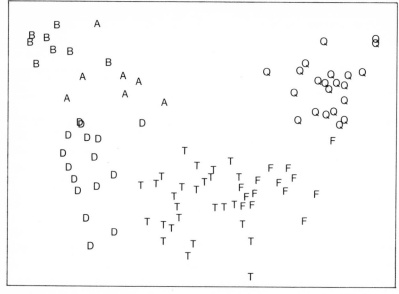

Fig 5.2 Result of canonical variates analysis on 96 Mousterian assemblages:
Key: A = M.A.T. 'A'   F = Ferrassie
     B = M.A.T. 'B'   Q = Quina
     D = denticulate   T = Typical.
From Callow and Webb (1977).

subjective typology or a cluster analysis. It cannot, however, be used
to divide a body of material into groups from scratch: there must
always be some initial idea of possible grouping to be checked.

DISTRIBUTION PATTERNS OF ARTEFACTS ON A SITE

(i) Recording

We can now return to the various techniques of spatial analysis which
can be used to study distributions of artefacts on a site. The choice of
technique will depend on the degree of precision with which the
location of artefacts has been measured. It is a reasonably common
practice to measure in the position of more important finds (for
example coins on a Roman site) exactly – that is to the nearest cen-
timetre – but to record the position of more common finds more
loosely, perhaps in terms of metre squares. The latter method is
employed partly in order to reduce the inordinate amount of work
that would be involved in measuring the position of every find
exactly. Some very small finds might only be detected when the spoil

is sieved (an increasingly common practice), and clearly they will never have more than a very general location. On the other hand, the requirements of the various statistical methods can influence the way in which a site is excavated and the finds recorded. Recently a compromise has been proposed by Johnson, who suggests recording the location of finds in cells, that is squares of side twenty to thirty centimetres.[1] Locating a find within a particular cell is much more precise than locating it within a metre square (there could be up to twenty-five cells in each square), but much less work than recording the position exactly. In Johnson's opinion, the level of accuracy obtained by recording loose artefacts by cells is enough for most archaeological purposes, and the extra precision of an exact location may well represent nothing more than 'noise', such as post-deposition disturbance (worm action, frost movements, etc.). Obviously relationships between closely associated finds would still have to be recorded separately, say in a sketch plan.

(ii) Methods based on grid squares

Firstly, suppose the locations have been recorded by grid squares, and remembering that we are interested in detecting associations between the distribution patterns of two (or more) different artefacts, what do we do with this information? Methods that can be used here are known as quadrat methods (quadrats are just the units of our grid, e.g. metre squares). The most common approach is to note the presence or absence of the two artefact types, say A and B, in each of the quadrats. There will be four sorts of quadrats – those with both A and B, those with A but not B, those with B but not A, and those with neither. Their numbers can be counted and a 2×2 table drawn up. A simple hypothetical example is shown in *fig 5.3*.

This approach has been extensively used in plant ecology, and many different measures of association have been suggested. The three most common are known respectively as χ^2 (pronounced chi-squared), Q and V. The chi-squared statistic can be used in the famous chi-squared test of association, while Q and V measure how strong the association is. In this example, χ^2 is about 5, Q is -0.8 (Q $= +1$ would indicate complete association, and Q $= -1$ complete disassociation) and V is -0.5 (like Q, V ranges from $+1$ to -1 with the same interpretation). Clearly the distributions are dissociated, as one would expect from *fig 5.3(a)*.

However useful they may be in plant ecology, simple quadrat methods have not proved useful in archaeology. Even without going

Fig 5.3 (b)

-	A	B	B	B
A	A	A,B	B	B
A	A	A,B	B	B
A	A	A,B	B	-

Fig 5.3 (c)

type A

		present	absent	total
	present	3	8	11
type B	absent	7	2	9
	total	10	10	20

Fig 5.3 (a) plan of trench, 5 m by 4 m, showing location of artefacts of types A (●) and B (○). Quadrats are metre squares.
(b) the same trench. Letters show the presence or absence of types A and B in each quadrat.
(c) 2 × 2 table, showing numbers of quadrats with (i) both A and B, (ii) A only, (iii) B only, (iv) neither A nor B, in this example.

Fig 5.4 (a)

-	-	-	-	-	-	-
-	-	A	B	B	B	-
-	A	A	A,B	B	B	-
-	A	A	A,B	B	B	-
-	A	A	A,B	B	-	-
-	-	-	-	-	-	-

Fig 5.4 (b)

type A

		present	absent	total
	present	3	8	11
type B	absent	7	24	31
	total	10	32	42

Fig 5.4 (a) trench shown in *fig 5.3(a)*, extended by 1 m in each direction. No more artefacts of either type are found.
(b) 2 × 2 table, based on the extended trench. *See fig 5.3(c)*.

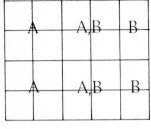

Fig 5.5 (b)

type A

		present	absent	total
	present	2	2	4
type B	absent	2	0	2
	total	4	2	6

Fig 5.5 (a) trench shown in *fig 5.3(a)*, but recorded in 2 m squares as far as possible.
(b) 2 × 2 table, based on trench as recorded in (c). *See fig 5.3(c)*.

into the statistical details, one can see why from a purely common-sense point of view:

(i) much of the information is wasted: no account is taken of how many artefacts are present in each cell, or of which quadrats are next to each other,

(ii) the result is very sensitive to the size of the site. *Fig 5.4* shows the effect of increasing the size of the trench in *fig 5.3* by one metre in each direction. We suppose that no more artefacts of either type are found. The new values of Q and V are now +0.1 and +0.5, indicating a very weak association between A and B rather than a fairly strong dissociation as before.

(iii) the result is also very sensitive to the size of quadrat. For example, suppose that two-metre squares had been used instead of one-metre squares: the pattern of associations would then become that shown in *fig 5.5*.

If the enlarged trench is recorded in the same way, we have Q = +0.3 and V = +0.2, the strongest evidence yet for association of the two types.

You may conclude (quite rightly) that we can get almost any answer by a suitable choice of site boundary and quadrat size.

One way out of this dilemma has been proposed by Whallon.[2] His idea, briefly, was to study how the degree of association varied as the size of the quadrat was varied, and to draw conclusions from the pattern that this produced. Before looking at his approach, it will be useful to see what simple methods are available when the location of each artefact is recorded.

(iii) Methods based on the exact positions of artefacts

These methods are based on the idea of the 'nearest neighbour'. The nearest neighbour of a chosen artefact, called the base point, is simply the artefact which is nearest to it. Some examples are shown in *fig 5.6*.

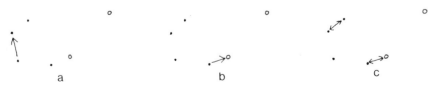

Fig 5.6   Hypothetical patterns of artefacts of type A (●) and B (○). The arrows point from 'base point' to its 'nearest neighbour'.
(a) nearest neighbour of the chosen 'A' is another 'A',
(b) nearest neighbour of the chosen 'A' is a 'B',
(c) two 'nearest-neighbour pairs' (i.e. pairs of artefacts, each of which is nearest neighbour to the other).

145

The simplest approach to this sort of information is to count how many times the nearest neighbour of an 'A' is another 'A', and how many times it is a 'B', then how many times the nearest neighbour of a 'B' is another 'B', and how many times it is an 'A'. The results can be presented as a 2 × 2 table (see *fig 5.7*), which for our example shows an apparently strong dissociation. Our old friend chi-squared has been used to test the significance of the association. A coefficient of segregation, called S, can be used to measure its strength. S varies from +1 where the distributions are completely segregated to −1 when A and B are associated in isolated pairs made up of one A and one B. S equals 0 when the two types are randomly intermingled. In this example, S = +0.6, indicating a fairly strong level of dissociation.

		base point		
		type A	type B	total
nearest neighbour	type A	20	5	25
	type B	7	24	31
	total	27	29	56

Fig 5.7 Nearest neighbour table for artefact distribution patterns shown in *fig 5.3(a)*.

The main problems with this approach are its sensitivity to small-scale patterning, in other words small changes in the position of a few 'key' artefacts could have a disproportionate effect on the value of S, and the amount of work involved in recording all the positions and examining for nearest neighbours. The first point can be partially overcome by taking second and even third, fourth or fifth nearest-neighbours into account, but this exacerbates the second problem.

A different approach, using nearest-neighbour *distances*, was proposed by Whallon,[3] but has not had a favourable reception.[4]

(iv) Dimensional analysis of variance

Whallon's other technique, which uses data collected by the quadrat method, is known as dimensional analysis of variance – something of a misnomer since it bears little relationship to the well-known statistical technique of analysis of variance (or anova for short). We have seen that one of the major difficulties of using quadrat methods is the choice of quadrat size, which can have an overwhelming effect on the results of the study. Dimanova (as I shall call the technique, for short) looks at the spatial patterns through a range of quadrat sizes, from the basic recording unit (for example metre squares) up to the whole site. Successive quadrat sizes are shown in *fig 5.8*.

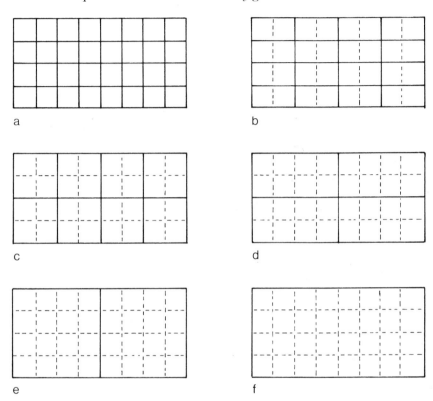

Fig 5.8   Quadrat sizes for successive stages of dimanova. The solid lines represent the edges of quadrats used at each stage, and the broken lines represent quadrats not used at that stage.

(a) original site grid, 8 m by 4 m. Quadrats are metre squares.

(b) second stage of analysis: the metre squares are grouped together in pairs to form quadrats 2 m by 1 m.

(c) third stage of analysis: the metre squares are grouped together in 'fours' to form quadrats 2 m by 2 m.

(d) fourth stage: the metre squares are grouped together in 'eights' to form quadrats 4 m by 2 m.

(e) fifth stage: the metre squares are grouped together in 'sixteens' to form quadrats 4 m by 4 m.

(f) sixth and final stage: metre squares grouped into 'thirty-two', i.e. quadrat is whole site.

The degree of concentration of each artefact type is calculated for each quadrat size, and the concentrations compared, in graphical or tabular form. If the artefact distribution does in fact form a distinct pattern, the measure of concentration rises to a peak at a particular quadrat size, indicating the scale of the pattern in that distribution. An example is shown in *fig 5.9*. The original quadrats were metre squares; the 'block-size' is the number of them grouped together at each stage. The mean square represents the degree to which the nuts (not, I suppose, artefacts, but their presence is the result of human activity) are concentrated in some blocks but relatively absent in others: the peak is clearly seen at block size 8 (that is, eight square metres). The conclusion was that there was a definite pattern in the distribution of the nuts, which seemed to be aggregated in areas of about eight square metres each. (Note, however, that other results might not be so easy to interpret: the very clear and well-defined peak observed here is not always present.)

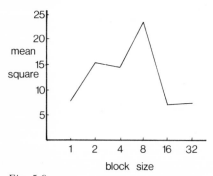

block size	mean square
1	7.6
2	14.5
4	13.6
8	23.4
16	6.9
32	7.6

Fig. 5.9   *Fig 5.9(a)*

Dimensional analysis of variance for *Jatropha,* or Susi Nuts, from Zone C, Guila Naquitz Cave, Oaxaca, Mexico *(after Whallon, 1973).*

This result by itself is not of tremendous interest, but Whallon went on to examine the distribution of another seventeen sorts of find – flints, faunal and plant remains, and found that all of them exhibited this peak at the 8-quadrant block size. This suggested strongly that the 'best' size of quadrat for an association analysis (see p 143 above) is the eight square metre quadrat. When this was carried out, definite groups of associated finds were discovered. Whallon interpreted these groups as follows: 'each group represented either the products fruiting together within a single environmental zone or items exploited and/or processed by distinct work groups. Products from the upland forest were separate from products of the piedmont, and products of the hunt were distinct from collected vegetal foods'. In other words, the mathematically determined groups of finds do have a real physical meaning and a reasonable archaeological interpretation. In a sense, the results of the study merely confirm common-sense expectations as to which sorts of finds would occur together on the site, but it does show that dimanova can pick out this sort of pattern mathematically, and might therefore be expected to do so in a more difficult situation, like the question of flint artefacts with which we started this chapter.

'   Or does it? Whallon rightly pointed out the main limitations of the technique. If you have been following this account carefully, they should be fairly obvious. They are:

(i) it imposes severe restrictions on the shape of the site, which in theory should be either square or rectangular (2 × 1 ratio of sides). In practice one might be able to fudge a little, perhaps by omitting the odd peripheral quadrat, or adding a few 'dummy' squares, or by dividing the site up into separate squares or rectangles. But many sites will be an unsuitable shape.

(ii) the smallest scale of pattern which it can reliably detect is of the order of twice the size of the original quadrats. Concentrations in areas smaller than this will not be reliably revealed.[5]

(iii) the range of shapes of areas within which concentrations may be detected is limited, since the analysis is based on squares and rectangles. 'Irregularly shaped, linear, or curved concentrations will be poorly or not at all defined by a method which operates on strictly regular, geometrically shaped areas.'[6]

(iv) since the block size is doubled at each step, the precision with which the scale of patterns can be detected decreases as the scale increases.

The method of dimensional analysis of variance is thus limited in (i) the shape of site for which it can be used, (ii) the scale of patterning sought, in relation to the grid size in which the finds were recorded, (iii) the shapes of patterns present and (iv) the precision with which large-scale patterns can be detected. Its main advantages seem to lie in its simplicity: it does not rely on sophisticated site recording, but only simple recording by (for example) metre squares, and the mathematical calculations are relatively easy to carry out. A desk calculator should suffice unless the number of different types of artefacts is large. Therefore it is probably best seen as a fairly crude but inexpensive exploratory tool.

(v) Local density analysis

The search for techniques more suited to real archaeological data has led (so far) to development of two new approaches: Johnson's local density analysis and Hodder's index of association A. Both methods were intended for use with the measurements of exact locations of artefacts (known as co-ordinate data), but Johnson found that his also worked if the locations were recorded in terms of cells – small grid units twenty or twenty-five centimetres square. It is therefore more flexible in its applications than Hodder's index.

The basic principle of Johnson's method is to measure the local density of artefacts of type A (say) in the vicinity of artefacts of type B. By this local density he means the number of artefacts of type A in a circle centred on an artefact of type B, divided by the area of the circle, and averaged over all the artefacts of type B. In passing, note that the local density depends (usually) on the size of the circle – we shall come back to this later. The idea is illustrated in *fig 5.10.*

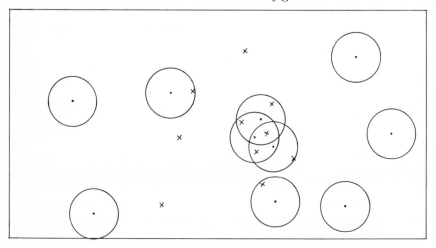

Fig 5.10   Measuring the local density of artefacts of type A (crosses) in the vicinity of artefacts of type B (dots). Each circle is centred on a type B artefact, and has an area of 1 unit. The rectangle represents the edge of the site.

Here there are ten artefacts of each type. The numbers of type As in the circles are (reading from left to right): 0, 0, 1, 3, 3, 3, 1, 0, 0, 0, giving an average local density of 1.1 type A artefacts per unit area. What does this mean? By itself, very little. But if we compare this local density of type As in the vicinity of type Bs to the density of type As over whole size (called the global density) we can see whether the As appear to be associated with the Bs in some way, or not. In this case, the area of the whole site is about sixty units, so the global density of type As is 10 ÷ 60 or 0.17. In this case, the comparison between the local density of 1.1 and the global density of 0.17 suggests that there is an association between the two distributions, i.e. the two different types of artefacts are closer to each other than one could reasonably expect if either (or both) were distributed randomly across the site.

The next step in Johnson's method is therefore to calculate the index of co-clustering, C, which is the local density divided by the global density (in our example nearly 7). It is a strange mathematical fact that the same answer is found whether one calculates the index for artefacts of type A in circles around artefacts of type B, or vice versa. In general, one will be working with many different types of artefacts (say N in all), not just two, and each pair will have its own index of co-clustering. To a mathematician, this immediately suggests a matrix, and just such as is shown in *fig 5.11*.

		artefact types		
		A	B	N
	A	index for A and A	index for A and B ... index for A and N	
	B	index for B and A	index for B and B ... index for B and N	
artefact	C	index for C and A	index for C and B ... index for C and N	
	.			
types	.			
	.			
	N	index for N and A	index for N and B ... index for N and N	

Fig 5.11 Matrix of indices of co-clustering for artefact types A, B, ... , N
[See text for explanation.]

Something here that has not been mentioned before is the 'index for A and A', which is the local density of type A in the vicinity of type As – a measure of how much an individual distribution is clustered. For example, the local density for B with B in *fig 5.10* is $0 + 0 + 0 + 2 + 1 + 1 + 0 + 0 + 0 + 0 \div 10 = 0.4$, which, compared with the global density of $10 \div 60 = 0.17$, gives an index of about 2.4.

If you remember what happened to the quadrat methods (see *fig 5.4* again), you may feel like asking 'what about the site area?' Usually the edges of the site, and therefore its area, are arbitrary, and often they are determined by non-archaeological factors (time available to excavate the site, existing buildings, etc.). But the area of the site is used to find the global densities, which in turn help make up the indices. So the indices of co-clustering that we calculate will depend on what we consider, or are forced to accept, as the edges of our site. This is a valid point, to which Johnson has discovered a very elegant answer. What he does is to calculate the correlation coefficient between all the 'A and another' indices and all the 'B and another' indices, to give a new coefficient of the association between the distribution of A and the distribution of B, and so on for all pairs of distributions. This has a number of advantages: firstly, the coefficient for A and B will be the same whatever the area of the site is considered to be; secondly, the coefficient for A and B takes into account not only the index for A and B, but also the indices of A and C, B and C and so on. The coefficient therefore tells us a great deal about the respective distributions, and the whole matrix of coefficients even more. I apologise to anyone who has felt lost in this rather heavy piece of mathematics – the important thing to grasp is the idea of local density of type B near type A, what it means and how it can be compared with the global density. I have gone into such detail here because it does seem to be a potentially very useful idea and method.

Nevertheless, it would be wrong to gloss over the problems. The first is the choice of the size of the circle used in measuring local

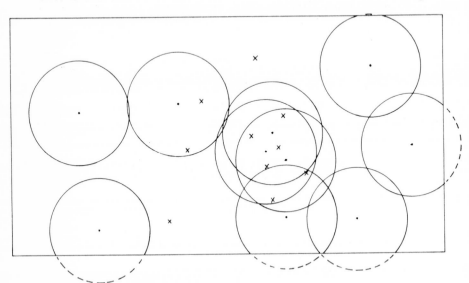

Fig 5.12   See *fig 5.10*. The radius of the circles has been doubled, i.e. their area is now 4 units each.

density. Comparison of *figs 5.10* and *5.12* shows that the density will vary according to the size of circle chosen, and we suppose that for any particular site there will probably be a 'best' size of circle. But how to find it?

Some sizes are clearly too small: they will give low densities and erratic results, while large circles have problems because they will often overlap the edges of the site (edge-effects) (*see fig 5.12*). In between, the choice is probably not too crucial (my guess): Johnson recommends a process of trial-and-error illuminated by mathematical intuition – not the sort of thing for an archaeologist to try unaided. The 'best' size of circle is itself a useful piece of information, as it indicates the likely scale of the patterns present in the distributions.

Secondly, the statistical tests necessary to determine the significance of the correlation coefficients have not yet been worked out. Work is in progress on this and the difficulties should not prove insuperable.

It is now worth looking at the situation when the artefacts are recorded by cells (see p 143) and not located exactly, as this is perhaps more realistic archaeologically. Johnson recommends treating the record as if all artefacts in a cell were located at the centre of that cell. Looked at another way, this means that instead of true circles we measure the local density in shape made up of cells all of whose centres are less than a certain distance (the 'radius') from the centre of the chosen cell (see *fig 5.13* for some examples). The calculations are then basically the same as before, using the areas of the outlined shapes instead of the areas of circles.

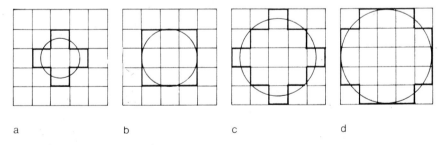

a   b   c   d

Fig 5.13   Four examples of the use of square 'cells' instead of exact measurements of the position of artefacts. In each case, the cells that make up the area used to measure local density are outlined heavily.
(a) circle's radius = cell side
(b) circle's radius = 1 ½ × cell side
(c) circle's radius = 2 × cell side
(d) circle's radius = 2½ × cell side

Johnson reported the use of this method on four sites. In all cases it gave good results: in one case much better than a simple quadrat analysis (see p 143) that had been carried out earlier. Results using exact locations and the cell method (on the same site) gave results which were in close agreement, confirming the reliability of the cell approach.

All in all, this is a very promising new technique, and could well make an important contribution to the study of the spatial distribution of artefacts on sites.

(vi) The index of association

Another new method is Hodder's index of association A. Hodder wanted to use more of the information contained in distribution plans or maps than is used in either quadrat or nearest-neighbour methods (see also chapter 7). He did this by calculating the average distance from type A points (in our example, points where artefacts of type A have been found) to other type A points, and to type B points, and also the average distance from type B points to other type B points. His index is then calculated as the average A to A distance divided by the average A to B distance, multiplied by the average B to B distance divided by the average A to B distance. When the distributions of types A and B are randomly mingled, with no association or dissocia-tion, A will have a value of about 1: closely packed but separate distributions have low values of A, and if As and Bs tend to occur together, then A will be greater than 1 (see *fig 5.14*).

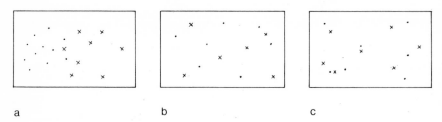

a   b   c

Fig 5.14   Examples of distribution patterns with different values of A.
(a) A is less than 1
(b) A is about 1
(c) A is greater than 1.

Hodder has argued that methods based on exact positions are likely to be more useful in archaeology than quadrat methods (which is the conclusion we have come to), and that his A index seems more sensitive (i.e. better at detecting) the sort of patterns one is likely to be

looking for in archaeology. It can be used for studying both distributions of artefacts on sites and distributions of sites in a geographical
area (see chapter 7). Its main disadvantage seems to be that the calculations of average distances are very time-consuming, particularly if
there are many points in the distributions. Also, as yet we know little
about how the index behaves, that is how large does a large value of A
have to be to indicate significant association of the As and Bs, and
how small does a value have to be to indicate significant dissociation?

Summary

The idea that the function of artefacts, particularly flints, could be
studied systematically via their associations in patterns – either distribution patterns in one layer of a site, or patterns involving more
than one layer or more than one site – is a relatively new one. Of
course, observant archaeologists have always noticed apparently
significant associations of individual artefacts in situ: what is new is the
systematic approach and the mathematical techniques borrowed or
devised in order to cope with it. It is becoming clear that under
favourable circumstances much useful information can be contained
in these patterns. This information is not always easy to extract
subjectively, nor were early methods (borrowed from other disciplines) particularly successful. More recent methods, developed with
archaeological problems in mind, promise to become a very useful
tool in the archaeologist's kit.

1. *Johnson 1977*
2. *Whallon 1973 a and b*
3. *Whallon 1974*
4. *Hodder and Orton 1976, 207*
5. *Kershaw 1957, 123*
6. *Whallon 1973a, 123*

CHAPTER SIX

Bits and Pieces

The problem of measuring quantity

Earlier chapters have relied heavily on the idea of the number of artefacts of a certain type at a certain site, or in a certain context. In chapter 3 we saw how the number of artefacts had been used by Kendall as a basis for his seriation technique (p 82), and later in the chapter the number of (for example) samian vessels in a context was important for constructing the dating probability curve of the context. In chapter 4 we made extensive use of the idea of the proportion of the pottery at a site (for example '25% of the pottery at X in the fourth century is Oxfordshire ware'), and used regression and trend surface analysis to study how it varied from site to site. Finally, in chapter 5 we moved on from the simple idea of presence or absence of a type of artefact in a quadrat to the more complicated idea of the density of a type of artefact in the neighbourhood of an example of another type.

All this supposes that we know what we mean by the number, or, in more general terms, quantity, of a certain type of artefact. Some artefacts do not cause us any problem of course – a flint is a flint and a coin is a coin, and there's not much doubt about that. But what can we do about artefacts that are found broken more often than not? Some interesting work on classifying such objects – in this case bone combs – has recently been reported by Galloway.[1] The biggest problem, that faces almost every excavator, is pottery. How do we measure quantities of pottery when we are faced, not with nice whole pots, but large numbers of sherds, many of them completely anonymous? What can we do with the body sherds? The problem is especially acute if we encounter a kiln site, with literally tons of broken 'waste' vessels – is there an alternative to the laborious reconstruction of each and every vessel?

Pottery – what can we tell from sherds?

Before trying to answer these questions we should think carefully about the idea of a pot 'type'. Every pot has two general characteristics – its fabric (what it is made of) and its form (what shape it is). The fabric is described in terms of the physical characteristics of the clay – hardness, colour, nature, size and quantity of inclusions (i.e. the filler added to the clay, if any) – and the technological aspects – wheel-thrown or hand-made, burnished, wiped, etc. A sherd, however small, still has an identifiable fabric: it may or may not have a recognizable shape. So however broken the pottery is, we can always sort it into different fabrics, but only some of it into different forms. Fortunately, this is just what we need for chapter 4, because we hope to be able to identify one (or a group of) fabric(s) with the products of one or more kilns – so we can say that a certain group of sherds comes from (a) certain kiln(s), even if we cannot tell what forms they are. In chapter 3, however, we might be interested in finer detail – does a certain rim form vary over time, for instance? Chapter 5, being concerned with function, also points towards form, but in a more general sense.

Firstly, then, can we say anthing about the form of a vessel from a sherd? Clearly it all depends on the sherd, but a bit of simple geometry will help us make the best use of such information as is available. The first step is to orient the sherd, that is find the angle at which it would sit if it were still part of its parent vessel, resting naturally on a horizontal surface. For rims or bases this is easy, unless the sherd is extremely small, as the free edge must be horizontal. This can be checked on a horizontal surface (see *pl 11*).

For a body sherd, we have to look for clues. Fortunately, most wheel-made and some hand-made vessels (if they have been finished on a turntable), possess fine rilling marks, caused by the coarser particles in the clay and irregularities of the potter's hands, on one or both surfaces. A simple geometric thought tells us that these marks (sometimes known as throwing- or wheel-marks) must be horizontal or very slightly spiral. If we rotate the sherd until the lines are horizontal, the orientation is correct. Except, of course, that it might be exactly upside-down. Can we do anything about this? Well, if the grooves are deep they are probably asymmetrical (see *fig 6.1*). If so, then the deep part of the groove will be uppermost, showing the upward pull of the potter's hand. If not, then we shall have to live with the possibility that the sherd is upside-down.

Having oriented the sherd, and possibly keeping it in place with a

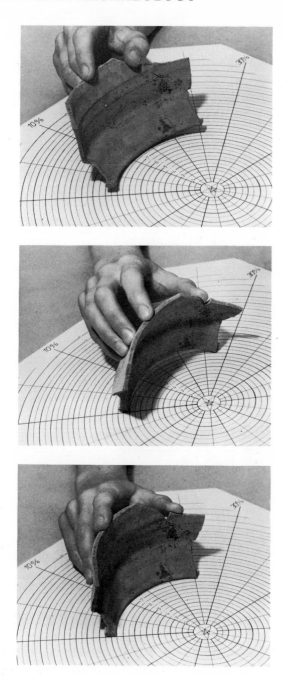

Plate 11 Orienting a rim sherd relative to a horizontal flat surface.

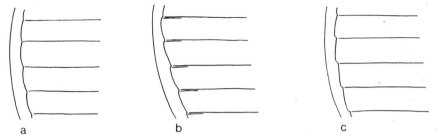

Fig 6.1 Throwing marks on the interior of sherds.
  (a) symmetrical grooves
  (b) asymmetrical grooves
  (c) asymmetrical grooves – upside down.

piece of plasticine, what next? We can measure its diameter, either external or internal, with a template made from very stiff card, or better still, the synthetic 'Plastikard' (the thirty thousandths of an inch grade is suitable) (see *pl 12*).

A set of internal (convex) and external (concave) templates, in a wide range of sizes at say one cm of radius (two cm of diameter) intervals is a very useful piece of equipment.

We can also sometimes tell whether the vessel form is open or flat (i.e. widest at the top) or closed or hollow (i.e. widest below the top) – see *fig 6.2*.

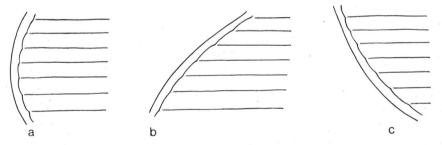

Fig 6.2 Open (or flat) and closed (or hollow) vessel forms.
  (a) sherd has smaller diameter at 'top' and 'bottom' than at some point between. *Closed* form.
  (b) sherd has smaller diameter at 'top' than at 'bottom'. *Closed* form.
  (c) sherd has smaller diameter at 'bottom' than at 'top'. *Closed* or *open* form.

Finally we can look at the steepness and vertical curvature of the sherd. Putting these together with the size (diameter) and open/closed, we can often get a surprisingly good idea of the overall shape of the vessel.

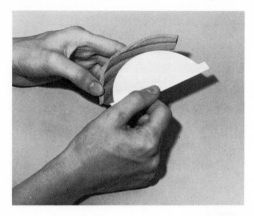

(i) wrong diameter –
   template too small
   in radius

(ii) wrong diameter –
   template too large
   in radius

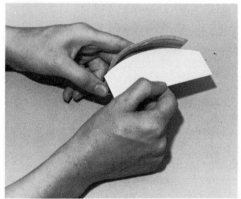

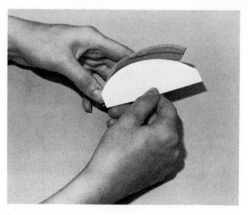

(iii) correct diameter –
   template has same
   radius as sherd along
   line of contact.

Plate 12   Measuring the internal diameter of a sherd by means of
   templates.
Note: both the line of contact and the template must be horizontal.

Problems of quantifying pottery

Now, suppose we have classified all our sherds by fabric, and as many as possible by form. We next want to be able to quantify them, and say that in such-and-such a context, x% of the pottery is Oxfordshire ware, y% is New Forest ware and so on. Unfortunately there is no best way of doing so, nor is there likely to be one. Even if we had excavated a complete site, and had found only whole pots, there would still be room for disagreement. Most archaeologists in this position would simply count each pot as 'one', but Hulthén has suggested giving more weight to the large vessels (see *pl 13*).[2] The choice seems to depend on the use to which one intends to put the percentages (see also p 163 below), but I would support the simple count unless a very good case could be made to the contrary.

Plate 13　Comparison of a large pottery vessel (Roman amphora) with a small one (samian ware cup). Measured in terms of weight, the amphora is many times greater than the cup; measured in terms of vessels, they are exactly the same.

A more realistic situation would be the complete excavation of a site, but with relatively few complete vessels present. In a sense, a division of pottery into proportions of different types probably tells us relatively little about the activities at their time of use that they represent. For example, a preponderance of coarse cooking-pots over fine tableware is more likely to mean that the tableware was well cared for – 'curated' to use Binford's term – while the cooking pots were treated with less care and thrown away when cracked or foul, than that there were more cooking pots than table vessels in use at any one time. Nevertheless, we would expect variations between sites (or between different phases of the same site), to mirror a real difference in activity. For example, if a higher proportion of fine ware was found at site A than at site B, we would probably infer that a higher proportion of fine ware was in use at A than at B – though we could just as logically infer

161

that they were just more careless with their fine ware at A. This question of the relationship between the pottery in use at a site at a certain time (the population), and the pottery actually found (the sample) is a difficult one, and much work remains to be done in this area. At this stage we should note that unless we are prepared to make some assumptions about the relationship, we can say nothing quantitative about the pottery at all. Unfortunately these assumptions tend to be of a very statistical nature, but what they seem to come down to is that it is reasonable to compare the proportions between one group of pottery and another, but not (generally) reasonable to make archaeological interpretations of the proportions in just one group in isolation.

Completely excavated sites

Let us return to our completely excavated site. We suppose that all pots used at the site are, sooner or later, broken and deposited there. It is a curious fact that even in such cases it is rare to find all the sherds from one vessel. There always seem to be some missing. Where do they go? Possibly some are broken down into unrecognizably small fragments, and possibly some are just missed in excavation. Certainly, recovery can increase dramatically when sieving is employed. Whatever the reason, one just has to live with this problem. The best one can do is to estimate how many vessels there were originally, that is, how many vessels our sherds represent. This is not always as easy as it sounds – some vessels may be represented by their entirety, other by only a sherd or two. The problem is then to judge whether a sherd belongs to one of the existing vessels, or whether it represents a new vessel. In this case, the best measure of quantity is the number of vessels represented.

Partially excavated sites

(i) Number of vessels represented

For a partially excavated site – and this includes almost all urban sites, since a town is really one big site – the situation is rather different. What we have now is a sample – perhaps as much as 50%, perhaps less than 1% – of the whole site and correspondingly a sample of the finds available at the site. The number of vessels represented can now be seriously misleading, because (for example) 10% of the sherds do not necessarily come from 10% of the vessels. A few hypothetical examples should clarify this point. The argument is based on the statistical theory of sampling, so it will have to be taken as read here. First think of just one pot type (called A), which (for simplicity's sake) we suppose always breaks into five sherds. Suppose that there are 100 of them on the site so that in all there are 500 sherds. We excavate 1% of the site, and find five sherds, which (probably) represent five different vessels. Extending to 10% of the site, we increase our haul to fifty sherds. But now there are only forty vessels represented, as more than one sherd of some are present (this is a statistical average figure). Increasing to 50% of the site, our 250 sherds represent ninety-two vessels in all, and finally when the whole site is excavated we have 500 sherds = 100 vessels (at least, we do in theory). So there is no simple relationship between the number of sherds and the number of vessels represented. Moreover, suppose a second type (B) does not break up at all (I am using simple figures of 1 and 5 sherds per pot to keep the arithmetic simple: more realistic figures might be 20 and 100). If there are again 100 of them on the site, the true ratio of type A to type B is 1:1, i.e. each is 50% of the total), but at different stages of excavation the ratios are very different, as shown in *fig 6.3*.

percentage of site excavated	type 'A'		type 'B'		estimate of proportion of type 'A'
	sherds found	vessels rep'd	sherds found	vessels rep'd	
1	5	5	1	1	83%
10	50	40	10	10	80%
50	250	92	50	50	65%
100	500	100	100	100	50%

Fig 6.3   The effect of partial excavation on estimates of relative proportions of different sorts of pottery. The estimate of proportion of type A is the number of vessels of type A represented (i.e. column 2) divided by the total number of vessels represented (i.e. column 2 plus column 4).

This simple example makes two points: (i) unless both types break into the same number of sherds the estimate of the relative proportions is seriously affected by the proportion of the site that has been excavated (ii) unless the whole site has been excavated, vessels that break up into many sherds will be over-represented relative to those that break into few. In practice, this means that the estimated proportion of type A could vary between one site and another simply because different proportions of the two sites had been dug. Also (this is not so obvious but can be shown mathematically), the estimate of the proportion is affected by the degree of breakage: a ratio of 1 sherd to 5 sherds per vessel in, say, a pit will give a different result to a ratio of 20 sherds to 100 sherds per vessel in, say, a garden soil. The use of 'number of vessels represented' is therefore positively dangerous unless all (or almost all) of the site has been excavated. A great deal of effort can be wasted in trying to calculate this misleading statistic – unless of course one needs it for another purpose, like plotting a dating probability curve (see p 99).

(ii) Counting and weighing sherds

What can one do instead? The simplest and possibly the most common approach is to count the sherds. This method avoids the practical difficulties inherent in estimating the number of vessels represented, and overcomes one of the types of bias noted above (i). Using again the data in *fig 6.3*, a sherd count would give an estimate of 83% in the final column in each case – which means that the estimate could not vary from site to site just because different proportions of the sites had been dug. Any variations that do occur are likely actually to mean something. We still have point (ii) to contend with – some types will always be less well represented simply because they break into fewer pieces. But this is a less important objection than (i), as we are more interested in site-to-site comparisons.

A more subtle approach, and one which seems to be gaining in favour, is to weigh the sherds, or measure their displacement volume. In terms of the two points made above sherd weight is on an equal footing with sherd count – it overcomes (i) but does not overcome (ii). If one favoured a Hulthén-type count of vessels (see p 161) it would be particularly appropriate. Also, it is probably the more stable, since sherd count can be influenced greatly by variations in sherd size.

(iii) Vessel–equivalents

Approaching the problem from a statistical point of view, and using sampling theory, has led me to favour the idea of vessel-equivalents, an idea that has been around for some time but which seemed to lack theoretical support. If one has one sherd, its vessel-equivalent (or v.e. for short) is simply the proportion of the vessel that it constitutes: a small sherd might be less than 1%, a large sherd more than 10% of the vessel. It is probably best to think of this percentage in terms of weight, although an interpretation in terms of surface area has also been suggested. If one has more than one sherd, the percentages are simply added together to give a total v.e. (of, for example, a certain fabric, or all the pottery, in a context). It can be argued that this is a meaningless statistic, since one cannot add together parts of different pots. But since if one counts whole pots one is adding together different pots, and no one has objected to that, the argument carries no real weight, although it may represent a genuine gut reaction. The advantage is that if proportions are calculated using v.e.s, both of the above problems (i) and (ii) are overcome. In fact, it is the only count which will do this.

Unfortunately, the theoretical advantages are balanced by practical difficulties. How does one estimate the proportion of the whole vessel that the sherd is? If we are very lucky and can recognize the form, and if the form is sufficiently standardized, one might be prepared to weigh another, complete example and express the weight as a percentage of that. In general, however, we will be forced back to cruder methods. What we can measure is the percentage of a whole rim taken up by a rim sherd, and similarly for bases, by using a special rim radius chart (see *pl 14*).

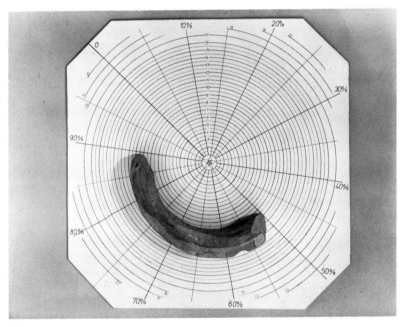

Plate 14   Chart for measuring radius of rim sherds, and percentage of whole rim present.

The rim sherd is placed on the chart and moved in or out until it matches one of the circles exactly (giving the radius in the usual way). If one end is now lined up on the 0% line, the other end will give the percentage that the sherd is of the complete rim – in this example about 17%. This is called the rim-equivalent (or r.e.). The simple formula, estimated vessel equivalent (e.v.e.) = (rim requivalent + base equivalent) ÷ 2, can be used for most, but not all, types of vessel. An obvious exception would be round-bottomed vessels (for which one would just use r.e.), but a more difficult problem is posed by types in which the rim breaks up into far more sherds than the base (or vice versa). A good example is the Roman colour-coated beaker (*pl 15*): the rim is thin and often breaks into ten or twenty very small frag-

Plate 15   A Roman colour-coated beaker. Note the thin fragile rim and thick robust base.

ments, while the base is solid and chunky, and may not break at all. As a result the base is easily found, but the rim fragments can be easily missed. For example, the Nene Valley beakers studied from a recent excavation in London, carried out under difficult waterlogged conditions, had a base-equivalent about ten times the rim equivalent. Much more work, both theoretical and empirical, is needed to discover the best way of dealing with such types. In general, we do not yet know in detail how various sorts of e.v.e.s behave in practice, and what adjustments and corrections may be necessary. In view of the amount of quantitative work in progress these problems should be tackled as a matter of urgency.

(iv) Summary

Meanwhile, what is the poor excavator to do? The pottery is there, crying out to be studied, and he cannot wait for the theoreticians to come up with the 'best' method. The advice offered here is to consider carefully both the nature of the site – complete or sample excavation? – and the uses to which the numerical summaries of the pottery will be put. With these firmly in mind, he should be able to assess the four main contenders – sherd count, sherd weight, vessels represented and estimated vessel equivalent – in the light of the above and related discussions. If in doubt, use more than one method (even if only one is eventually published) and always say exactly what was done, so that the work can be reassessed in the future.

Reconstruction of vessel shape from sherds

Another topic that has aroused some interest is the mathematical reconstruction of pots from sherds, seen as an alternative to the laborious business of physically piecing together the actual sherds. I became involved in this problem through the excavation of a Romano-British kiln site at Highgate Wood in London. To some extent the interest that this work generated at other sites may be misplaced, because it has become clear that Highgate was in a statistical sense a rather special site, and that the conditions necessary for the technique to work just happened to exist there. Nevertheless, it seems worthwhile to (i) indicate the conditions under which mathematical reconstruction is likely to work, (ii) summarize the method for those not familiar with it and (iii) suggest how it should have been done.

What was special about Highgate? Well, first it was a kiln site, which meant that although there were large quantities of pottery present, relatively few different types were represented. Also, almost all the types were found repeatedly in association with each other over large areas of the site. There were therefore enough data, of sufficient quality, for a mathematical approach to be feasible. Many domestic sites would not fulfil this condition. Secondly, the pottery was thoroughly broken, so that reconstruction was necessary. What is more it had apparently been moved about after it had been thrown away – perhaps the Roman potters, like modern archaeologists, found that their spoil heaps were always in the wrong place, and it seems that heaps of sherds were piled over some of the kilns (to keep the frost out during winter?). Whatever the reason, the sherds had become so mixed that the physical reconstruction of more than a few favoured vessels would have been an incredibly costly and space-consuming task. Thirdly – and this only emerged from the statistical work – the sherds were not so mixed that no relationships remained. Sherds from the same vessel probably ended up, on average, closer to each other than sherds from different vessels. Had this not happened the statistical answer would have been nonsense.

The site was excavated as a grid of square trenches – mostly ten feet square but some twenty feet square, and interrupted by the presence of trees. The statistical work was concentrated on what later became known as the 'Phase III' pottery (*ca* 100–140 AD), which formed the bulk of the pottery on the site. In this phase there were five main types of rim form, known as A2, A3, A4, A6 and A7, and three types of base, known as B1, B2 and B3 (see *fig 6.4*).

The problem seemed to break down into three stages: (i) to find out which rim and base categories co-existed on the same vessels, so that we could talk about vessel categories, (ii) to relate the size of rim to size of base in each vessel category, and (iii) to reconstruct the entire profile of vessels of a certain category and chosen size.

The data initially available consisted of the numbers and diameters of rim and base sherds in (a) one pit, (b) two parts of a ditch, (c) the flue and chamber of one of the kilns and (d) four parts of a large waster dump (the parts of it found in four different trenches) – making nine groups or lots in all, with about 2500 rim and 900 base sherds. More became available during the course of the work. In a sense, the lots were bigger than necessary: from a statistical point of view it would have been better to have had more lots, with less sherds in each. In practice, this would have meant recording the pottery from the dump in smaller units than ten feet squares – for example metre squares.

The solution to stage (i) was based on the simple intuitive idea that if a certain category of base is always common in lots where a certain

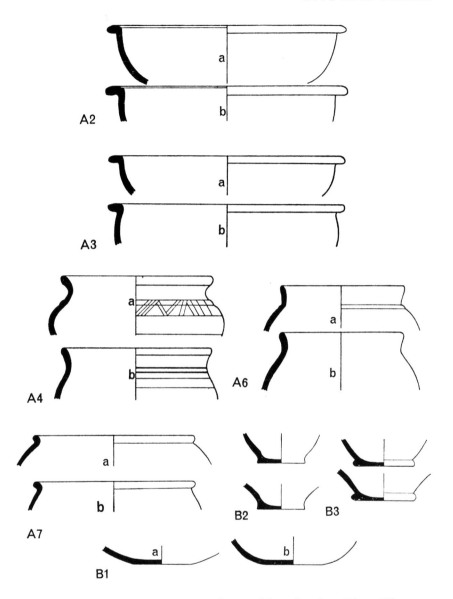

Fig 6.4 Examples of the main types of rim and base found on 'Phase III' pottery at Highgate Wood. *From Orton (1974).*

category of rim is also common, and rare where that category of rim is rare, they are likely to belong to the same category of vessel. If you have already read chapter 5, you will probably see immediately the relevance of the methods of within-site spatial analysis described there (pp 142–55). Unfortunately, chapter 5 had not been written at that time (1970) and spatial techniques in general were little used in archaeology. So the well-known but not completely appropriate technique of multiple regression was used, to find out which categories of rim appeared to vary in step with each base category. The results established six categories of vessel – rim A2 with base B1 (called A2B1), A3B1, A4B3, A6B3 and A7B2. From a purely archaeological point of view all seemed perfectly reasonable except possibly for A6B2.

The first part of this chapter should have alerted you to the hidden snag – our use of simple sherd counts (modified in that two joining sherds counted as one) was less reliable than the use of rim-and-base-equivalents, which I now much prefer. The only excuse is that the value of these measures was not generally appreciated in 1968, when the sorting and measuring of the rims started. If any similar work is done in the future it would be very desirable to use rim-and-base-equivalents.

The approach to stage (ii) was based on a comparison of the cumulative frequency curves of rim and base diameters (see *fig 6.5*). These are curves which show the percentage of the sherds with diameters less than a certain size.

Put at its simplest, the idea is that if rim category A and base category B belong to the same vessel category, and if x% of rims A are smaller than say six inches, while x% of bases B are smaller than say three inches, then the six-inch rim should go with the three-inch base. It may require some thought to grasp the point: remember that it is based on the assumption that within a vessel category, bases get bigger as rims get bigger.

I think much improved results would have been achieved here by the use of rim-and-base-equivalents. Because large rims tend to break into more pieces than smaller rims, while bases of categories B2 and B3 often do not break at all, whatever their size, counting sherds will over-represent the large jar rims. This probably led to the top-heavy appearance of some of the larger jars (see below). The use of r.e.s and b.e.s would have eliminated this source of bias.

The final task was to fill in the vessel profile between a rim and a base sherd which the first two stages had indicated as belonging together. It was done by a simple geometric technique of curve-fitting

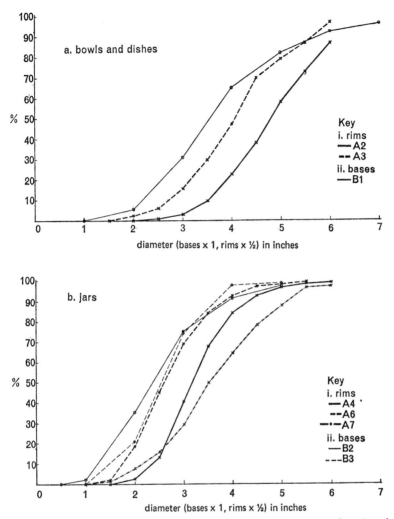

Fig 6.5 Cumulative frequency curves of rim and base diameters, showing the percentage of the sherds with diameters less than a certain size. *From Orton (1974).*

– finding a mathematical equation which describes the shape of the rim or base profile. If the curves are then continued beyond the broken edge, that is, downwards for rim sherds and upwards for base sherds, they will meet somewhere in between. The height can be adjusted so that the curves meet smoothly, thus giving a pot-like profile, and not one with a nasty kink. *Fig 6.6* shows (a) a real profile of category A2B1, (b) curves fitted to the rim and base and continued beyond, (c)

171

the correct reconstruction, (d) an example of an incorrect reconstruction.

Here the crucial point is the choice of the sort of curve that one tries to fit – there are so many possibilities that one has to restrict oneself to a family of related curves. The best family to choose is still an open question – at the time I chose quadratic curves because they were the simplest, but much work remains to be done in finding the most suitable family.

What did the results look like? Some typical results are shown in *fig 6.7*. These are in fact the average-sized vessels of each category, and on the whole they look archaeologically reasonable. But the smaller and larger vessels (not shown here) do look rather older, and some of the jars shown here do look too big for their bases – particularly those with A6 rims. The probable reason has been suggested above.

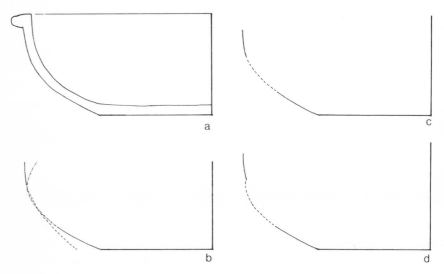

Fig 6.6   Example of curve-fitting to reconstruct the profile of a pot.
(a) complete profile of vessel of Highgate category A2B1.
(b) as an experiment, we pretend we have only the top third ('rim') and bottom third ('base') of the profile (shown as solid lines). Mathematical curves are fitted to them and extended – the rim curve is the dashed line and the base curve is alternate dots and dashes.
(c) a slight adjustment in height gives a smooth reconstructed profile. The height of the vessel is now about 7% less than we know it should be (see (a)).
(d) the height is wrong, giving a distinct 'kink' to the reconstructed profile.
From Orton (1974).

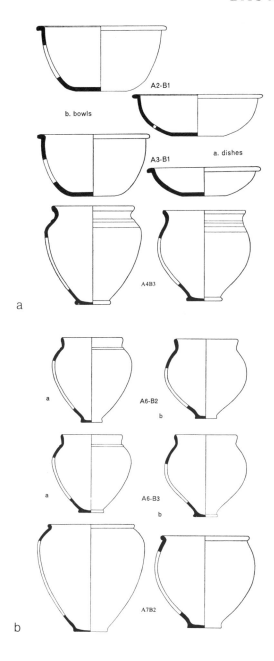

Fig 6.7   Examples of shapes of Highgate pots, as reconstructed by the 'curve-fitting' method. *From Orton (1974).*

173

Despite the deficiencies in the methods, the results are encouraging and suggest that this approach could make a useful contribution to the post-excavation work on sites which have similar problems. But it would be wrong to use such an approach on sites which do not share the characteristics of Highgate Wood, as described at the beginning of this section.

Another question: the standardization of pottery

Another aspect of pottery which has been studied in recent years is standardization – the idea that a scale of standard units was used by pottery manufacturers. Thus, when vessels of a similar shape but different size are made, they fall into one of a limited number of standard sizes, and are not just any size between the smallest and greatest. Size, in this context, usually refers to rim diameter but can refer to height. For example, modern flowerpots come in three inch, four inch, five inch, six inch sizes and so on, but one cannot buy a three and a half inch or a four and a half inch pot, and it has been argued that the production of certain classes of Roman pottery followed a similar pattern. In the jargon, the pot size was quantised – in this example the quantum (basic unit) being the inch. The topic seems to fall most naturally in chapter 8, where we shall be looking at other attempts to find quanta in archaeological data.

The study of bones

Another field of study where the problems of fragmentary data loom large is that of animal bones. The finding of a complete animal skeleton is even rarer than the finding of complete pots, and always seems to excite comment and speculation, just because it is so unusual. This is not at all surprising when one considers the processing to which animal bones is subjected – butchery, cooking, and industrial uses like glue-making or carving. Waste not, want not may mean that very little of the skeleton is thrown away in recognizable form. Even then, the evidence is not safe. Bone is far more vulnerable to adverse soil conditions than pottery and can even disappear altogether (e.g. in very acid soils).

Nevertheless, the archaeologist will want to make what use he can of the surviving evidence. Of particular interest will be the species represented on his site, their relative importance, their population structures and their economic position and importance in the community. The statistical information needed to support this type of study includes (i) estimates of proportions of different species represented on the site, (ii) estimates of the age and sex distribution of each species, (iii) estimates of the bone-type distribution. The last is particularly important on urban sites, where different parts of the same animal could have been used in different areas of a town for domestic, commercial or industrial purposes.

Here we shall look briefly at the problems of estimating the relative proportions of different species from a sample of animal bones, as this is a subject which has attracted statistical attention in recent years. The old-fashioned approach is simply to count bone fragments and to use these numbers as a basis for the proportions. It has been realized for some time that this is at best unreliable and at most downright misleading – an example of the sort of error that can arise is shown in *fig 6.8*.

	Skull	Mandible	Single teeth	Vertebrae	Scapula	Humerus	Radius	Ulna	Metacarpal	Pelvis	Femur	Tibia	Metatarsal	Astragalus	Calcaneum	Tarsals	Phalanges	No. of spec.	%
Bos			5	1		5	3		2			3	4	1				24	29
Sheep/goat		3	16	2		2	2	1	4			4	1			1	1	37	45
Pig	1	4	3		1	3						2						14	17
Horse		1	5															6	7
Others: Domestic fowl					Wing bone													1	1
																		82	99

Fig 6.8 Table of numbers of animal bone fragments from a site in Winchester. *From Cunliffe (1964).*

Here a relatively large number of teeth, quite possibly from the same animal, bias the results in favour of sheep as the predominant species. Attempts have been made to improve the method – the approach now most in favour is to estimate the minimum number of animals of each species represented in the bone sample, and to base the

175

proportions on these numbers. Minimum number means the smallest number of animals that the bones could possibly belong to, assuming that if there is no hard evidence that two bones belong to different animals (e.g. on grounds of age or size), then they belong to the same one. The rules for sorting bones so as to ascertain the minimum number can be quite complicated.

This type of estimate is clearly related to the estimate of vessels represented described earlier. It is however, a lower limit rather than an actual estimate: there may or may not be more animals than the minimum number, but there cannot be fewer. The question of the validity of these numbers as a basis for relative proportions raises all sorts of statistical problems, which are far from solved. We have already seen that a 'vessels represented' approach can lead to serious bias unless substantially the whole site is excavated: a true 'animals represented' approach would do the same, and the use of lower limits instead of genuine estimates seems likely to increase bias rather than diminish it. The advantage of using a minimum approach is that it is repeatable and reproducible: since there is a definite set of rules to follow, different workers (or the same worker on different occasions) are likely to get the same answer from the same sample of bones. An estimate of the number of animals represented is more subjective and could vary from worker to worker. Nevertheless, there are serious theoretical difficulties associated with the use of the minimum numbers approach, especially for excavations that are not total (which includes virtually all urban excavations).

An alternative approach has been put forward recently by Altham. Since our main interest lies in estimating proportions of species rather than the absolute numbers of animals as such, she has devised a method for going directly to the relative proportions without first estimating numbers of animals. The mathematics are too complicated to go into here, but an important point to note is that the method depended on the assumption that the number of surviving fragments per bone depended only on the type of bone, and not also on the species. The method was tried out on data from a Roman site at Aldborough, Yorks. The numbers of bones available for study are shown in *fig 6.9* – there are 770 bones in all, which is a reasonable number for a statistical study of this kind. Some results (e.g. that mentioned from Winchester) are unreliable partly because they are based on a sample that is too small. The first attempt gave proportions of 44% pigs, 38% sheep and 17% cows, but an examination of the results showed that the crucial assumption did not hold: on going back to the bones it was found that the pig scapulae generally occurred in

	Scapula	Humerus	Radius	Ulna	Pelvis	Femur	Tibula	Metacarpal	Metatarsal	Phalanges	Astragalus	Calcaneum	Mandible	Total
Pigs	96	40	30	36	46	26	34	3	16	6	8	16	11	368
Sheep	23	20	23	15	36	24	35	26	24	21	5	7	19	278
Cows	18	7	5	5	7	9	3	14	6	35	1	2	12	124
Total	137	67	58	56	89	59	72	43	46	62	14	25	42	770

Fig 6.9 Table of numbers of animal bone fragments from a site at Aldborough. *From Altham (unpublished).*

smaller fragments than either sheep or cow scapulae, while the sheep mandibles generally occurred in larger fragments than either pig or cow mandibles. Altham got round this difficulty by sorting the bones into four groups – whole bones, 75% complete bones, 50% complete bones, and 25% complete bones. These were then given weights of 1, ¾, ½ and ¼ respectively per fragment – corresponding roughly to the vessel equivalent concept mentioned earlier. This reduced the numbers of bones to those shown in *fig 6.10*. If these numbers are used, the estimated proportions become 49% pigs, 40% sheep and 11% cows, and the data now fit Altham's statistical model better than before.

	Scapula	Humerus	Radius	Ulna	Pelvis	Femur	Tibula	Astragalus	Calcaneum	Mandible	Total
Pigs	26.5	12.5	11.5	12.5	13.5	8.5	9.75	7.5	12.75	4.5	119.5
Sheep	7.25	8	14.25	6.5	10.75	7.75	13.75	5	7	15.5	95.75
Cows	6.25	1.75	2.75	1.25	1.75	3.00	1.5	1	1.25	6	26.5
Total	40	22.25	28.5	20.25	26	19.25	25	13.5	21	26	241.75

Fig 6.10 Table of numbers of animal bones from the Aldborough site, adjusted to allow roughly for the proportion of each bone present. *From Altham (unpublished).*

This method is really only a start on the problem, and Altham admits that further research is needed to produce methods with a sounder theoretical basis. In particular, the adjustment for fragment size is rather ad hoc, although intuitively reasonable. Nevertheless, the results are sufficiently encouraging to suggest that more mathematical work could usefully be put into this problem. (It is interesting to note that the results are closer to the old-fashioned bone count than the more modern minimum numbers approach.) Perhaps the real lesson is that large numbers of bones are needed if one is to draw numerical conclusions.

Conclusion

We have seen in this chapter how the need to deal with finds which are usually discovered in a fragmentary state raises a number of problems which are of interest to the statistician. The urgent need is for statistical models of these situations which are sufficiently detailed to be reasonably true to life yet sufficiently simple to be mathematically tractable. The application of such models could have consequences for the practice of archaeology, in both excavation and post-excavation work, even down to such basic matters as the size of the grid used for recording on site.

1. *Galloway 1976*
2. *Hulthén 1974*

CHAPTER SEVEN

Distribution Maps

Introduction

Some of the uses of the techniques of spatial analysis for studying distribution patterns have already been discussed in chapters 4 and 5. In chapter 4 we looked at artefact distribution maps, and saw how regression and trend surface analyses could help us to interpret these patterns in terms of trade outwards from a centre of production. In chapter 5 we turned to a smaller scale, and saw how distribution patterns on a single site could be studied by means of quadrat and nearest-neighbour analyses, dimensional analysis of variance and local density analysis, often leading to a functional interpretation of the artefacts found.

Problem of site survival

We now turn to the topic of distribution patterns of sites, or settlement patterns, as they are often called. At once we run into a fundamental problem: if on the map there is no site of the type we are studying in a certain area, this could mean either (a) there never was a site of that type there, (b) there was once such a site in the area, but it has since been destroyed, (c) there is a site there, but it has not been found. We may have no way of knowing which is the case. This doubt, particularly if it is repeated over the map, will put our analysis in jeopardy.

There are basically two problems – differential survival and differential detection. Both will depend on the nature of the site itself and the uses to which its locality has been put. For example, a large hillfort could suffer much damage and remain recognizable, while a small barrow could be obliterated relatively easily. It is significant that recent analytical studies have tended to concentrate on the larger monuments, for example multivallate hill forts,[1] Roman walled towns,[2] or Mayan ceremonial centres.[3] Land use can affect survival in

179

a number of ways – intensive agriculture could destroy surface traces but leave crop-marks (patterns formed by crops growing either unusually badly – e.g. over walls – or unusually well – e.g. over ditches – and showing up as a difference in colour or height of crop) which might be easily visible from the air, or only apparent in exceptional years (like 1976, when owing to the drought many previously unknown sites were discovered by aerial photography). *Pl 16* shows the same site at the same time in two successive years. Crop-marks can clearly be seen in one, but not at all in the other. Urban development might be thought to obliterate all traces, but surprising amounts of evidence can be detected by aerial photography of sports grounds and

other open areas in towns. Differential survival, by its very nature, cannot usually be studied directly. An interesting example where it has been possible to do just this, has arisen recently. It concerns the use of oil jars as shop signs in London. *Fig 7.1* shows the locations of twenty-four surviving examples in Greater London.

This represents the surviving archaeological evidence for oilmen's shops (the *sites* of those examples) of the eighteenth, nineteenth and early twentieth centuries, and would form an insubstantial basis for a study of the distribution of oilmen's shops, and its economic and social implications. Fortunately, we have contemporary evidence in the form of Tallis' *London Street Views 1838–40*. This is a directory of

Plate 16   The same site at the same time in two successive years: crop-marks can be seen clearly in (ii) but not at all in (i).

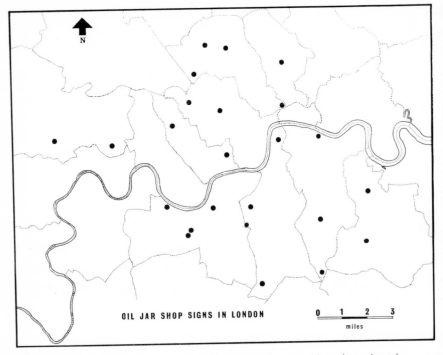

OIL JAR SHOP SIGNS IN LONDON

0   1   2   3
miles

Fig 7.1   Distribution of surviving and known oil jars used as shop signs in London. *From Ashdown (1974) with additions from Ashdown (1975).*

tradesmen in what is now central London, and includes many street views with representations of actual buildings. Backman has identified over 100 oilmen recorded here (in an area much more restricted than Ashdown's),[4] and published illustrations of thirteen shop-fronts with oil jars visible, none of which survived in 1973. Only two of Ashdown's listed shops were in the area studied by Backman, and both date to after 1840. A map of all known shops and those with jars is shown in *fig 7.2*. The data are now adequate to support economic and social arguments – for example, Backman points out the lack of oilmen's shops in the fashionable Mayfair area and the predominantly business City area. This example may seem rather divorced from more usual fields of archaeological study, but it does show that the link between the original pattern and what actually survives may be surprisingly tenuous, and that working backwards from present-day survivals can be a dangerous game. Fortunately, the evidence in this example was so thin that no one actually tried to do so.

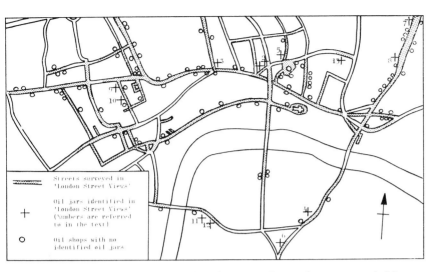

Fig 7.2 Distribution of oil jars used as shop signs in London, as recorded in Tallis' *London Street Views* (1838–40). *From Backman (1977).*

Differential fieldwork

The problem of differential fieldwork has been widely acknowledged, to the extent that 'distribution maps show the distribution of archaeologists not of sites' has become a widespread saying among archaeologists. It has been demonstrated vividly in recent years by the work done in advance of motorway building – in particular the M5 and M40. Site densities far in excess of those previously known have been recorded by intensive fieldwork on proposed motorway routes. For example, seventy-five miles of the M5 yielded 150 sites, mostly previously unknown, while a preliminary survey of the eleven miles of the Northampton-Wellingborough Expressway suggested the presence of seven major and seven minor sites.[5] Either motorway builders have a strange attraction towards archaeological sites or the density of sites (as yet undiscovered) in other areas must be as great. If the latter is true, it is clearly going to be very difficult to make any sort of general statement about the distribution of all except the most major monuments. But how can one tell? Are any sorts of independent checks available? It is necessary to go beyond purely archaeological evidence to find them, and place-name evidence is one possibility.

Fig 7.3 shows all the Saxon or medieval sites excavated in Greater London from 1972 to 1975. Although short, this period was one of

183

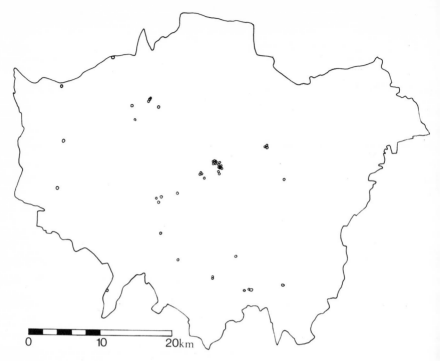

Fig 7.3   Greater London, showing all Saxon or medieval sites excavated from 1972 to 1975.

intense archaeological activity, with probably more excavation taking place than at any other comparable period. Taking the pattern of sites at its face value, what does it show? The core of medieval occupation – the City of London, Southwark, and Westminster – is clear enough, but what beyond that? A rash man might see a sort of Putney – Stratford axis running SSW-NNE through the centre of London, a southern arc running out to Keston, a north west cluster in the Hendon area and an outer arc beyond that. A more cautious interpreter might see a central core of occupation, a gap or belt round it and then a zone of dispersed settlement, more concentrated to the south and west. How valid would such an interpretation be? *Fig 7.4* shows the distribution of the Saxon and medieval place names in Greater London recorded by Ekwall.[6] A few, relating to rivers, have been omitted as they do not in themselves represent settlement. Some of the names plotted may not represent Saxon or medieval settlement, and for some the archaeological evidence may have been completely des-

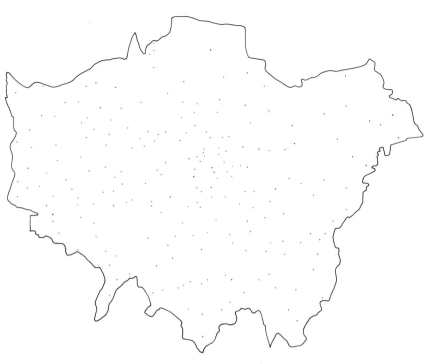

Fig 7.4   Greater London, showing distribution of Saxon and medieval place
names (see *fig 7.3* for scale).

troyed by later development, but against this there are probably many
sites not represented by place-name evidence. Even so, the picture
given is completely different. The density of sites is much higher –
approaching a one-kilometre spacing in some areas – and blank areas
are explicable in terms of parks, heaths or woods (e.g. Richmond
Park). Any coincidence between the two patterns appears to be more
or less accidental (except for the City itself). Elsewhere the pattern of
excavated sites does not provide a reliable guide to the apparent
pattern of settlement (which could be amplified by evidence for size of
settlement). But it does show, with some accuracy, the activities of the
archaeological units (in the City, Southwark, Inner London [North],
South West London), and the more active local societies and
museums. It could be argued that the excavation map shows only
short-term activity, and that over a longer period a more even and
representative pattern could emerge. Local society activity tends to go
in waves, which in the long run would tend to cancel each other out

185

and give a reasonably fair overall picture. In some areas, and for some periods of study, this may be true, but generally, and for London in particular, it seems to be wishful thinking without much firm evidence.

You would be justified in asking – is it ever worth doing anything with distribution maps? Or is it all a waste of time? But the position is improving; much survey work has been done recently by the new archaeological units, and many areas now maintain a Sites and Monuments record, which is kept up-to-date. A frank acknowledgement of the problems of differential fieldwork may in itself be a spur to greater, and better-directed, effort. In some areas, and for some classes of site, it may be possible to be reasonably certain that the record is adequate to support the sort of analysis that can now be brought to bear on distribution maps.

What are these techniques? and what sort of pattern are they looking for? The usual approach is to start from a null hypothesis of a random pattern in the area under study, and to try to detect, by means of various tests which will be described below, deviations from this neutral sort of pattern. By a random pattern I mean in mathematical terms independent occurrences from a uniform distribution – in other words, every part of our map has an equal chance of being selected for a settlement, and this chance is not altered by the location of existing settlements. The null hypothesis in this case is a sort of 'Aunt Sally': we do not expect that such an unrealistically simple situation will actually exist, but we set it up in order to knock it down and see which way it falls – in which direction the real situation diverges from the simple model. We hope that what we observe will generate useful ideas about the settlement pattern – how it may have developed, perhaps, or what social forces gave rise to its own particular form.

In what ways could a settlement pattern diverge from the random? The two general types of non-random patterns are called regular and aggregated. In a regular pattern the settlements are spaced more evenly than in a random pattern – few are close together but few are very far from their nearest neighbouring site. It is as if some force of repulsion were acting between the sites. An aggregated pattern is just the opposite: sites tend to be grouped together in clusters, separated by areas with few sites, if any. To use a physical analogy, one might say there is a process of attraction between the sites.

Settlement patterns

In a rural area, centres are needed to provide services which individual farms or villages cannot perform for themselves, like markets. They need to be located so that every farm or village has easy access to a centre, while the centres must not be so close to each other that there is not enough trade for each market. In practice, this will be achieved if the centres are spaced evenly in a regular pattern. Patterns which fit this model in general have been observed under surprisingly widely differing conditions – from Roman Essex to south western Wisconsin.[7] The spacing is about ten kilometres between settlements, giving rise to a greatest distance from the nearest market of about seven kilometres or four miles, a reasonable day's return trip before the advent of modern transport. This idea of a regular spacing of small centres forms the first stage of the geographical model known as Central Place Theory.

On the other hand, there are circumstances in which one might expect aggregated patterns to arise. For example, if natural resources are not uniformly distributed across the area, as is assumed in the basic Central Place Theory, then settlements may be expected to cluster in the most favoured areas. These might be on (or near) the best agricultural soil, near to a water supply, or mineral resources. Even in these circumstances one might be able to detect some regularity of spacing of settlement within the favoured area: the remarkably regular spacing of Roman villas in the Darent valley comes to mind. Aggregated patterns can also arise as the result of increasing density of settlement in an area. Suppose the area is initially thinly settled, with a settlement pattern apparently 'random'. As population increases the settlements may, to avoid becoming too large themselves or to take in new land, set up 'daughter' settlements relatively nearby – nearer to the 'mother' settlement than to the other primary settlement. At this stage the pattern may well appear aggregated. If the process continues until the whole area is covered, the pattern may tend to become more regular. It can be shown that these two very different processes can give rise to very similar patterns.[8]

Techniques

It is clear by now, without going further into the geographical or archaeological theory, that techniques are needed to detect tendencies towards regularity or aggregation in settlement patterns. The human eye, although good at picking out some spatial patterns (e.g. linearity) is not very good at distinguishing between aggregated, random and regular patterns. As a rule, one's subjective idea of a random pattern is on the regular side of true randomness. To put it another way, the eye is prone to see clusters where none may exist. Before thinking about the mathematical techniques, it is a good idea to look at some typical, if hypothetical, patterns (see *fig 7.5*).

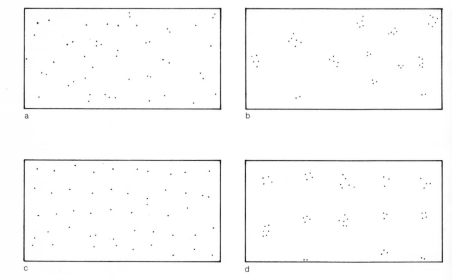

Fig 7.5   Examples of different sorts of patterns of points:
(a) random
(b) aggregated
(c) regular
(d) aggregated in small scale but uniform in large scale.

It is worth noting that a pattern can be both regular *and* aggregated, if looked at in different scales. For example, pattern (d) is aggregated in the small scale (the sites form clusters) but regular in the large scale (the clusters themselves have a regular pattern).

Quadrat methods

The simplest sort of techniques are the quadrat methods (see p 143). Simplest of all is the variance-to-mean-ratio. This compared the variability (V) in the number of sites per quadrat with the mean number (m): regular patterns tend to have roughly equal numbers of sites per quadrat, and thus a low V/m ratio, while aggregated patterns tend to have a few quadrats with many sites and many quadrats with no sites at all, giving rise to a high ratio. For example, pattern (b) in *fig 7.5* has a V/m ratio of 3.64, while for (c) it is only 0.09. Pattern (a), the 'random' pattern, has a ratio of 0.9, close to the theoretical 'random' value of 1.0. The main objection to this method is that the answer depends heavily on the size of the quadrat chosen. For this reason Whallon's dimensional analysis of variance (see p 146) is sometimes used instead, but even this is limited in its application. In particular, the area of study must be square or rectangular (p 149).

Distance methods

In general, then, quadrat techniques are not suited for this kind of study, and what are called 'distance' techniques are preferred. They all have one thing in common – they make use of the distances between each site and the other sites – but vary widely in their complexity. The simplest, and probably the best known, is nearest-neighbour analysis (see p 145). It uses only the distance from each site to the site nearest to it (its 'nearest neighbour'): the average distance is calculated and divided by the theoretical average distance for a random pattern. The result for a random pattern will be about 1: it will be greater for a regular pattern (up to a value of just over 2) and less for an aggregated pattern (only just greater than 0 in extreme cases). This technique is usually more sensitive than quadrat methods, and can be applied without too laborious calculations. However, it has two main defects. Firstly, it can only pick up patterns at the very smallest scale – for example, in *fig 7.5(d)* it would not detect the regular patterning of the clusters but only the grouping of the sites into clusters. This suggests it may be more useful in studying regular patterns than aggregated patterns, and, in particular, patterns in which sites appear to have a zone round them in which no other sites are permitted (the so-called 'hard core' model). In general, though, it is better to study not just the nearest neighbour, but the second, third, etc. nearest neighbours, although this does increase the work. A recent development is the idea of studying the distances from each site to all other sites. This advance, which cannot be used without the aid of a computer, has not yet been applied in archaeology.

The second problem is that areas or regions have edges. Sites near the edge of the area (e.g. near the coast) have less chance of having another site within a certain distance of them than do more centrally located sites (because they have less land within that distance). The usual way of overcoming this difficulty is to impose a 'collar' on the area, so that only sites whose nearest neighbour is closer to them than the edge of the area are actually studied (see *fig 7.6*). Of course, one loses information because not all the sites can be used, and this could be serious if there were relatively few to start with. It may be possible to overcome this problem by an adjustment factor which in effect gives more weight to distances from peripheral sites. A correction factor is now available for dealing with edge-effects of relatively simple shapes, like rectangles and circles.

Two examples

Two practical examples – one of a regular and one of an aggregated pattern – will serve to illustrate this way of looking at distribution

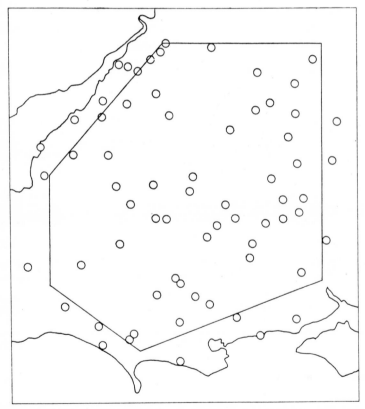

Fig 7.6   A distribution map (of Iron Age hill forts in south-west England), with 'collar' imposed to exclude sites not suitable for nearest-neighbour analysis. *From Hodder and Orton (1976).*

maps. The first example is a study made of the spacing of Romano-British walled towns in central and southern England. The map on which the study is based is shown in *fig 7.7*. Look first at the towns and ignore the pattern of lines and circles that has been imposed on them. Apart from London, three sorts of town are shown: the Colonia (2, 21 and 25), the cantonal capitals (5, 7, 20, 22, 24, 30, 34, 35 and 37) and the lesser walled towns – all the others. Note the regular spacing of the cantonal capitals (5, 7, 22, 24) at about 100–110 kilometre intervals, and also the spacing of the lesser towns on the 'borders' of hypothetical areas drawn around the cantonal capitals, at a distance of about fifty kilometres from them, and about thirty kilometres from each other. This pattern suggested various hypotheses about the

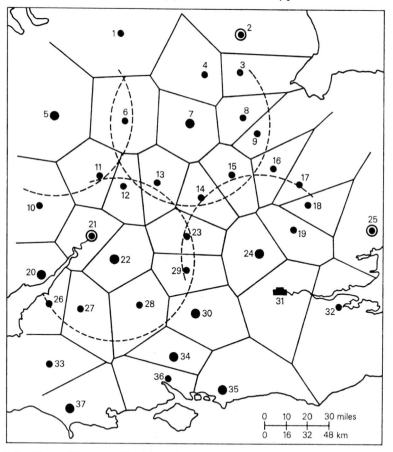

Fig 7.7   Map of Romano-British walled towns in central and southern England. *From Hodder and Orton (1976).*

reasons for the location of the towns: first, the lesser walled towns developed half-way between the large centres because there was both the least competition from them there, and the greatest need for additional centres; second, the spacing was similar but influenced by the relative size of the major centres, so that a large cantonal capital would have a larger territory around it, and the lesser towns would tend to be found nearer to the smaller cantonal capitals than the larger; and third, the lesser towns are market centres which grew up at the boundaries of tribal areas of the immediately pre-Roman period. The mathematical evidence contained in the map did not significantly favour one hypothesis above the others.

Implicit in this work is the idea of a 'territory' or 'service area' around a centre, reflecting the need for centralized services to aid the functioning of a rural area – markets for food, craft and specialized products, and administrative, military or religious services. In this example hypothetical service areas have been drawn around each centre (see *fig* 7.7) known as Thiessen polygons (also as Dirichlet cells, or Voronoi polygons); they are constructed simply by drawing lines at right angles through the mid-points of the lines joining neighbouring centres. Every point in a service area is nearer to its centre than to any other. It is an instructive exercise to invent a pattern, draw its Thiessen polygons and verify this fact.

Further study of *fig* 7.7 might provoke more questions – for instance, why does the pattern described above hold in central England, but not in the south or East Anglia? Is it an 'edge effect', or are there geographical or even social reasons? At present, the main value of such maps seems to be to generate questions which may open up fruitful lines of research.

An example of aggregated settlement patterns occurs in a study of neolithic settlement in a small part of southern Poland. Some results are presented as three maps of succeeding phases – the Bandkeramik, Lengyel and TRB. The first is shown as *fig* 7.8. The settlement pattern appears to be strongly clustered, and a simple quadrat analysis shows this to be so. This poses the question – how did the pattern come about? Does it reflect localized resources, or does it show groups of related settlements, perhaps around a primary 'mother' settlement (see p 187 above). A rather complicated statistical analysis is needed to distinguish between these two possibilities, known respectively as spurious contagion and true contagion, but it can be done if the data are adequate. The test indicated that the pattern was one of clusters of sites around the initial colonizers, that is the true contagion model. In the subsequent Lengyel phase the true contagion model again fits the

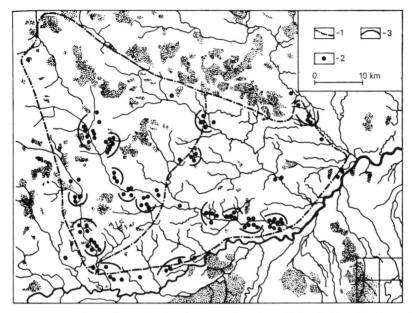

Fig 7.8 Map of Bandkeramik sites in part of southern Poland. *From Hodder and Orton (1976).*

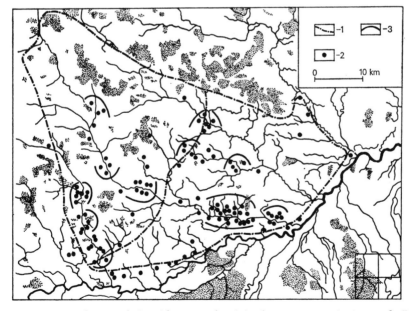

Fig 7.9 Map of Lengyel sites (the next phase) in the same area. Source as *fig 7.8*.

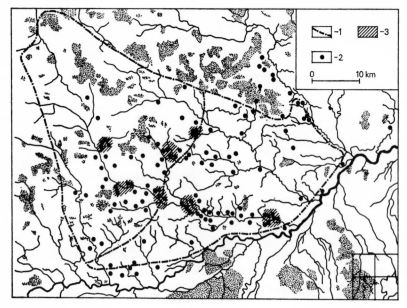

Fig 7.10   Map of TRB sites (third phase) in the same area. Source as *fig 7.8*.

pattern, while the spurious contagion does not. But in the final, TRB, phase both models fit the settlement pattern fairly well. This suggests a trend away from the true contagion picture as the density of settlement increases.

Summary

The systematic mathematical study of settlement patterns is still in its infancy. An introductory idea of its potential has been given by the examples described above. The analytical power of the techniques that are available highlights the need for reliable and comprehensive information on settlement patterns. Whole areas or regions will need to be thoroughly examined for sites of a particular type or period. But if the work is done the rewards will be there.

1. *Cunliffe 1971*
2. *Hodder and Hassall 1971*
3. *Hammond 1974*
4. *Ashdown 1974*

5. *Williams 1972*
6. *Ekwall 1960*
7. *Drury 1972, 8; Brush and Bracey 1955*
8. *Hodder and Orton 1976, 85–8*

CHAPTER EIGHT

Is There a
Case to Answer?

Jumping to conclusions

In the preceding chapters we have seen how mathematics can help the archaeologist to detect patterns in his results. In chapter 2 they were patterns of similarity between objects or groups of objects, in chapter 3 they were chronological patterns and in chapters 4, 5 and 7 they were spatial patterns. All the time we have been using the power of mathematics to detect patterns which, for one reason or another, are not easily picked out by the human eye or brain. But we know that archaeologists spend much of their time looking for just such patterns, and finding them, too. The question then arises – how valid are these patterns? Do they mean anything? This is, so to speak, the other side of the coin, and mathematics has a role to play here. Presented with a certain body of information – perhaps the results of an excavation he has just conducted – the archaeologist may be tempted to jump to a conclusion, and even the most prudent may feel forced to do so for the sake of a well-rounded report. The urge to interpret is always with us, and rightly so. The danger is that we may interpret an inadequate body of data, or go further than the evidence allows. The 'pending' tray is not a popular place to leave one's ideas. To illustrate this point I shall take one example from my own work.

During work on the pottery from a Romano-British kiln site at Highgate Wood, London (see p 167), the diameters of a large number of rim sherds, from a number of contexts, were measured. Four main categories of rim were studied – categories 1 (jars), 2 (beakers), 4 (bowls) and 5 (different bowls) – and the sizes were measured in one-inch ranges (e.g. six inches to seven inches), so that the results could be presented either as histograms (see *fig 8.1*) or cumulative frequency diagrams (*fig 8.2*).

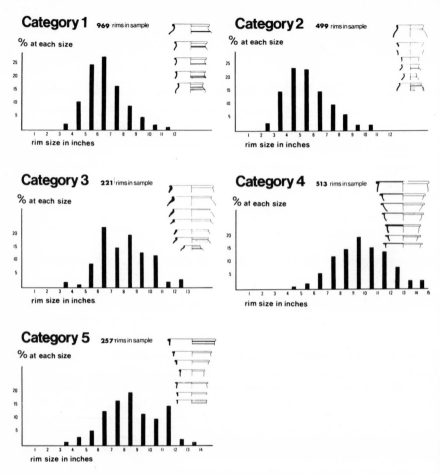

Fig 8.1 Histogram of sizes of jars produced at Highgate Wood Romano-British kiln site. *From Brown and Sheldon (1969).*

The former is probably quite familiar: the height of each column represents the number of rim sherds that fall into each size range. The latter may be less familiar: it shows the percentage of rim sherds that are smaller than a certain size. For example, *fig 8.2* shows that about 60% of the category 1 rim sherds in L33 were smaller than six inches in diameter, while only about 20% of those in L2 were. The cumulative frequency diagrams for the remaining three categories of rim are shown in *figs 8.3–5*.

Here at once we have an observed pattern: we can see that there are large differences in the relative proportions of the size-ranges rep-

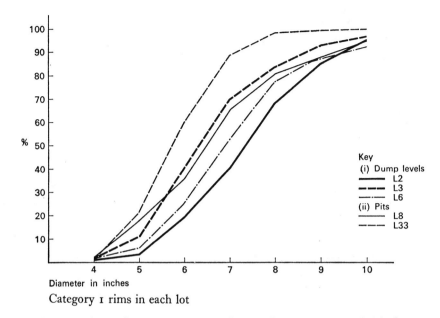

Category 1 rims in each lot

Fig 8.2   Cumulative frequency diagram of sizes of category 1 rim sherds from vessels produced at Highgate (compare *fig 8.1*). *From Orton (1970).*

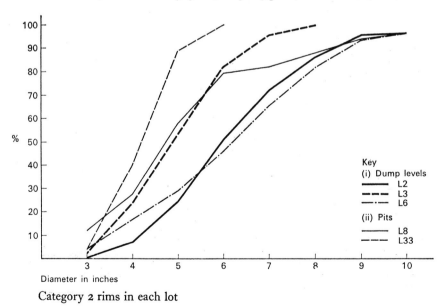

Category 2 rims in each lot

Fig 8.3   Cumulative frequency diagram of sizes of category 2 rim sherds from vessels produced at Highgate. *From Orton (1970).*

197

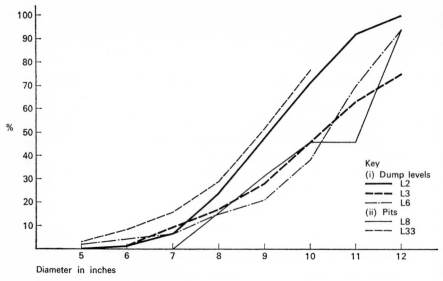

Category 4 rims in each lot

Fig 8.4   Cumulative frequency diagram of size of category 4 rim sherds from vessels produced at Highgate. *From Orton (1970).*

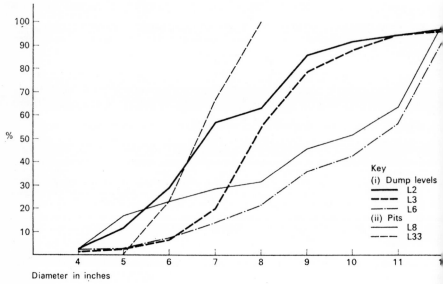

Category 5 rims in each lot

Fig 8.5   Cumulative frequency diagram of category 5 rim sherds from vessels produced at Highgate. *From Orton (1970).*

resented in the five contexts. If we look more closely, we can see that the patterns for categories 1 and 2 are quite similar. In particular, the median sizes (i.e. the sizes exceeded by 50% of the rim sherds) follow the same pattern: L33 has the smallest, L3 and L8 come next in order of size, and L2 and L6 have the largest. Categories 4 and 5 do not follow the same pattern: for them L2 and L33 have the smallest median rim, then L3, L6 and L8. Category 5 has the fewest rims (about 200, compared with 1000 of category 1, 500 of category 2, and 400 of category 4), which may help to explain the wide spread in *fig 8.5*.

Interpretation

So much for the basic data: what was the interpretation? The tentative conclusion was that two potters had been at work, one making category 1 and 2 and the other 4 and 5, and that fluctuations in average size could be related to demand for certain products. But we could look at the problem in an entirely different light. The counts are of individual rim sherds, and on the whole large pots tend to break up into more sherds than smaller ones. This in itself would not affect the argument, but suppose that pottery from some parts of the site (e.g. surface dumps) is more broken than the pottery from other parts of the site (e.g. pits). This could occur if some of the pottery had been moved about after being dumped, and there are indications that this did happen. One could argue that the larger pots would be affected more than the smaller, so that the greater average rim diameter in one context might mean, not that the pots were larger, but that they were more broken. Counting sherds would then have been the wrong thing to do: we should have used rim-equivalents (see p 166).

We therefore have two rival interpretations: one in terms of the history of the site and the other in terms of excavation and post-excavation technique. It is difficult to choose between them. The point is that the historical interpretation may be an attempt to explain phenomena which are nothing to do with the production of pottery. Because the method of recording was wrong – and a simple mathematical argument could have told us that before we started – we simply cannot make the sort of interpretation we would like. In this case, it would be possible (if tedious) to re-measure all the sherds and start again, but this may not always be possible. For example, in chapter 6 (p 163) we saw how certain statistics reflect the proportion of the site that has been excavated, and often there is little one can do about that.

What sorts of interpretation are possible?

Another pitfall is the attempt to interpret data that are mathematically 'random'. In chapter 7 we looked at distribution maps of settlements, and saw how one could interpret regular and aggregated patterns. But we also saw how to distinguish between these and apparently 'random' patterns (p 188). Although we do not believe that a settlement pattern can really be random, in the sense that every point on the map has an equal chance of being chosen for settlement, we would be unwilling to interpret as either regular or aggregated a pattern which cannot be distinguished mathematically from random.

Before going on and making our interpretation, we clearly have to ask 'is there a case to answer? Is it *permissible* to interpret these data in this way?' In the rest of this chapter we shall look at some particular cases that arise in archaeology, and which have not already been dealt with under specific topics.

Size of cattle horn cores

A simple example is taken from a report on the animal bones from a site in Southwark. Of particular interest from a statistical point of view is a group of sixty-eight cattle horn cores from a late seventeenth century rubbish pit. They were divided into three types – D, E and F, and the base circumference of each specimen was measured. Chaplin explained that 'the reason for classifying these horn cores into types is to locate in time and place livestock showing common characteristics. Horn cores have an inherent variability in their size and form which makes them particularly useful in such studies.

'The size and form of an individual's horns in a herd of cattle of common origin is due to both individual variation and to the sex of the animal. Horns are moderately sexually dimorphic in most *Bovidae*. The horns of the females are normally slighter than those of the male.'

Chaplin gave the base circumferences for the forty examples of type D, the four of type E and the twenty-four of type F. The figures for types D and F were presented visually (as in *fig 8.6* here).

From this figure, Chaplin deduced that 'the coincidence of the measurements between groups D and F strongly suggests that these are distinct varieties of cattle and not the sex classes of a single type. The dispersal of the measurements within each type shows no clear evidence that two sex classes are present.' But suppose we were not satisfied with this apparently subjective view, and thought that perhaps there really was a difference between the two types. How

Pit III P

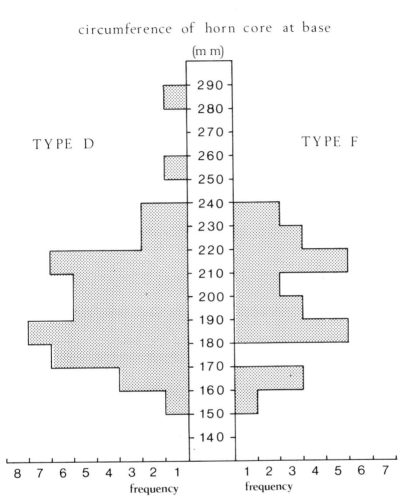

Fig 8.6 Double histogram showing base circumference of horn cores of types D and F from a pit in Southwark. *From Chaplin in Turner and Orton (1980).*

would we go about testing our ideas mathematically? The classical statistical approach would go as follows.

We suppose that there are two populations of cattle, one with type D horn cores and one with type F, and that our cores are in some sense random samples from these two populations. We form the null hypothesis (see p 186) that there is no difference between the sizes of horn cores in the two populations as a whole: any differences apparent in our samples arise simply because they are samples – and small ones at that – and may not accurately reflect the characteristics of the populations. Next we measure the difference between the two sets of circumferences. There are many possible ways of doing this: the one used here is known as the 'D' statistic and can be read off from the cumulative frequency diagram (*fig 8.7*). This shows the percentages of each type with circumferences less than each of the measurements, for example 55% of type D have a circumference of less than 200 millimetres.

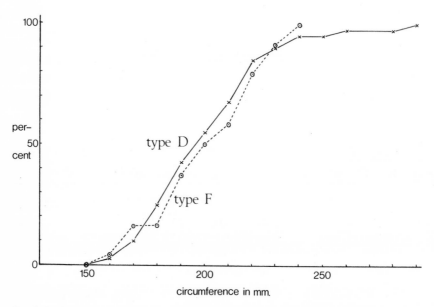

Fig 8.7   Cumulative frequency diagram, showing percentages of horn cores of types 'D' and 'F' with circumference less than the number shown.

Our test statistic, D, is just the greatest vertical distance between the two lines. It occurs at a circumference of 210 millimetres and has a value of about 0.09 (i.e. 9%). We now ask – if the null hypothesis were true, how likely is it that we would find a value of D as large, or larger, than 0.09? One has to look this up in statistical tables, which tell us that there is a one in five chance of getting a 'D' larger than 0.28, and a one in twenty chance of getting a 'D' larger than 0.35. The chance of D being larger than 0.09 is thus very high. In other words, our value of

'D' is just the sort of value we could reasonably expect if the null hypothesis were in fact true. It would therefore be most unwise to try to interpret any differences we might be able to find between the two types, since we cannot show that they are due to anything more than sampling effects.

If, on the other hand, the value of 'D' was so large that it had only a small chance of being exceeded if the null hypothesis were true, we might begin to have doubts about the validity of the null hypothesis. Conventionally, statisticians seem to start worrying when the chance falls to one in twenty (the famous 5% level) and are seriously worried when it falls to one in one hundred (the 1% level). In practice, it depends to some extent whether we take the null hypothesis seriously (as we do here) or whether we are just using it as an 'Aunt Sally' (as in chapter 7).

Significance tests – some problems

This is a much simplified account of the statistical technique of hypothesis testing. There are snags, however, both practical and statistical. Firstly, we have to assume that our measurements are random samples from some hypothetical population. In what sense can horn cores from one pit be considered to be a random sample from – what? All cattle killed in or near Southwark *ca* 1680? And if we cannot make this assumption, what validity does the test have? All these questions are easily overlooked by the archaeologist in his urge to come to grips with his newly found statistical technology.

Secondly, the acceptance or rejection of the null hypothesis depends not only on the difference (if any) between the populations, but on the size of the samples. If the samples are small, differences between the populations will have to be large for the null hypothesis to be (rightly) rejected, and we face the danger of clinging to a false hypothesis for sheer lack of evidence. On the other hand, if the samples are very large, the null hypothesis may be rejected although the difference between the two populations is really quite small – perhaps too small to be of practical (as opposed to statistical) significance. The practical implications, as well as statistical theory, must always be kept in mind.

Nevertheless, hypothesis testing does seem to be a useful tool for sorting out whether an observed phenomenon really needs explaining, or whether it merely reflects chance variation. The conclusion may often be that more data are needed before anything definite can be said.

Ley lines

A more interesting and controversial example concerns the existence, or otherwise, of ley lines. This term was coined in 1925 by Alfred Watkins, who put forward the idea that ancient sites could be found in alignments, or leys, which he interpreted as prehistoric tracks. More recent writers have abandoned the idea of tracks in favour of transmission lines of ley energy – a sort of prehistoric national grid. Basing his thinking on some rather simple experiments with random points on a map, Watkins decided that three-point leys (i.e. three sites in a row) could be expected to occur naturally even if sites were located at random, while four-point leys would be uncommon and five-point leys (five sites in a row) distinctly unlikely. Therefore, if five-point (or more) leys were found they would be strong evidence that the sites had been deliberately aligned on each other. His success in finding such leys created a considerable following, even to the extent of a journal, *The Ley Hunter*. Enormous numbers of leys have been published, up to eight-and nine-point ones, the odds against which were claimed to be enormous unless deliberate alignment was postulated.

Meanwhile, conventional archaeologists either ignored these findings or treated them as a joke. Little rigorous work was done on establishing the validity of these claims: the ley hunter tended to rely on Watkin's five-point rule of thumb, and anyway they believed in leys so what was there to prove? The archaeologists thought such ideas ridiculous, so why go to the effort of formally disproving them?

However, attempts have recently been made to tackle the problem with an open but rigorous mind, using the hypothesis-testing approach outlined above. The null hypothesis was that there were no deliberate alignments, and the sites were simply located at random. This puts the onus of proof on the ley hunters, which seems reasonable enough because (a) theirs is the original claim which needs to be substantiated, (b) it would be logically impossible to prove that leys did *not* exist. The test of this null hypothesis will show how much the evidence supports the ley hypothesis.

The first task, then, is to establish a reliable body of data. This is not as easy as it sounds, as there seems to be no common definition of what constitutes a valid ley point (i.e. a site through which a ley line can pass). Some hunters include only bona fide ancient sites and standing stones, while others accept crossroads, milestones, moats, churches and 'significant' places (even, with tongue in cheek, Post Offices!). Also, the area of study must be checked, so that no sites are missed, or sceptics could claim that careful selection of sites had biased the outcome.

There is a formula for the number of leys of different sizes that one could expect to find on a certain map, if the sites were located at random. These expected numbers of leys depended on various factors – the number of sites on the map, the area of the map, the average length of leys (which depends on the area and shape of the map), and the width of leys. Mostly these points are obvious – the more sites there are, the greater the chance of alignments, and so on. But ley width may need some explaining. Since sites are not mathematical points, but have a width, there is not just one line through two sites, but a whole 'bundle' of lines (see *fig 8.8*). The larger the sites, or the closer together they are, the wider this bundle will be.

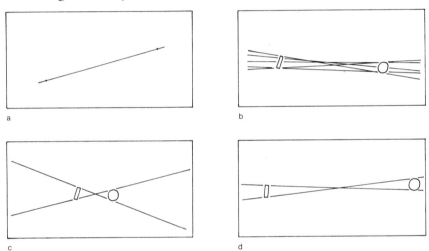

Fig 8.8 Ley lines: some problems of definition.
(a) the mathematical ideal: just one line passing exactly through two points.
(b) archaeological reality: many lines passing through two sites (the rectangle and the circle).
(c) sites close to each other have a wider 'bundle' of lines passing through both of them than do.
(d) sites further apart from each other.

If we want to see if a third site lines up on the first two, we have to take *all* the bundle of lines into account. This involves an impossible amount of work if there are more than very few sites, so the approach is usually to give the ley lines a width, but to have only one between any two sites. The width is usually taken to correspond to the average width of sites. This reduces the problem to manageable proportions (see *fig 8.9*).

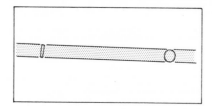

Fig 8.9   Ley lines – a simplified approach. A ley of constant width passing through two sites.

A case study

Some work recently done by Forrest will give the flavour of this method.[1] He gives an example of four leys – nine-, eight-, seven- and five-point ones found on one one inch Ordnance Survey map. His survey of the map found 600 suitable sites (468 churches, ninety-seven moats and thirty-five other earthworks). Taking a ley width of thirty-five yards he found the expected number of leys to be as follows:

five-point: 1144
seven-point: 15
eight-point: 1
nine-point: 0.1

Clearly there is nothing surprising about the five-, seven- or eight-pointer, but surely the nine-pointer is significant? Unfortunately not, because it only skirts two large sites (i.e. larger than the ley width) and if due allowance is made for their size, its significance is greatly reduced.

After examining fifteen such case studies, Forrest concludes that the ley hypothesis is 'not proven'. None of the examples provides convincing statistical evidence. He also makes the valuable point that one statistically significant result is not good enough if it is obtained by inspecting and rejecting a large number of maps – a point that is often overlooked in this and other contexts.

The approach of Gadsby and Hutton-Squire is more sophisticated. They chose what they considered to be a reliable set of data – the locations of fifty-three standing stone sites in a small area of Cornwall[2] – and checked it carefully to verify the twenty-two alignments discovered by Michell. Twenty of them were found to be correct, including one five-point and three four-point lines. In addition, by using a computer, they found two more four-point lines and twenty-nine new three-point lines, making fifty-one in all. Using the same statistical formula as Forrest, the expected numbers of leys were:

three-point: 34
four-point: 0.4
five-point: 0.004

On these grounds, the null hypothesis would be rejected. But the hypothesis was of random location of sites, and it was apparent that the sites were in fact clustered. How does this affect the likely number of leys? This cannot be calculated theoretically, so the writers used a computer to generate an artificial set of fifty-three sites which were clustered in the same way but had an otherwise random pattern (this technique in general is known as *simulation*). Ideally, they should have carried out many simulations (i.e. many different artificial sets of sites following these rules) to see how often a set with a five-point ley etc. occurred. Unfortunately each simulation would have taken them about two and a half hours' computer time, and the analysis the same again, so they published (as an interim statement) the results of only one simulation, which scored:

three-point: 36
four-point: 1
five-point: 0

suggesting that, even allowing for the clustering of sites, the observed alignments are still statistically significant.

There remains one weak link in the argument. An archaeological survey of the area has revealed a further sixty sites not used by Michell in his study.[3] How do they affect the analysis? How significant would the results have been if all the sites had been used? Michell's case is wide open because the sceptic can always claim that sites which did not align were deliberately not used. While there is no evidence that this is the case, it is a difficult argument to refute. The writers hoped to study this enlarged body of data when more computer time became available. So far, though, the results look distinctly interesting.

The value of computer simulation to tackle problems too difficult for a straight theoretical approach is worth noting. It is becoming more widely used in archaeology and it could be very helpful.

My purpose here is neither to prove nor 'disprove' the idea of ley lines, but to show how such problems might be approached in a reasonably objective way. Before going on to wonder about what they might be, and what function they might serve, one has first to stop and consider whether the data give adequate support to their existence: in other words, is there a case to answer?

The 'Megalithic yard'

A second fruitful field for speculation in recent years has been the search for ancient units of measurement, from surviving monuments and artefacts. The best known example is probably the Megalithic yard, an idea put forward by Thom and used by many other writers. The statistical side of the problem has been expertly assessed by Kendall, who coined the term 'quanta-hunting' for this sort of work.

The basic idea is simple enough – one has to study a certain dimension of a class of artefact (e.g. diameters of stone circles, height of pots) in order to discover whether there is a consistent grouping of the different measurements around multiples of some basic unit – for example the Megalithic yard. If so, this is evidence for the deliberate use of such a unit in the construction of the monument or artefact. One can then go on to interpret this in terms of standardization of units of measurement, perhaps over long distances or long periods of time, with implications for the degree of social organization involved. If on the other hand, a statistical examination shows that an apparent 'bunching' of (say) heights in this way is not significant, it is safer not to start building such theories on this foundation.

The standardization of Roman pottery

As an example of this sort of problem, I shall look at a simpler and less well-known example: the supposed standardization of Roman pottery. This idea has been put forward and developed by Rottländer. The fundamental idea on which all else is built, is that certain 'key' dimensions of the Roman pots he studied were 'standardized', that is, they tended to come in certain sizes – just as modern shoes or socks do – and not any old size. A good example of his work is based on the beaker form Gose 190, the shape of which is shown in *fig 8.10*. Four dimensions were measured – the maximum girth (a), the rim diameter (d) – note that it is measured to the highest most outer point (P), not the top of the rim, as is more usual – the base diameter (f) and the height (h), measured up to point P. All measurement were made to the nearest millimetre.

If the dimensions are standardized, then they must be related to a Roman unit of measurement. Suitable candidates are the digitus (1/16 of a Roman pes, or foot, and equal to about 18.5 millimetres) and the

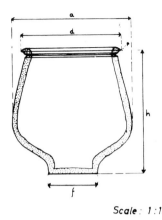

Fig 8.10   Beaker of form Gose 190,
showing the four dimensions
used by Rottländer.

Scale : 1 :1   *From Rottländer (1966).*

uncia (1/12 of a Roman pes, equal to about 24.6 millimetres). Rottländer called them d and u for short, and we shall do the same.

Rottländer measured a, d, f and h for 31 beakers (all from different potteries) and plotted the values he obtained against scales of d (*fig 8.11*) and u (*fig 8.12*) (a few dimensions could not be measured).

On these graphs, the four measurements taken off any one beaker can be found by taking the beaker number on the horizontal axis, and drawing a line vertically upwards and reading off the d values where it crosses the four graphs. For example, beaker no. 11 has (from bottom to top): f = 1½d, d = 3.2d, a = 3.9d and h = 4d. The beakers are numbered in order of ascending size. Rottländer claimed that these graphs showed a strong correspondence between the key dimensions of the pots and the Roman units of measurement d and u (either exact or quarter units). In fact, if both units were used at the same time, almost all the dimensions corresponded to the units.

I was sceptical and decided to put his claim to the test. The obvious null hypothesis to choose was that there was no correspondence between the dimensions and the Roman units: although very small and very large beakers might be less common than medium-sized ones, measurements close to each other (e.g. eighty millimetres, 100 millimetres) should have about the same chance of being chosen for a key dimension. If this hypothesis holds, the dimensions should be more or less evenly spread along the scale of measurements. Now, we can divide the scale into two parts: those within ± one millimetre of the d and ¼d units (shown shaded on *fig 8.13*) and those not (unshaded). The margin of one millimetre was chosen because Rottländer allowed this margin for errors of measurement. The shaded

209

areas occupy 42% of the scale of measurements. On the other hand, eighty-two of the 112 plotted points (i.e. 73%) fall into the shaded area. If the null hypothesis were true, one would expect only 42% of the points to fall in the shaded area. But there are only thirty-one pots and 112 measurements: could not sampling variation account for this discrepancy? The answer is no – a statistical test shows that the chance of obtaining a discrepancy as large as this, given the null hypothesis to be true, is very small indeed (less than one in 1000). So, to my surprise, I had to reject the null hypothesis in favour of Rottländer's idea.

On the uncia scale, the shaded area occupies 32% of the scale, but 45% of the points fall in it. Although this is a smaller discrepancy, the chance of one as large occurring by chance (if the null hypothesis is true) is still small – less than one in 100. Once again the null hypothesis must be rejected.

These results may look a bit odd – there appear to be correspondences between the dimensions and both sets of units. However, if both d and u are taken together in a common system of units, we find that the shaded area occupies 57 ½% of the scale, but 97% of the points (all except three in fact) fall in it. This is a very strong correspondence.

Rottländer obtained similar results for other forms – Gose 185 and 187, Dragendorff 33 and others – 259 vessels in all. As well as the correspondence with d, u and their quarter-units, an especially strong correspondence with the whole units was noted.

Subsequent work studied the questions of the design of vessels, particularly from the point of their stacking, the effects of shrinkage during firing and the historical origins of the units of measurement. The implications for the organization of the Roman pottery industry are considerable, in terms of the organization of both supply and demand. Also, one has a solid statistical basis on which to build. Interpretations may vary but the underlying statistical phenomenen remains, almost begging us to explain it.

Rival hypotheses

In all these examples we have seen how the need for a new, more elaborate hypothesis can be established by taking a neutral position (our null hypothesis) and seeing whether the available evidence is strong enough to shift us from it. Usually there is just one alternative that we are interested in, but sometimes it happens that two rival hypotheses compete for our support. Such a case arose in a study of the location of the Romano-British lesser walled towns. *Fig 7.7* shows the locations of the Roman cantonal capitals (large circles) and lesser

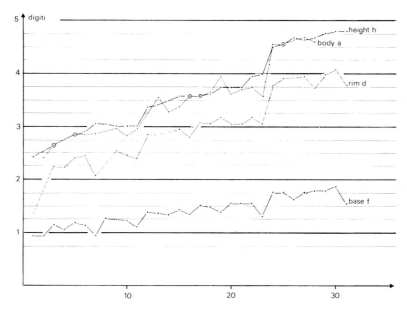

Fig 8.11   Values of the four measurements shown on *fig 8.10*, for 31 beakers, plotted on a scale of *digiti*. *From Rottländer (1966).*

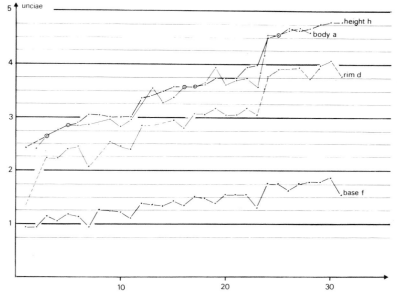

Fig 8.12   The same measurements as in *fig 8.11*, but plotted on a scale of *unciae*. *From Rottländer (1966).*

211

walled towns (small circles) in central southern England.

An examination of this map suggests that the lesser towns are not distributed at random around the cantonal capitals, but are spaced between them, in some sense as far from them as possible (see p 191). A statistical test of the null hypothesis of a random pattern would support this subjective interpretation. But what does it mean? – how, and why, are the towns spaced?

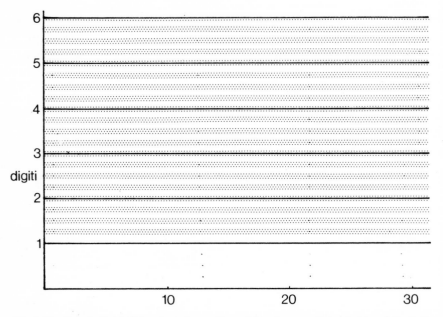

Fig 8.13 See *fig 8.11*. The shaded area lies within 1 mm of the *digiti* and ¼ *digiti* units, and occupies 42% of the possible measurements.

Of the many reasons that could be advanced, we shall look at two. The first is that the lesser towns grew up halfway between the major towns, perhaps originally for reasons of military controls, later developing into civil settlements. The second is that the lesser towns grew up naturally to provide services for the areas remote from the major centres. In this hypothesis the larger of the major centres would provide services to larger areas than the smaller, so that the lesser towns would tend to be nearer the smaller cantonal capitals than the larger. In other words, the first hypothesis stresses military and/or administrative control, while the second stresses the normal economic servicing of an area.

It was decided to test the relative merits of these two hypotheses by measuring the distances along Roman roads from one cantonal capital to the intermediate lesser town and on to the next cantonal town. The results are shown in *fig 8.14*. If the first hypothesis were the superior, we would expect the observed results (x) to be closer to the predicted outcome of the first hypothesis (p1), i.e. the lesser town would tend to be situated halfway between the major towns. If the second were better, the observed results would be closer to p2, i.e. each lesser town would tend to be nearer to the smaller of the two neighbouring major towns, because the smaller major town would have a smaller marketing area around it. A comparison of the figures suggests that there is little to choose between the two: a proper statistical test (a *likelihood-ratio* or *L.R.* test) would say the same.

Road	Town	Total distance	Distances			Proportions		
			p1	p2	x	p1	p2	x
1. Cirencester to St Albans	Alchester	11.7	5.8	6.1	6.0	0.5	0.52	0.51
2. Cirencester to Silchester	Mildenhall	8.6	4.3	5.1	4.1	0.5	0.59	0.48
3. Cirencester to Dorchester	Bath	13.4	6.7	8.8	4.6	0.5	0.66	0.34
3a. Cirencester to Dorchester	Ilchester	13.4	6.7	8.8	9.4	0.5	0.66	0.70
4. Cirencester to Leicester	Chesterton	11.8	5.9	7.1	6.7	0.5	0.60	0.57
5. Cirencester to Wroxeter	Droitwich	13.6	6.8	7.3	7.2	0.5	0.54	0.53
6. Cirencester to Wroxeter	Kenchester	14.7	7.4	7.9	7.6	0.5	0.54	0.52
7. St Albans to Leicester	Towcester	12.4	6.2	7.2	6.0	0.5	0.58	0.48

Fig 8.14 Table showing distances from 'intermediate' lesser town to the nearest cantonal capital in each direction. *From Hodder and Orton (1976).*

Where do we go from here? For the time being at least, the case has to rest. On the available evidence, the two hypotheses are, roughly speaking, equally likely. This leaves us with a problem; we cannot go and collect more data (the statistician's usual remedy for such situations), because Roman towns cannot be found to order. The best chance of resolving the question seems to be to look for a consequence of the 'military/administrative' and 'economic' hypothesis that is more sensitive than those considered above. But we may have to say that we simply cannot decide on purely locational reasoning.

Conclusion

The attempt to explain or interpret an archaeological phenomenon should be preceded by tests to establish, as far as possible, its objective validity. Sometimes apparently interesting patterns can arise purely by chance (possibly a product of site survival and detection) or as a by-product of particular techniques of excavation or recording. The statistical technique of hypothesis testing can be a useful tool in the attempt to establish a phenomenon as worthy of interpretation, and in suggesting areas where further work might be needed. The merits of rival hypotheses of equal standing can also be compared statistically.

1. *Forrest 1976*
2. *Michell 1974*
3. *Russell 1974*

CHAPTER NINE

Summing Up and Looking Ahead

In the preceding chapters we have looked at many different aspects of archaeology in which mathematics has a role to play. It has not been possible to mention all the different sorts of applications that have been made, particularly the more technical and specific ones. Examples of these occur in subjects like archaeological surveying, and can be surprisingly sophisticated. The use of a technique known as Fourier analysis to help in the interpretation of resistivity surveys is a good example.

Catastrophe theory

Mathematical models are beginning to be used at a higher level of archaeological study, to represent the fate of whole cultures or civilizations. One problem has always been to explain the collapse of a civilization, or some other culture discontinuity, without having necessarily to invoke some major disruption from outside (e.g. invasion, earthquake or tidal wave). The mathematical Theory of Elementary Catastrophes, which seems to have been initially applied to engineering problems, has recently been put forward to provide such a model. Its attraction is its ability to explain a sudden discontinuity (machine failure, civilization collapse) in terms of gradual changes in the variables that underly the system, without the need for a large external impulse. It is too soon to say how widely this model will become accepted in archaeology.

The role of mathematics

The topics chosen have been intended to show the breadth of application of mathematics in archaeological work, and to illustrate the point made in chapter 1, that mathematics is far more than a technique (or even many techniques), that can be used 'off the shelf' when required. In this way, it differs essentially from the many scientific techniques (e.g. radiocarbon, trace element analysis) with which it is often lumped. If we restrict it to the data analysis stage of study we are only using one fraction of the statistical cycle (see p 20). Nothing is more frustrating to the statistician than to be presented with a great heap of figures, laboriously collected (perhaps in a vague belief that figures are a 'Good Thing'), and to be asked to 'do some statistics on them, please'. Very often there is little that can be done with them at this stage, because they are the wrong figures, or have been collected wrongly, or answer a question that the archaeologist is not asking. The archaeologist then thinks that mathematics has nothing to offer him. If, however, the statistician had been actively involved from the outset, and had studied the problem in depth before work started, he would be in a position to offer advice as to what data are needed, how much and so on. For example, a detailed study of what sort of answers one hoped to obtain from the Highgate kilns (see p 167) would certainly have altered the post-excavation work on the pottery, and might even have influenced the method of excavation.

The archaeological response

Archaeologists respond to this situation in various ways. At one extreme is the 'record everything' school of thought: one cannot predict just which data will turn out to be useful, so if all are recorded, then one will have the right bits when the need arises. This is an expensive approach and falls down because, in real life, one cannot record literally everything. Archaeology has been described as the systematic throwing away of information, and all along one must make decisions affecting which information is retained and which lost. Does one wet-sieve every bucketful of the site? Is every find to be three-dimensionally recorded? and so on. Better to think in advance of the useful limits of accuracy, suitable for the analysis one might subsequently employ. For example, the technique of local density analysis (p 150) can be used if the location of finds is recorded to within a grid of cells of perhaps twenty centimetres by twenty centimetres and is probably superior to nearest-neighbour analysis, which requires the location of each find to be measured exactly. There is no point in creating work by generating redundant data.

At the other end of the spectrum is the 'archaeology is an art not a science' school of thought, which appears to deny the validity of mathematics as an archaeological tool. The idea seems to be that archaeology is a humanity and therefore not within the scope of 'the scientific method'. As a reaction to some of the odder expressions of scientific archaeology, this is fair enough, but it is misunderstanding the nature of the sort of approach outlined in chapter 1 to label it (along with computers, the chief bête noire) as 'dehumanizing'. Indeed, mathematics itself has been described as an art and the model-building phase of the statistical cycle (p 120) can rank among the great creative arts. The tedious and automatic parts of the cycle can be dehumanizing to whoever has to do the requisite 'number-crunching' but the advent of the computer and the cheap electronic desk calculator has done much to lift the burden – although we are still left with some responsibility for the poor punch-card operator.

But this, I suspect, is not what the self-styled humanist is getting at. More likely, he is objecting to the very idea that something as exact as mathematics or science has anything to say about something as numinous and imprecise as human activity. This can only stem from an incomplete idea of the extent of mathematics. Since at least the seventeenth century, when French noblemen employed mathematicians to calculate their gambling odds, mathematicians have been grappling with ideas of imprecision and uncertainty. The outcome, the theory of probability, has been with us for some time, and more recently the new approach of 'fuzzy subsets' has made an impact on the study of medicine and other humane disciplines (see p 220 below). It does seem that the gulf is more imaginary than real, and is the result largely of an incomplete picture of the modus operandi of the other side.

Computers

Where do computers, the other great stumbling block, fit into this argument? Although there is considerable overlap, the positions of mathematics and the computer are not the same. On the one hand, the computer has a non-mathematical role as a recorder, storer and presenter of information of any sort – tasks which could (at a cost) be done manually with card indices or similar systems. Wilcock has shown how the results of geophysical surveys (in this case a proton magnetometer survey at South Cadbury) can be prepared more quickly and more accurately by computer than by hand.[1] In the field of graphics, computers can easily produce maps, plans and sections as well as more ambitious visual representations, like the moving three-

217

dimensional pictures of artefacts recently demonstrated by Diment and Biek.[2] All three aspects have been brought together in work at Danebury and York.

On the other hand, it is perfectly possible – as if it needed saying – to perform a statistical analysis without the aid of a computer. Obviously, some techniques (e.g. most forms of cluster analysis) are so tedious to do by hand, and the chance of an undetected error is so high, that they are not really practicable unless one has access to a computer. As far as the performance of repetitive calculations is concerned, the difference is in degree rather than kind – the computer is quicker and usually more accurate than the human, but performs the same calculation although possibly in a different way. This speed is particularly important if the solution has to be reached by successive trial and error, or by simulation (p 130). On the other hand, there are occasions when a problem involving six months' programming and computer time could have been solved by a competent mathematician equipped only with pencil and paper, in less than half an hour. Reliable access to a computer can lead to a change in emphasis: one tends to look for a good, if approximate, numerical solution, rather than an exact algebraic solution to a problem. The computer can be used to break through a mathematical barrier, but this sledge-hammer approach has its dangers, as the example above shows.

The real danger in the use of computers comes from the availability of a large number of statistical packages. All one has to do is to select the programme that seems most appropriate to one's problem, feed in one's data, press the button and hey presto! – the answer. The problem is that most of these packages were not designed for archaeological problems and their programmes may well be based on assumptions that do not match archaeological reality. The archaeologist probably does not know enough statistics to realize this, and if he is fortunate enough to be able to get advice from a statistician or computer expert they will probably not fully understand his problems. Fortunately, there is now at least one package which has been designed with the archaeologist in mind – PLUTARCH, short for Programs Likely to be Useful to Archaeologists.

Before leaving computers, it is worth mentioning the idea that the study of computing science itself could have useful applications in prehistoric archaeology. Computer programmes have been written to carry out non-numerical reasoning of a type similar to that appearing in many archaeological reports (of the 'if A and B are accepted, then C follows, but on the other hand X argues that . . .' variety).

The future

In a sense, the future has loomed large in earlier chapters, which have been as full of unsolved problems as of useful and well-tried techniques. However, I would like to finish with three pieces of personal speculation: ideas which may or may not lead anywhere, but which I think deserve exploration.

The first speculation concerns the idea of fuzziness, which has already been mentioned (p 217). To see why a new way of looking at uncertainty could be useful, it is worth taking a quick look at the basis of conventional statistical approaches. Unfortunately, the subject itself is divided: there are two ways of looking at the fundamental concept of probability, which colour the statistician's approach to a problem (although in practical terms, the answer is often very much the same).

Classical statistics

The classical or frequentist approach links the idea of probability to that of an indefinitely repeatable event or experiment. For example, if I toss a coin, what is the probability that it comes down heads? The classical interpretation of this question is 'if I toss the coin very many times, what proportion of the times will it come down heads?' If, for example, 1000 tosses of the coin produce 600 heads, the probability of heads is somewhere near (but not necessarily exactly) 0.6. The more often we toss the coin, the better our idea of the probability. This sort of approach works very well for certain sorts of problems – for example, in questions of quality control. If an engineer has a large consignment of screws, and wants to know the probability that one will be faulty when he comes to use it, he can test a sample and estimate the probability from it. The screws are sufficiently alike and anonymous for a sample to stand for the whole – they can be seen as repetition of the same event.

This sort of situation is not common in archaeology. Suppose the archaeologist finds a burnt layer in a Roman town and suspects that it may have something to do with the Boudiccan rebellion. He may ask himself 'what is the probability that this layer is a Boudiccan destruction deposit?' Here probability does not have the classical meaning: he does not mean 'suppose I dug up 1000 layers just like this one, how many of them would be Boudiccan?' For one thing, no other layer is just like this one (in the sense that two screws in a box are alike). What he means is 'how strongly do I believe this layer to be Boudiccan?' and it is from this point of view that he will examine the evidence.

Bayesian statistics

Difficulties like these arise in many other fields, and an alternative view of statistics has been put forward to try to come to terms with them. Known as Bayesian statistics (from the Rev. Thomas Bayes, who is something of a posthumous founding father of the subject), it deals with subjective probabilities: the beliefs that you or I might hold about a particular event. Our question 'what is the probability that the coin will come down heads?' now means 'how strongly do I believe, in the light of the available evidence, that the coin will come down heads?' We all start with a prior belief or probability about an event (for example, we might believe that the probability of the coin coming down heads is 0.5). We then acquire some data, which naturally affect what we believe about the coin (if we were told it had produced nine heads in ten throws, we might change our beliefs). In fact, this approach has been described as 'the orderly influencing of opinions by data', and I think that is a good description: we all have opinions, they are all influenced by data, so what better than a way of ensuring that this happens in an orderly and systematic fashion. The outcome, that is prior opinions plus data, is the posterior probability: our 'final' state of mind – at least for the time being.

This is much more like the archaeological situation. The excavator may have his hunch that the deposit is a Boudiccan destruction layer (his prior probability). Then data, say in the form of coin and samian dates, arrive from the specialists, and modify his opinions, producing his posterior probabilities (which may be that the deposit is very likely/likely/ not likely/most unlikely to be Boudiccan). This way of looking at the problem, although still statistical, is likely to be much more in tune with the average archaeologist's approach.

There is however, still a snag. Although Bayesian statistics is a way of handling uncertainty, some things in it are certain. There is no question about the data – they are just accepted and that is that. But archaeological data often are not like that. In our examples, the coin dates may be throughly reliable, but what about the samian? Not even the most sanguine samian expert will pretend that a piece of samian, now dated to *ca* 50–70 AD (and note the *circa*), will *always* be given that date in the future. The uncertainty is all-pervasive.

Fuzziness

This, at last, is where fuzziness comes in. This new mathematical concept goes right back to the basic mathematical building block, the set, and injects an element of uncertainty into that. In mathematical terms, a set is 'any collection of definite, distinguishable objects of our intuition or of our intellect, to be conceived as a whole'.[3] In other words, what defines a set is its members: we can have the set of English counties, of four-letter words or of prime numbers – all are equally valid as sets. A set can have sub-sets, which consist of any collection of its members (including all or none of them). Given a set (or sub-set) and an object, it is possible to determine whether or not that object belongs to the set (or sub-set). This approach, now known as 'intuitive' or 'naive' set theory, has been found to lead to contradictions, but for the sorts of mathematics we are dealing with it serves remarkably well, and in fact it forms the basis of mathematics as it is commonly known and used. In archaeological terms, 'the sub-set of group 1 palstaves' or 'the sub-set of the Flavian period' (i.e. the years 69, 70 . . . up to 96 AD) are two examples.

The first example gives a clue to the problem: given a real palstave, we may not be quite sure to which group (sub-set) it belongs. We may be able to force it into group 1, but the doubt remains: we say that it more or less belongs to group 1. How confidently can we proceed with our analyses when the fundamental doubt remains at the back of our minds? If the idea of a sub-set does not hold, can we use mathematics at all? These are the sorts of questions that can assail one in the darker moments. Imagine my delight when I first encountered the idea of a fuzzy sub-set. In this theory, the objects only more or less belong (or not) to the sub-set. We can say this is more or less a group 1 palstave yet still be mathematical about it. The mathematics is much closer to reality as we appreciate it, and an element of uncertainty can be injected into the roots without killing the tree, as it were.

This is only the beginning: if we allow our sub-sets to be fuzzy, then the rest of out mathematics can be too – making it even more like real life. One simple example will have to suffice: in mathematical terms, the dating of objects would be called a 'mapping' – we are mapping a set of objects, for example coins on to another set of objects, for example years. *Fig 9.1* should make this clear.

A slightly more complicated map would associate a range of years, instead of a single year, with each coin, as in *fig 9.2*.

So far so good, but what about the samian? Well, if we have fuzzy sub-sets, we also have fuzzy maps, which express mathematically just what we mean when we give a date as (e.g. *ca* 50–70 AD). More generally, we can reconcile our own imprecise ideas and thoughts with the power of mathematical analysis. The applications of this radically new approach are still in their infancy: an impact has been

221

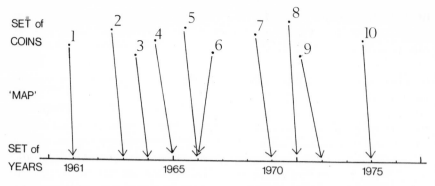

Fig 9.1   Simple example of a 'map' (in the mathematical sense). A set of coins is mapped onto a set of years. In this case, the map gives the date of coin 1 as 1961, of coin 2 as 1963, etc.

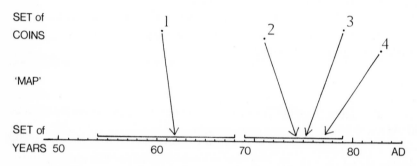

Fig 9.2   Slightly more complicated 'map', in which each coin is mapped onto a range of years. The map gives the date of coin 1 as 54–68 AD ('Neronian'), and of coins 2, 3 and 4 as 69–79 AD ('Vespasianic').

made on engineering, medicine, linguistics and other disciplines, but not yet in archaeology. Obviously much hard work remains to be done, and maybe there is a snag that will limit the applications, but I think it should be tried.

Limits to the accuracy of archaeological dating

The second idea follows on from where we left off in chapter 3 (p 105). We saw there that the precision with which an object could be dated in itself tended to be offset by a relatively long useful life, so that its value in dating a context was not as great as first appeared (coins are a good example). Conversely, objects which might have a very short useful life tend to be difficult to date themselves (e.g. coarse pottery). This suggests to me that the amount of dating information contained in any one find is limited. It follows that there is a limit to what we can reasonably say about the date of a context from the object(s) found in it. This is not just a practical limitation, stemming from our ignorance, but a fundamental theoretical limitation which cannot be overcome by archaeological means. It is really only common sense that there must be such a limit: the point is that we might be able to form some idea of what this limit actually is. The precision we can practically achieve in dating may be a good deal less than this theoretically 'best' precision, and may improve as we learn more, but never beyond this limit. As we saw in chapter 3, the precision with which we can date a context is the greater the more dateable objects are found in it, so the limit to what we can say about the date improves – but remains a limit. This is a difficult idea, so a simple hypothetical example may help.

Suppose coins can be dated exactly but have an average useful life of fifty years (this approximates to the results of the work on the coins described in chapter 3). If one only is found in a context, which we are to date with a 95% chance of being correct (see p 91), then some maths shows that we have to give a range of coin date to coin date plus 150 years as the date of the context. For example, if the coin can be dated to 100 AD, we would have to give a range of 100–250 AD to have a 95% chance of being correct. This may not seem satisfactory but there is nothing we can do about it. Two coins would halve the range (in this example, to 100–175 AD, if they were of the same date), but we cannot find another to order.

Samian seems to follow a similar pattern: the average life might be about thirty years (see p 102) but to this must be added a range of uncertainty in the original dating of perhaps twenty years (e.g. 60–80 AD). We can add these two together (this does not always apply, but fortunately it does for this particular problem) to get an 'effective average life' of fifty years – the same as the coin!

Of course, it is not that simple. Contexts do not exist in isolation, and adjoining contexts might be able to improve the precision (see p 105). Conversely, disturbance by later features might decrease the precision. Nevertheless, if the hypothesis holds, it should be possible, given a site, its stratigraphy and its finds, to set a theoretical limit to the precision with which one will ever be able to date a chosen context. This only applies to strictly archaeological evidence. Historical evidence – for example dated inscriptions, or documentary evidence for buildings, completely changes the picture. But is this more than a mathematical game? I think it is, for two reasons. Firstly, a sober appraisal of the possibilities of one's dating evidence could have considerable influence on the way in which one tries to interpret a site. If one knows that it will not be possible to say with any certainty which of two features is the earlier, one does not build an interpretation that relies on one being earlier than the other. Secondly, it would be a great help in assessing priorities. By comparing our knowledge with the theoretical limits we could see where our efforts could bring the greatest rewards. Conversely, other fields of study might be approaching the point of vanishing returns, at least as far as obtaining extra dating evidence is concerned.

The third idea, and the vaguest, is to extend this general approach beyond the field of dating evidence. As an example, take the study of artefact distribution patterns by regression analysis (p 116). An examination of the precision of the data (e.g. percentages of different types of pottery at different sites) could lead to a better idea of the reliance that could be placed on the estimated parameters α and b (see p 120). This in turn could aid interpretation of the different parameters found for different classes of artefact – how different do two parameters have to be before one can safely interpret the differences, for instance?

What seems to be emerging here is a sort of general theory of archaeological interpretation – what sort of things can one reasonably expect to be able to say about a given body of data? The implications for the direction of archaeological research could be enormous. However, at the moment it is all speculation, and only time will tell whether there is really anything in it. And that will be another story.

1. *Wilcock 1970*
2. *Diment and Biek 1977*
3. *Stoll, 2*

SUGGESTIONS FOR FURTHER READING

CHAPTER 1

It is impossible to recommend a single text-book on statistics for the general reader – so much depends on the reader's own background, aptitudes and preferences. Wherever possible, I have restricted references on purely statistical techniques to only two text-books – Davies and Goldsmith (1972) and Davies (1963) – because I believe that the reader with a little mathematics should be able to cope with them, and because it seemed useful to have standard books that can be referred to throughout, rather than flitting hither and thither. An alternative text-book, which is often recommended, is Moroney (1969). More mathematical topics can be found in Kendall (1975).

For an approach to the problems of manuscript linkage (p 16) see Haigh (1971).

There are many examples of the use of models in archaeology (p 20), see especially Clarke (1972) and Renfrew (1973). For a coherent theoretical approach to archaeology see Clarke (1968, revised 1978), Gardin (1979).

The explicit use of sampling methods in archaeology (p 22) is a more recent development. A comprehensive view can be obtained from Cherry, Gamble and Shennan (eds.) (1978).

CHAPTER 2

The best reference for archaeological classification in general is Doran and Hodson (1975), which can be supplemented by selected reading from Hodson, Kendall and Tautu (1971, 3–116). The former has a particularly useful and comprehensive bibliography. Also useful, although written for biologists, is Sokal and Sneath (1963, revised 1973).

There are many references for the description of shapes of objects in mathematical terms (p 38). Some are:

Brooches:	Hodson, Sneath and Doran (1966)
Metal Weapons:	Barker (1975), Densem (1976)
Stone axes:	Roe (1964, 1968), Allsworth-Jones and Wilcock (1974), Celoria and Wilcock (1975)

Pottery: Clarke (1962), Ericson and Stickel (1973),
        Hardy-Smith (1974), Shennan and Wilcock (1975)
General: Gardin (1967)

Similarity coefficients (p 43) have been discussed in detail by Sokal and Sneath, Cormack (1971), Doran and Hodson and many other writers. Cormack gives an extensive bibliography on classification in general, though it is by now a little dated.

The recent development of clustering methods in archaeology (p 46) can be followed through a series of papers – Hodson, Sneath and Doran, Hodson (1969, 1970, 1971), Doran and Hodson. Many individual case-studies have also been published.

The basic ideas of multidimensional scaling (p 55) are given by Shepard (1962) and Kruskal (1964). There are a number of archaeological applications in Hodson, Kendall and Tautu (pp 119–169), and others by Bonsall and Leach (1974), Shennan and Wilcock (1975). For an up-to-date view see Springall (1978).

Accounts of principal components analysis (p 56) can be found in many statistical text-books, for example Kendall (1975, 13–30).

CHAPTER 3

There is no single reference to cover the whole of this chapter. Recent general works on dating include Michels (1973) and Fleming (1976).

A brief account of Meadow Taylor's work is given by Wheeler (1956, 22–3), while Harris' work on stratigraphy (p 66) is summarized by Harris (1975a and b, 1977). Barker (1977) is well worth reading on this subject. For an account of context sorting by computer see Bishop and Wilcock (1976).

The earliest recorded attempt at seriation (p 81) was Flinders Petrie's (1899), discussed mathematically by Kendall (1963). Kroeber's work (1940) attracted relatively little attention at the time and the recent interest in the subject can be said to date from work by Brainerd and Robinson (both 1951). Many developments followed – for example Dempsey and Baumhoff (1963), Hole and Shaw (1967) – and a section of Hodson, Kendall and Tautu (pp 173–287) is devoted to a wide range of techniques and applications, including Kendall's HORSHU method (pp 215–52). Doubts have been voiced by Kruskal (1971) and McNutt (1973): an up-to-date view, including doubts, is given by Doran and Hodson (pp 267–84).

Straightforward basic accounts of radiocarbon dating and other techniques (p 89) – the fission track technique, obsidian dating, archaeomagnetism, potassium-argon dating and thermoluminescence – can be found in Brothwell and Higgs (1969). Watkins (1975) gives a fairly up-to-date, but slightly one-sided, account of the current state of play on radiocarbon dating, including the calibration debate. The 'smoothy' side of the debate has been put by Wendland and Donley (1971), Damon, Long and Wallick (1972), Switsur (1973) and Clark and Renfrew (1973), and the 'wiggly' side by Suess (1970),

Ralph *et al* (1973) and McKerrell (1975). Personally, I favour the position expressed by Clark (1975) – a modified 'smoothy' argument. The debate continues with Clark (1979).

Good accounts of the problems of 'external' dating (p 89) have been given by Hurst (1964) and Barker (pp 193–6). The uses of coin evidence have been discussed in Casey and Reece (1974). For an introduction to renewal theory (p 100) see Cox (1962). The work on the samian from Highgate and Top-pings Wharf (p 101) is described in Orton and Orton (1975), and that on the samian from 93/5 Borough High Street (p 102) in Bird *et al* (1978).

The development of the argument about statistical methods for dating clay tobacco pipes has been set out by Walker (1970) and Oswald (1975, 92).

CHAPTER 4

The basic reference for scientific examination of materials is Brothwell and Higgs (1969) although interesting (and more recent) papers are to be found in the journals *Archaeometry, Journal of Archaeological Science, Science and Archaeology* and elsewhere.

The use of trace element analysis on European bronzes (p 108) has been discussed by Doran and Hodson (pp 246–51). For a use of heavy mineral analysis in pottery studies (p 108) see Peacock (1973).

An account of discriminant analysis (p 110) can be found in many text-books on multivariate statistics, including Kendall (1975, 145–169).

The account given here (pp 107–24) of the techniques available for study-ing distribution patterns of artefacts relies heavily on Hodder and Orton (1976, 98–197), from which the case-studies on pp 121 and 122 are taken, and which also contains a useful bibliography.

Most text-books on statistics include regression analysis (p 116) among their topics: fewer include trend surface analysis (p 124). One that includes both and is relatively easy to read is Davies and Goldsmith (1972, 178–303). A more detailed explanation of the latter can be found in Davies (1963, 495–531), which assumes some familiarity with Davies and Goldsmith (known in earlier editions as Davies 1947, 1949 and 1957).

Hodder's experiments in the simulation of artefact dispersal (p 130) are described in Hodder and Orton (pp 126–54), which also gives a more detailed discussion of the interpretations of fall-off curves (pp 144–6), and their value in distinguishing between redistributive and other forms of artefact dispersal (p 153). Wider aspects in simulation can be found in Hodder (1978).

CHAPTER 5

The debate about the functional interpretation of Mousterian flints (p 135) is summed up in three papers in Renfrew (1973) – Bordes (pp 217–26), Binford (pp 227–54) and Mellars (pp 255–276) and amplified by Binford and Binford

(1966). Factor analysis (p 138) is a difficult statistical technique to understand: perhaps the most straightforward account is that given by Lawley and Maxwell (1971). For other archaeological applications see Cowgill (1968).

Examples of the techniques adapted from geography and ecology (p 140) can be found in Stewart and Warntz (1958) and Greig-Smith (1964) respectively. Callow and Webb's use of canonical variates analysis (p 141) is described in Callow and Webb (1977). The technique itself is explained by Kendall (pp 61–70) and others: Callow and Webb recommend Blackith and Reyment (1971).

The calculation of the Q and V statistics (p 143) is explained, and their value discussed, by Pielou (1969, 160–5) and Hodder and Orton (pp 201–4): the former from an ecological and the latter from an archaeological point of view. The coefficient of segregation, S, (p 146) was suggested by Pielou (1961).

Dimensional analysis of variance (p 146) is described by Whallon (1973a and b) from whom the example on p 148 is taken. The mathematical theory is set out by Mead (1974). Local density analysis (p 150) is described by Johnson (1977) and the index of association, A, (p 154) by Hodder and Okell (1978). Dacey (1973) is also useful.

The correlation coefficient (p 152) can be found in almost any statistical text-book: see Davies and Goldsmith pp 229–35, for example.

The reader should note that the statistical techniques mentioned in this chapter are, on the whole, more difficult that those in other chapters.

CHAPTER 6

No single reference covers all, or most, of the topics in this chapter. An up-to-date account of methods of handling excavated pottery is given in Young (forthcoming). For a way of describing pottery fabrics (p 157) see Rhodes (1977) or Orton (1977). Useful accounts of the technical aspects of potting, from an archaeological point of view, can be found in Hodges (1964) and van der Leeuw (1975).

Ways of measuring the quantity of pottery (pp 161–7) have been discussed by Solheim (1960), Willey (1961), Evans (1973), Hulthén (1974) and Orton (1975). For an example of the effects of sieving (p 162) see Keighley (1973). The statistical argument about pottery from partially excavated sites (pp 162–7) is taken from Orton (1975).

The final report on the Highgate Wood excavations (pp 167–74) is not yet published, the most recent interim is Brown and Sheldon (1974). The statistical work described here (pp 168–74) can be found in more detail in Orton (1974). It should be noted that, if this work were being done now, the approach would be rather different (see p 170).

The section on bones (pp 174–8) draws heavily on unpublished work by Altham (1973). A modern text-book on the subject, which includes rules for calculating the minimum number of animals represented, is Chaplin (1971).

CHAPTER 7

The general reference for this chapter is again, Hodder and Orton (pp 17–97), augmented by Clarke (1972) and Clarke (1977). For an example of a site survey in a basically urban area (p 180) see Longley (1976). The distribution map of oil jars used as shop signs (p 182) is taken from Ashdown (1974 and 1975). Tallis' *Street Views* has been re-published (1969), and the study of oil jars shown in it is by Backman (1977).

There are a number of reports on the finding of sites on motorway routes (p 183) e.g. Fowler (1969), Rowley and Davies (1972), Williams (1972), Johnson (1975). The locations of Saxon and Medieval sites excavated in Greater London (p 184) are taken from Bloice (1973 to 1976).

The literature on Central Place Theory (p 187) is extensive: the original idea seems to be due to Christaller (1933), while standard academic works are Haggett (1965), Berry (1967) and Morrill (1970). A simpler account, written for sixth-formers, is given by Briggs (1974). The archaeological implications are discussed in Hodder and Orton (54–85).

The variance-to-mean ratio (p 188) is described by Greig-Smith (1964, 63). Nearest-neighbour analysis (p 189) was introduced by Clark and Evans (1954) and has been used extensively in geography and ecology. Greig-Smith (1964) suggested studying second, third, etc. nearest neighbours (p 189), while Ripley (1977) suggested the idea of studying the distances from each site to all other sites. A mathematical survey of the available methods has been made by Diggle (1979).

A correction for edge-effects in nearest-neighbour has been found by Donnelly (1978): it is however only applicable for simple shapes, and not complex shapes like coastlines.

A standard mathematical work on this subject is Bartlett (1976).

The example of the Romano-British towns (p 191) is taken from Hodder and Hassall (1971) and Hodder (1972), while the second example – neolithic settlement in southern Poland (p 192) – is from Hodder and Orton (pp 89–97).

CHAPTER 8

This aspect of the work on the Highgate pottery (p 195) is described in Orton (1970) while the horn core (p 201) data are taken from Chaplin and Harmer (1980).

The topic of hypothesis testing (p 203) can be found in most text-books on statistics. In Davies and Goldsmith it occurs on pp 69–76: a fairly simple account is given by Moroney.

The original work on ley lines (p 204) is by Watkins (1925). Critical examinations have been made by Forrest (1976) (who quotes a formula for the 'expected' number of lines), Gadsby and Hutton-Squire (1976) and Broadbent (1980).

The basic references for the Megalithic yard (p 208) are by Thom (1967 and 1971). For critical mathematical examinations of the problem, see Kendall (1974) or Angell and Barber (1977). A summary of the current state of play is given by Porteous (1977). There are many papers on individual sites in the *Journal for the History of Astronomy*.

The work on the standardization of Roman pottery (p 208) is taken from Rottländer (1966), which was followed up by Rottländer (1967, 1969) and Holzhausen and Rottländer (1970).

The study on the location of the lesser Roman walled towns (p 210) is from Hodder and Orton (pp 77–84), itself based on Hodder and Hassall (1971).

CHAPTER 9

The use of Fourier analysis in resistivity surveys (p 215) can be found in Scollar (1974). A relatively simple account of the technique in general is given by Rayner (1971). The Theory of Elementary Catastrophe is due to Thom (1975): archaeological possibilities have been discussed by Renfrew (1978).

For the view of mathematics as an art (p 217) see Sullivan (1925).

For an introduction to the information retrieval, data reduction and graphic functions of the computer (p 218) see Wilcock (1971). Practical applications can be found in the Northern Archaeological Index (Clack, 1975), the Fife Archaeological Index (Stapleton and Kenworthy, 1975) and in the work of Main and Duncan (1977) on graphical routines.

The work at Danebury and York was reported on by Shackley, Macgregor and Duncan (1976). The PLUTARCH system has been described by Wilcock (1974). For some ideas on using computers to examine non-numerical problems see Doran (1970).

Bayesian statistics (p 220) will usually only be found in text-books committed to this point of view, e.g. Lindley (1965). A short account is given in Davies and Goldsmith (pp 76–88). For an intuitive archaeological approach, see Rahtz (1975).

The idea of fuzziness (p 220) has been taken from Kaufman (1975) which is however not recommended for the general reader.

BIBLIOGRAPHY

ALLSWORTH-JONES, P. and WILCOCK, J. D. 1974: A computer-assisted study of European Palaeolithic 'Leafpoints'. *Science and Archaeol.* 11, 25–46.

ALTHAM, P. M. E. 1973: Statistical Analysis of Bone Fragment Data. Unpublished.

ANGELL, I. O. and BARBER, J. S. 1977: The application of Curve-Fitting Techniques to the Study of Megalithic Stone Rings. *Computer Appl. Archaeol.* 10–20.

ASHDOWN, J. H. 1974: The Oil Jar as a London Shop Sign. *London Archaeol.* 2, No. 7, 166–70.

ASHDOWN, J. H. 1975: The Oil Jar as a Shop Sign: an addendum. *London Archaeol.* 2, No. 10, 239–40.

BACKMAN, P. 1977: London Oil Jars in the 1840s. *London Archaeol.* 3, No. 3, 77–9.

BARKER, P. A. 1977: *Techniques of Archaeological Excavation.*

BARKER, P. C. 1975: An Exact Method for Describing Metal Weapon Points. *Computer Appl. Archaeol.* 3–8.

BARTLETT, M. S. 1976: *The Statistical Analysis of Spatial Pattern.*

BERRY, B. J. L. 1967: *The Geography of Market Centres and Retail Distribution.*

BIEK, L. 1976: Lernie – Phase III. *Computer Appl. Archaeol.* 65–71.

BINFORD, L. R. 1962: A New Method of Calculating Dates from Kaolin Pipestem Samples. *South eastern Arch. Conf. Newsletter* 9, 19–21.

BINFORD, L. R. 1973: Interassemblage variability – the Mousterian and the 'functional' argument. In Renfrew, A. C. (ed.): *The Explanation of Culture Change: Models in Prehistory.* 227–54.

BINFORD, L. R. and BINFORD, S. R. 1966: A preliminary analysis of functional variability in the Mousterian of Levallois facies. In Clark, J. D. and Howell, F. C. (eds.) *Recent Studies in Palaeoanthropology. Amer. Anthrop.* 68, No. 2, part 2, 238–95.

BIRD, J., GRAHAM, A. H., SHELDON, H. L. and TOWNEND, P. (eds). 1978. *Southwark Excavations, 1972–4.* Joint Pub. of London and Middlesex Archaeol. Soc. and Surrey Archaeol. Soc. No. 1.

BISHOP, S. and WILCOCK, J. D. 1976: Archaeological context sorting by computer: the STRATA program. *Science and Archaeol.,* 17, 3–12.

BLACKITH, R. E. and REYMENT, R. A. 1971: *Multivariate Morphometrics.*

BLOICE, B. 1973: Excavation Round-up 1972. *London Archaeol.* 2, No. 2, 40–2.

BLOICE, B. 1974: Excavation Round-up 1973. *London Archaeol.* 2, No. 6, 133–5.

BLOICE, B. 1975: Excavation Round-up 1974. *London Archaeol.* 2, No. 10, 256–9.

BLOICE, B. 1976: Excavation Round-up 1975. *London Archaeol.* 2, No. 14, 370–2,5.

BONEVA, L. I., KENDALL, D. G. and STEFANOV, I. 1971: Spline transformations: three new diagnostic aids for the statistical data-analyst. *Journ. Royal Stat. Soc.* B, 33, 1–70.

BONSALL, J. C. and LEACH, C. 1974: Multidimensional Scaling Analysis of British Microlithic Assemblages. *Computer Appl. Archaeol.*, 16.

BORDES, F. 1973: On the chronology and contemporaneity of different palaeolithic cultures in France. In Renfrew, A. C. (ed). *The Explanation of culture change: models in prehistory.* 217–26.

BRADLEY, R. and ELLISON, A. 1975: Rams Hill – *a Bronze Age Defended Enclosure and its Landscape.* British Archaeol. Reps.

BRAINERD, G. W. 1951: The place of chronological ordering in archaeological analysis. *Amer. Antiquity,* 16, 301–13.

BRIGGS, K. 1974: *Introducing Towns and Cities.*

BROADBENT, S. 1980: Simulating the Ley Hunter. *Journ. Royal Stat. Soc. A* 143, 000–000.

BROTHWELL, D. 1969: Stones, Pots and People. In Brothwell, D. and Higgs, E. S. (eds.): *Science in Archaeology.* 669–80.

BROTHWELL, D. and HIGGS, E. S. (eds.) 1969: *Science in Archaeology,* second edition.

BROWN, A. E. and SHELDON, H. L. 1969: Post-excavation Work on the Pottery from Highgate. *London Archaeol.* 1, No. 3, 60–5.

BROWN, A. E. and SHELDON, H. L. 1974: Highgate Wood: the Pottery and its production. *London Archaeol.* 2, No. 9, 222–31.

BRUSH, J. E. and BRACY, H. E. 1955: Rural service centres in south-western Wisconsin and southern England. *Geographical Review,* 45, 559–69.

BURGESS, C. 1974: The bronze age. In Renfrew, A. C. (ed.) *British Prehistory,* 165–232.

BURLEIGH, R. 1975: Calibration of C–14 Dates: Some remaining uncertainties and limitations. In Watkins, T. (ed.) *Radiocarbon: Calibration and Prehistory,* 5–8.

CALLOW, P. and WEBB, R. E. 1977: Structure in the S.W. French Mousterian. *Computer Appl. Archaeol.*, 69–76.

CAMPBELL, J. A., BAXTER, M. S. and ALCOCK, Leslie, 1978: Radiocarbon dates for the Cadbury massacre. *Antiquity* 53, No. 207, 31–8.

CANN, J. R., DIXON, J. E. and RENFREW, A. C. 1969: Obsidian

Analysis and the Obsidian Trade. In Brothwell, D. and Higgs, E. S., *Science in Archaeology*, second edition, 578–91.

CASEY, J. and REECE, R. 1974: *Coins and the Archaeologist*. British Archaeol. Reps. 4.

CELORIA, F. S. C. and WILCOCK, J. D. 1975: A computer-assisted classification of British Neolithic axes and a comparison with some Mexican and Guatemalan axes. *Sciences and Archaeol.* 16, 11–29.

CHANG, K. C. 1967: *Rethinking Archaeology*.

CHAPLIN, R. E. 1971: *The Study of Animal Bones from Archaeological Sites*.

CHAPLIN, R. E. and HARMAN, M. (1980). Anatomical and economic studies of animal bones from post-medieval refuse deposits in Southwark. In Turner, D. J. and Orton, C. R., 199 Borough High Street, Southwark: Excavations in 1962, *Res. Vol.* 7 of *Surrey Archaeol. Soc.*

CHERRY, J., GAMBLE, C. and SHENNAN, S. J. 1978: *The Role of Sampling in Contemporary British Archaeology*. British Archaeol. Reps. 50.

CHRISTALLER, W. 1933: *Die Zentralen Orte in Süddeutschland*. Jena.

CLACK, P. A. G. 1975: The Northern Archaeological Index Information Retrieval System. *Computer Appl. Archaeol.*, 9–17.

CLARK, P. J. and EVANS, F. C. 1954: Distance to nearest neighbour as a measure of spatial relationships in populations. *Ecology*, 35, 445–53.

CLARK, R. M. 1975: A calibration curve for radiocarbon dates. *Antiquity*, 49, 251–66.

CLARK, R. M. 1979: Calibration, cross-validation and carbon-14. I. *Journ. Royal Statist. Soc.* A 142, 47–62.

CLARK, R. M. and RENFREW, C. 1973: The tree-ring calibration of radio-carbon and the chronology of ancient Egypt. *Nature*, 243, 266–70.

CLARKE, D. L. 1962: Matrix analysis and archaeology with particular reference to British Beaker pottery. *Proc. Prehist. Soc.*, 28, 371–82.

CLARKE, D. L. 1968: *Analytical Archaeology*.

CLARKE, D. L. (ed.) 1972: *Models in Archaeology*.

CLARKE, D. L. (ed.) 1977: *Spatial Archaeology*.

CORMACK, R. M. 1971: A review of classification. *Journ. Royal Stat. Soc.* A 134, 321–53.

COWGILL, G. L. 1968: Archaeological applications of factor, cluster and proximity analysis. *Amer. Antiquity*, 33, 367–75.

COX, D. R. 1962: *Renewal Theory*.

CUNLIFFE, B. W. 1964: *Winchester Excavations 1949–60, Volume I*. City of Winchester Museums and Libraries Committee.

CUNLIFFE, B. W. 1971: Some aspects of hill-forts and their cultural environments. In Jesson, M. and Hill, D., *The Iron Age and its hillforts*, 53–69.

DACEY, M. F. 1973: Statistical tests of spatial association in the locations of tool types. *Amer. Antiquity*, 38, No. 3, 320–8.

DAMON, P. E., LONG, A., and WALLICK, E. I. 1972: Dendrochronologic calibration of the carbon-14 timescale. In Rafter, T. A. and Grant-Taylor, T. (eds.) *Proc. 8th Int. Conf. on Radiocarbon Dating*, A29–43.

DAVIES, O. L. (ed.) 1963: *Design and Analysis of Industrial Experiments.* Second Edition.

DAVIES, O. L. and GOLDSMITH, P. L. (eds.). 1972: *Statistical Methods in Research and Production.* Fourth Edition.

DEMPSEY, P. and BAUMHOFF, M. 1963: The statistical use of artifact distributions to establish chronological sequences. *Amer. Antiquity, 28,* 496–509.

DENSEM, R. 1976: Roman military spearheads and projectiles from Britain. Unpublished undergraduate dissertation, Institute of Archaeology, University of London.

DIGGLE, P. J. 1979: On Parameter Estimation and Goodness-of-fit Testing for Spatial Point Patterns. *Biometrics, 35,* 87–101

DIMENT, A. R. and BIEK, L. 1977: Lernie – Phase IV. *Computer Appl. Archaeol.* 21–6.

DONNELLY, K. P. 1978: Simulations to determine the Variance and Edge Effect of Total Nearest Neighbour Distance. In Hodder, I. R. (ed.), *Simulation Studies in Archaeology,* 91–5.

DORAN, J. E. 1970: Archaeological Reasoning and Machine Reasoning. In *Archéologie et Calculateurs,* CNRS. 57–69.

DORAN, J. E. and HODSON, F. R. 1975: *Mathematics and Computers in Archaeology.*

DRURY, P. J. 1972: Preliminary report. The Romano-British settlement at Chelmsford, Essex: *Caesaromagos. Transactions of the Essex Archaeological Society,* No. 4.

EKWALL, E. 1960: *The Concise Oxford Dictionary of English Place-Names.* Fourth Edition.

ERICSON, J. E. and STICKEL, E. G. 1973: A proposed classification system for ceramics. *World Archaeol., 4,* No. 3, 357–67.

EVANS, J. D. (1973): Sherd Weights and Sherd Counts. In Strong, D. E. (ed). *Archaeological Theory and Practice,* 131–49.

EVENS, E. D., GRINSELL, L. V., PIGGOTT, S. and WALLIS, F. S. 1962: Fourth report of the sub-committee of the south-western group of museums and art galleries (England) on the petrological identification of stone axes. *Proc. Prehist. Soc., 28,* 209–66.

FLEMING, S. J. 1976: *Dating in Archaeology.*

FLINDERS PETRIE, W. M. 1899: Sequences in prehistoric remains. *J. Anthrop. Inst., N.S.* 29, 295–301.

FORREST, R. 1976: The Linear Dream. *Undercurrents,* No. 18, 33–5.

FOWLER, P. J. 1974: Motorways and archaeology. In Rahtz, P. A. (ed). *Rescue Archaeology,* 113–29.

FULFORD, M. G. 1975: *New Forest Roman Pottery.* British Archaeol. Reps. 17.

GADSBY, P. and HUTTON-SQUIRE, C. 1976: A Computer Study of Megalithic Alignments. *Undercurrents,* No. 17, 14–17.

GALLOWAY, P. 1976: Cluster Analysis using Fragmentary Data. *Computer Appl. Archaeol.,* 41–7.

GARDIN, J.-C. 1967: Methods for the descriptive analysis of archaeological material. *Amer. Antiquity*, 32, 13–30.

GARDIN, J.-C. 1979: *Archaeological Constructs.*

GARRARD, L. S. 1977: Was pottery made in the Isle of Man in medieval times? In Davey, P. J. (ed.). *Medieval pottery from excavations in the North-West*, 109–11.

GILLAM, J. P. 1970: *Types of Roman Coarse Pottery Vessels in Northern Britain.* Third Edition.

GREIG-SMITH, P. 1964: *Quantitative plant ecology.*

HAGGETT, P. 1965: *Locational analysis in human geography.*

HAIGH, J. 1971: The manuscript linkage problem. In Hodson, F. R., Kendall, D. G. and Tautu, P. (eds.), *Mathematics in the Archaeological and Historical Sciences*, 396–400.

HAMMOND, N. D. C. 1972: Locational models and the site of Lubaantun: a Classic Maya centre. In Clarke, D. L. (ed.) *Models in Archaeology*, 757–800.

HANSON, L. H., Jr. 1971: Kaolin Pipestems – Boring in on a Fallacy. *Hist. Site Arch.* 4, 2–15.

HARDY-SMITH, A. 1974: Post-medieval pot shapes: a quantitative analysis. *Science and Archaeol.* 11, 4–15.

HARKNESS, D. D. 1975: The Role of the Archaeologist in C–14 Age Measurement. In Watkins, T. (ed.) *Radiocarbon: Calibration and Prehistory*, 128–35.

HARRINGTON, J. C. 1954: Dating stem fragments of seventeenth and eighteenth century Tobacco Pipes. *Qrly. Bull. Arch. Soc. Virginia*, 9 (1), 6–8.

HARRIS, E. C. 1975a: Stratigraphic analyses and the computer. *Computer Appl. Archaeol.*, 33–40.

HARRIS, E. C. 1975b: The stratigraphic sequence: a question of time. *World Archaeol.* 7, No. 1, 109–121.

HARRIS, E. C. 1977: Units of Archaeological Stratification. *Norweg. Archaeol. Rev.* 10, No. 1–2, 84–106.

HARTLEY, K. F. 1973: The Marketing and Distribution of Mortaria. In Detsicas, A. (ed.) *Current Research on Romano-British Course Pottery.* CBA Res. Rep. No. 10, 39–51.

HENSHALL, A. S. 1974: Scottish chambered tombs and long mounds. In Renfrew, A. C. (ed.) *British Prehistory*, 137–64.

HODDER, I. R. 1972: Locational models and the study of Romano-British settlement. In Clarke, D. L. (ed.) *Models in Archaeology*, 887–909.

HODDER, I. R. 1977: Some New Directions in the Spatial Analysis of Archaeological Data at the Regional Scale. In Clarke, D. L. (ed.) *Spatial Archaeology*, 223–351.

HODDER, I. R. (ed.) 1978: *Simulation Studies in Archaeology.*

HODDER, I. R. and HASSALL, M. 1971: The non-random spacing of Romano-British walled towns. *Man*, 6, 391–407.

HODDER, I. R. and OKELL, E. 1978: An index for assessing the association between distributions of points in archaeology. In Hodder, I. R. (ed.) *Simulation Studies in Archaeology*, 97–107.

HODDER, I. R. and ORTON, C. R. 1976: *Spatial Analysis in Archaeology*.

HODGES, H. 1964: *Artifacts*.

HODSON, F. R. 1969: Searching for structure within multivariate archaeological data. *World Archaeol.* 1, no. 1, 90–105.

HODSON, F. R. 1970: Cluster analysis and archaeology: some new developments and applications. *World Archaeol.* 1, no. 3, 299–320.

HODSON, F. R. 1971: Numerical typology and prehistoric archaeology. In Hodson, F. R., Kendall, D. G. and Tautu, P. (eds.) *Mathematics in the Archaeological and Historical Sciences*, 30–45.

HODSON, F. R., KENDALL, D. G. and TAUTU, P. (eds.) 1971: *Mathematics in the Archaeological and Historical Sciences*.

HODSON, F. R., SNEATH, P. H. A. and DORAN, J. E. 1966: Some experiments in the numerical analysis of archaeological data. *Biometrika*, 53, 311–24.

HOLE, F. and SHAW, M. 1967: Computer analysis of chronological seriation. *Rice University Studies*, 53, no. 3.

HOLZHAUSEN, H. and ROTTLÄNDER, R. C. A. 1970: Standardization of Roman Provincial Pottery IV: The origin of standardization. *Archaeometry*, 12, no. 2, 191–7.

HULTHEN, B. 1974: On choice of element for determination of quantity of pottery. *Norwegian Arch. Rev.*, 7, 1–5.

HURST, J. G. 1964: White Castle and the dating of Medieval pottery. *Med. Archaeol.*, 6–7, 135–55.

JARDINE, C. J., JARDINE, N. and SIBSON, R. 1967: The structure and construction of taxonomic hierarchies. *Math. Biosci*, 1, 173–9.

JOHNSON, B. 1975: *Archaeology and the M.25, 1971–1975*. Surrey Archaeol. Soc.

JOHNSON, I. 1977: Local Density Analysis. *Computer Appl. Archaeol.*, 90–8.

JONES, D. M. 1980: *Excavations at Billingsgate Buildings ('Triangle'), Lower Thames Street, 1974*. London and Middlesex Archaeol. Soc. Special Paper No. 4.

KAUFMANN, A. 1975: *Introduction to the Theory of Fuzzy Subsets*.

KEIGHLEY, J. 1973: Some problems in the quantitative interpretation of ceramic data. In Renfrew, A. C. (ed.) *The explanation of culture change: models in prehistory*. 131–6.

KENDALL, D. G. 1963: A statistical approach to Flinders Petrie's sequence-dating. *Bull. I.S.I. 34th session, Ottawa*, 657–80.

KENDALL, D. G. 1971: Seriation from abundance matrices. In Hodson, F. R., Kendall, D. G. and Tautu, P. (eds.) *Mathematics in the Archaeological and Historical Sciences*, 229–64.

KENDALL, D. G. 1974: Hunting Quanta. *Phil. Trans. Royal. Soc.* A 276, 231–66.

KENDALL, M. G. 1975: *Multivariate Analysis*.

BIBLIOGRAPHY

KERSHAW, K. A. 1957: The use of cover and frequency in the detection of pattern in plant communities. *Ecology*, 38, 291–9.

KROEBER, A. L. 1940: Statistical classification. *Amer. Antiquity*, 6, no. 1 29–44.

KRUSKAL, J. B. 1964: Multidimensional scaling by optimising goodness of fit to a non-metric hypothesis. Nonmetric multidimensional scaling: a numerical method. *Psychometrika*, 29, 1–27 and 115–29.

KRUSKAL, J. B. 1971: Multidimensional scaling in archaeology: time is not the only dimension. In Hodson, F. R., Kendall, D. G. and Tautu, P. (eds.) *Mathematics in the Archaeological and Historical Sciences*, 119–32.

LAWLEY, D. N. and MAXWELL, A. E. 1971: *Factor Analysis as a Statistical Method*. Second Edition.

LINDLEY, D. V. 1965: *Introduction to Probability and Statistics from a Bayesian Viewpoint*.

LINDLEY, D. V. and MILLER, J. C. P. 1962: *Cambridge Elementary Statistical Tables*.

LONGLEY, D. 1976: The Archaeological Implications of Gravel Extraction in North-West Surrey. *Res. Vol. of Surrey Archaeol. Soc.*, 3, 1–36.

MAIN, P. L. and DUNCAN, J. M. 1977: Graphical Routines for Archaeological Plans and Sections. *Computer Appl. Archaeol.*, 55–60.

McKERRELL, H. 1975: Correction Procedures for C-14 Dates. In Watkins, T. (ed.) *Radiocarbon: Calibration and Prehistory*, 47–100.

McNUTT, C. H. 1973: On the methodological validity of frequency seriation. *Amer. Antiquity*, 38, 45–60.

MEAD, R. 1974: A test for spatial patterns at several scales using data from a grid of contiguous quadrats. *Biometrics*, 30, 295–307.

MELLARS, P. A. 1973: The character of the middle-upper palaeolithic transition in south-west France. In Renfrew, A. C. (ed.) *The explanation of culture change: models in prehistory*. 255–76.

MICHELL, J. 1974: *The Old Stones of Land's End*.

MICHELS, J. W. 1973: *Dating Methods in Archaeology*.

MORONEY, M. J. 1969: *Facts from Figures*.

MORRILL, R. L. 1970: *The spatial organisation of society*.

MORTENSEN, P. 1973: On the reflection of cultural changes in artifact materials, with special regard to the study of innovation contrasted with type stability. In Renfrew, A. C. (ed.) *The explanation of culture change: models in prehistory*. 155–60.

MUSTY, J. G. 1973: Medieval pottery kilns. In Evison, V. I., Hodges, M. and Hurst, J. G. (eds.) *Medieval Pottery from Excavations*. 41–66.

NOEL HUME, A. 1963: Clay Tobacco Pipe Dating in the light of recent Excavations. *Qrly. Bull. Arch. Soc. Virginia*, 18(2), 22–5.

ORTON, C. R. 1970: The production of pottery from a Romano-British kiln site: a statistical investigation. *World Archaeol.* 1, no. 3, 343–58.

ORTON, C. R. 1974: An Experiment in the Mathematical Reconstruction of the Pottery from a Romano-British Kiln Site at Highgate Wood, London. *Bull. of Inst. of Arch., London,* 11, 41–73.

ORTON, C. R. 1975: Quantitative pottery studies: some progress, problems and prospects. *Science and Archaeol.* 16, 30–5.

ORTON, C. R. 1977: Studying the City's Pottery. *London Archaeol.* 3, no. 4, 99–104.

ORTON, C. R. (forthcoming): Excavations at Burleigh Avenue, Wallington, 1921 and 1976. *Surrey Archaeol. Collections.*

ORTON, C. R. and ORTON, J. L. 1975: It's later than you think: a statistical look at an archaeological problem. *London Archaeol.,* 2, no. 11, 285–7.

OSWALD, A. 1975: *Clay Pipes for the Archaeologist.* Brit. Archaeol. Reps. 14.

PEACOCK, D. P. S. 1973: The black-burnished Pottery Industry in Dorset. In A. Detsicas (ed.) *Current Research in Romano-British Coarse Pottery.* CBA Res. Rep. 10, 63–5.

PIELOU, E. C. 1961: Segregation and symmetry in two species populations as studied by nearest neighbour methods. *Journ. of Ecology,* 49, 255–69.

PIELOU, E. C. 1969: *An introduction to mathematical ecology.*

PLOG, F. 1974: *The Study of Prehistoric Change.*

PORTEOUS, H. L. 1977: The Saga of the Megalithic Yard. *Bull. Appl. Stats.,* 4, no. 1, 28–39.

RAHTZ, P. A. 1975: How likely is likely? *Antiquity,* 49, 59–61.

RALPH, E. K., MICHAEL, H. N. and HAN, M. C. 1973: Radiocarbon dates and reality. *MASCA Newslett.,* 9, no. 1, 1–20.

RAYNER, J. N. 1971: *An Introduction to Spectral Analysis.*

RENFREW, A. C. (ed.) 1973: *The explanation of culture change: models in prehistory.*

RENFREW, A. C. 1978: Trajectory Discontinuity and Morphogenesis: The Implications of Catastrophe Theory for Archaeology, *Amer. Antiq.* 43, no. 2, 203–22.

RHODES, M. 1977: A Pottery Fabric Type-Series for London. *Mus. J.* 76, No. 4 150–2.

RIPLEY, B. D. 1977: Modelling Spatial Patterns. *Journ. Royal Stat. Soc.,* B, 39, 172–212.

ROBINSON, W. S. 1951: A method for chronologically ordering archaeological deposits. *Amer. Antiquity,* 16, 293–301.

ROE, D. A. 1964: The British Lower and Middle Palaeolithic: some problems, methods of study and preliminary results. *Proc. Prehist. Soc.,* 30, 245–67.

ROE, D. A. 1968: British Lower and Middle Palaeolithic handaxe groups. *Proc. Prehist. Soc.,* 34, 1–82.

ROTTLÄNDER, R. C. A. 1966: Is Provincial-Roman Pottery Standardized? *Archaeometry,* 9, 76–91.

ROTTLÄNDER, R. C. A. 1967: Standardization of Roman Provincial Pottery II: Function of the decorative collar on form Drag. 38. *Archaeometry,* 10, 35–45.

ROTTLÄNDER, R. C. A. 1969: Standardization of Roman Provincial Pottery III: The average total shrinkage rate and the Bills of La Graufesenque. *Archaeometry*, 11, 159–64.

ROWLEY, T. and DAVIES, M. (eds.) 1972: *Archaeology and the M40 Motorway*. Rescue.

RUSSELL, V. 1974: *West Penwith Survey*. Cornwall Archaeological Society.

SCOLLAR, I. 1974: Interactive Processing of Geophysical Data from Archaeological Sites. *Computer Appl. Archaeol*. 75–80.

SHACKLEY, M. L., MacGREGOR, A. and DUNCAN, J. M. 1976: Information retrieval and Graphics at Danebury and York. *Computer Appl. Archaeol.*, 72–9.

SHENNAN, S. J. and WILCOCK, J. D. 1975: Shape and style variation in Central German Bell Beakers: a computer-assisted study. *Science and Archaeol.*, 15, 17–31.

SHEPARD, R. N. 1962: The analysis of proximities: multidimensional scaling with an unknown distance function, I and II. *Psychometrika*, 27, 125–39 and 219–46.

SIEVEKING, G. de G., CRADDOCK, P. T., HUGHES, M. J., BUSCH, P. and FERGUSON, J. 1972: Prehistoric flint mines and their identification as sources for raw material. *Archaeometry*, 14, 151–76.

SOKAL, R. and SNEATH, P. H. A. 1973: *Numerical Taxonomy*. Originally published as *Principles of Numerical Taxonomy* (1963).

SOLHEIM, W. G. 1960: The use of sherd weights and counts in the handling of archaeological data. *Curr. Anthrop.*, 1, 325–9.

SPRINGALL, A. 1978: A Review of Multidimensional Scaling, *Bull. Appl. Stats.* 5, no. 2, 146–92.

STAPLETON, J. R. and KENWORTHY, J. B. 1975: The Fife Archaeological Index. *Computer Appl. Archaeol.*, 41–8.

STEWART, J. Q. and WARNTZ, W. 1958: Macrogeography and social science. *Geog. Rev.*, 48, 167–84.

STOLL, R. R. 1961: *Introduction to Set Theory and Logic*.

SUESS, H. E. 1970: Bristle-cone pine calibration of the radiocarbon timescale 5200 BC to the present. In Olsson, I. U. (ed.) *Radiocarbon Variations and Absolute Chronology*, 303–12.

SULLIVAN, J. W. N. 1925: *Aspects of Science*.

SWITSUR, R. 1973: The radiocarbon calendar recalibrated. *Antiquity*, 47, 131–7.

TALLIS, J. 1969: *London Street Views 1838–1840*. Nattali and Maurice and London Topographical Society.

THOM, A. 1967: *Megalithic Sites in Britain*.

THOM, A. 1971: *Megalithic Lunar Observatories*.

THOM, R. 1975: *Structural Stability and Morphogenesis*.

VAN DER LEEUW, S. E. 1975: Medieval Pottery from Haarlem; a Model. *Rotterdam Papers*, 2, 67–88.

WALKER, I. C. 1967: Statistical methods for dating clay pipe fragments. *Post-medieval Archaeol.* 1, 90–101.

WATKINS, A. 1925: *The Old Straight Track*.
WATKINS, T. (ed.) 1975: *Radiocarbon: Calibration and Prehistory*.
WEBSTER, G. (ed.) 1976: *Romano-British coarse pottery: a student's guide*. CBA Res. Rep. No. 6. Third edition.
WENDLAND, W. M. and DONLEY, D. L. 1971: Radiocarbon-calendar age relationship. *Earth Planet. Sci. Letts.* 9, 135–11.
WHALLON, R. 1973a: Spatial analysis of occupation floors: the application of dimensional analysis of variance. In Renfrew, A. C. (ed.) *The explanation of culture change: models in prehistory*. 115–30.
WHALLON, R. 1973b: Spatial analysis of occupation floors I: the application of dimensional analysis of variance. *Amer. Antiquity*, 38, 266–78.
WHALLON, R. 1974: Spatial analysis of occupation floors, II. The application of nearest-neighbour analysis. *Amer. Antiquity*, 39, 16–34.
WHEELER, R. E. M. 1956: *Archaeology from the Earth*.
WILCOCK, J. D. 1970: Prospecting at South Cadbury: an exercise in computer archaeology. *Science and Archaeol.*, 1, 9–11.
WILCOCK, J. D. 1971: Non-statistical applications of the computer in archaeology. In Hodson, F. R., Kendall, D. G. and Tautu, P. (eds.) *Mathematics in the Archaeological and Historical Sciences*, 470–81.
WILCOCK, J. D. 1974: The PLUTARCH system. *Computer Appl. Archaeol.*, 75–82.
WILCOCK, J. D. 1975: Archaeological Context Sorting by Computer. *Computer Appl. Archaeol.*, 93–7.
WILLEY, G. R. 1961: Volume in pottery and the selection of samples. *Amer. Antiquity*, 27, 230–41.
WILLIAMS, J. (ed.) 1972: *Northampton-Wellingborough Expressway: Archaeological Survey*. Rescue Publication No. 2.
YOUNG, C. J. 1973: The Pottery Industry of the Oxford Region. In Detsicas, A. (ed.) *Current Research in Romano-British Coarse Pottery*, CBA Res. Rep. No. 10, 105–15.
YOUNG, C. J. (forthcoming): *Processing and Publication of Roman Pottery*. Dept. of the Environment Occasional Paper No. 4.

INDEX
Italics indicate archaeological sites and pages on which
diagrams or photographs appear.